IMAGES
of America

Paris and Bourbon County

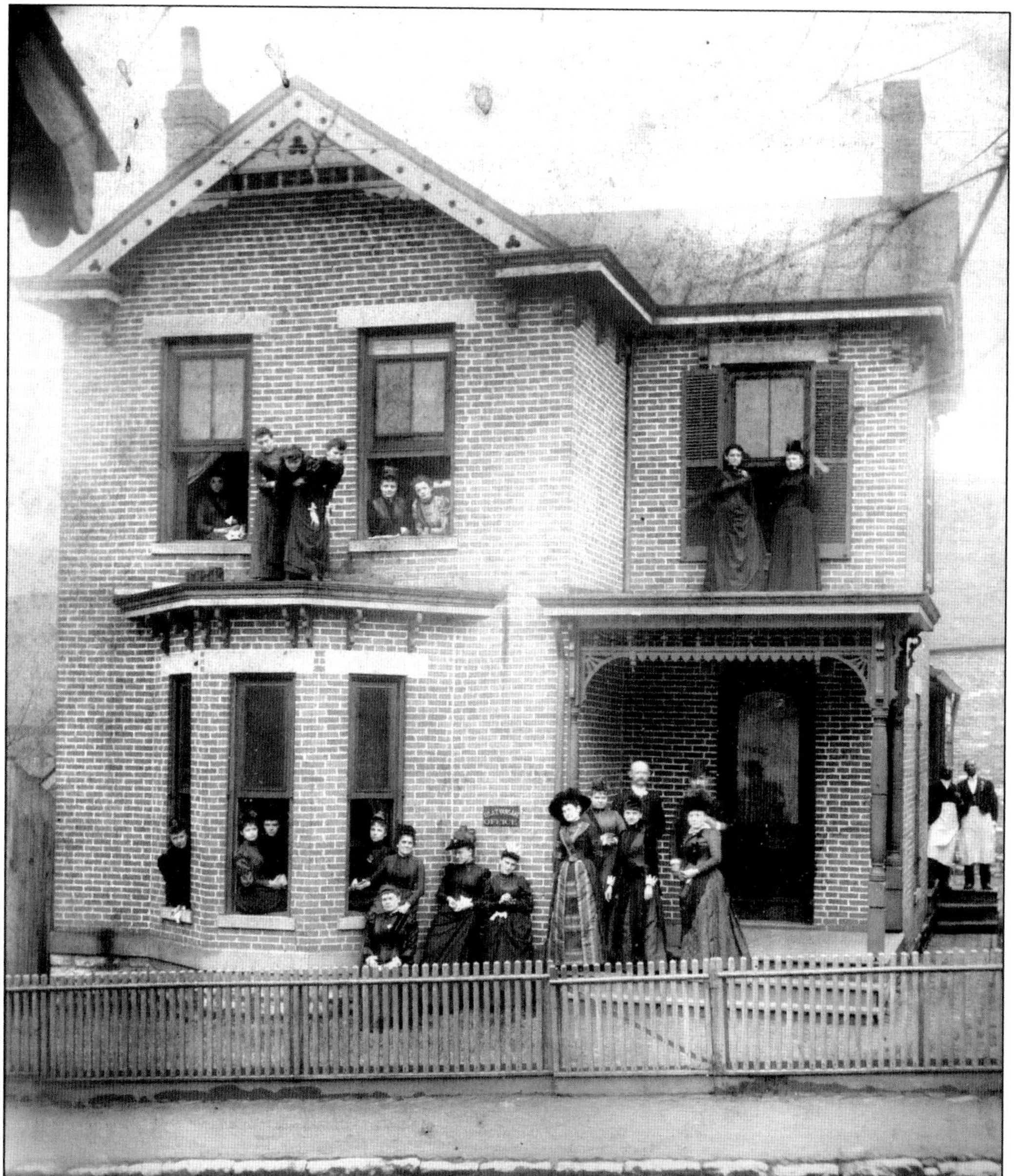

The Presbyterian Church's Matinee Club. The information on the back of this photo, taken in the fall of 1889, included the fact that the building was the Presbyterian manse and the group was identified as "The Matinee Club." Their object was said to have a "good time." The house was located on Fifth Street directly behind the large building near the corner of Fifth and Pleasant that was built for the New School Presbyterian Church and in use by the Presbyterian Church North at the time this photo was taken. The two men standing near the front door are identified as the Rev. T.J. Cheek and Dr. J.T. Vansant and one of the men at the back door is identified as Lias Anderson. The group was probably a church-sponsored social club that held meetings at the church manse. (U.K. Collection.)

IMAGES
of America

PARIS AND BOURBON COUNTY

Berkeley and Jeanine Scott

ARCADIA
PUBLISHING

ISBN 978-0-7385-1456-7

Published by Arcadia Publishing
Charleston, South Carolina

Printed in the United States of America

Library of Congress Catalog Card Number: 2002106722

For all general information contact Arcadia Publishing at:
Telephone 843-853-2070
Fax 843-853-0044
E-Mail sales@arcadiapublishing.com
For customer service and orders:
Toll-Free 1-888-313-2665

Visit us on the Internet at www.arcadiapublishing.com

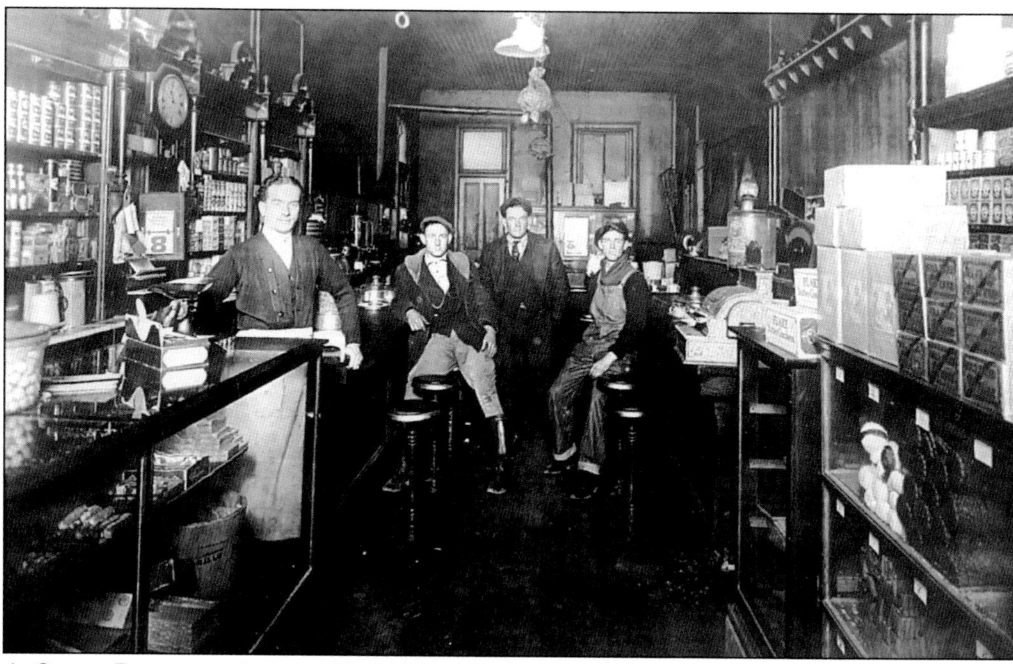

A Great Place for Lunch. This photo of Grant Owsley's store, which also appears on the cover, was probably taken in the 1920s and shows three customers along with Owsley. The store's shelves show a wide variety of items from cans of soups and vegetables to boxes of "Flake Butter Crackers" and two kinds of flour. In front of Owsley is a scale that was probably used to weigh candies like the "jaw breakers" in the big glass container on the counter. The rear area where the men are sitting was obviously a lunch counter with glass domes protecting homemade desserts and a shiny coffee machine in the back. The store, which was located on Main Street in Paris, is representative of the scores of similar establishments that could be found in Paris and in the county's small towns.

Contents

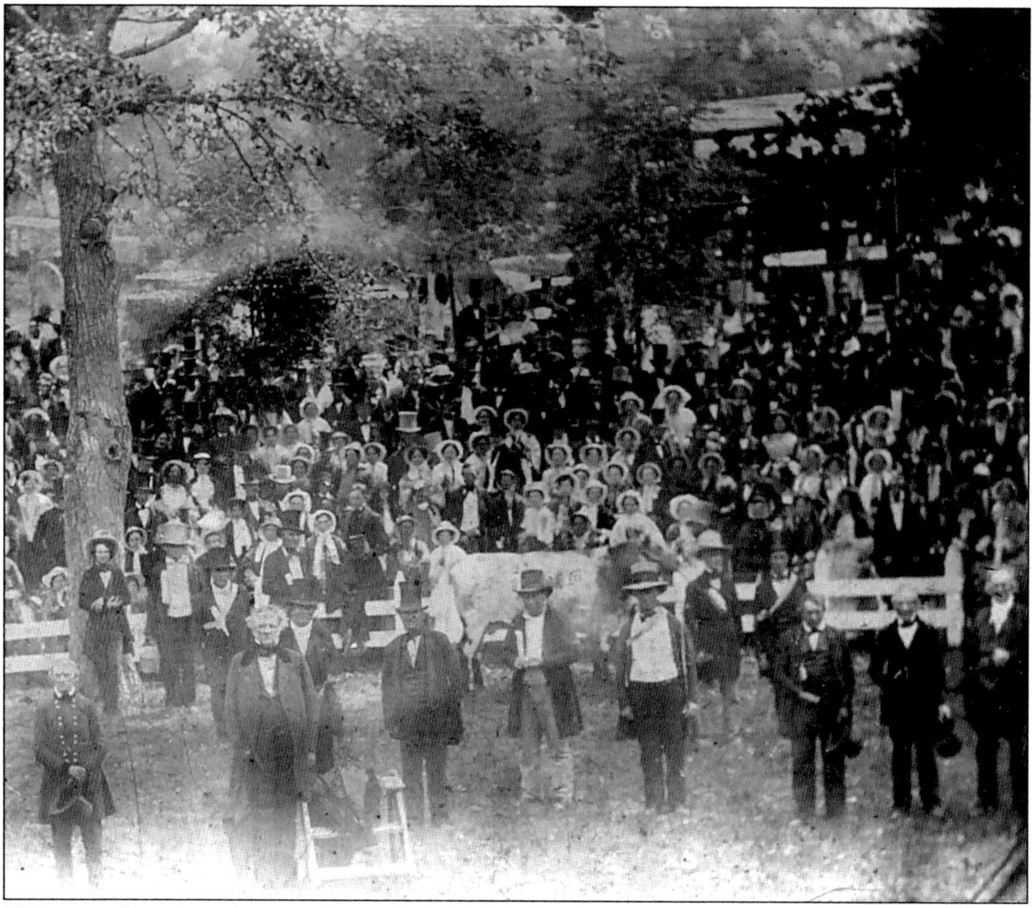

WINFIELD SCOTT AT BOURBON COUNTY FAIR IN 1852. This enhanced picture comes from a daguerreotype taken at the Bourbon County Fair in October of 1852. The gentleman near the center next to the steps is Gen. Winfield Scott, hero of the Mexican War, who was in the county campaigning as the Whig candidate for president. Scott gave a two-hour oration to the crowds assembled for the fair, not an unusual speech length for the day. He lost the election to Franklin Pierce but carried both Bourbon County and Kentucky. Pictured also are a number of the county's and state's leading citizens including U.S. Rep. Brutus J. Clay and future U.S. Sen. Garrett Davis, as well as one of the county's prime steers. The Bourbon County Fair began in 1817 and continues today to provide a showcase for local agricultural products.

Introduction

We have often thought how wonderful it would be to travel through time—to be able to go back to a pictured time and place and see what was going on in the world outside of the photo. Time travel would also give one the opportunity to smell the odors and hear the sounds of a world long gone—to be there and then.

Looking at vintage photographs is the closest we can come to time travel. From the comfort of our chairs, we can travel back to Bourbon County in the late 1800s and early 1900s. We can see the Opera House and wonder what is on the billboard just out of view; we can catch the Interurban as it rounds the corner at High onto Main; and we can go to church with men and women "dressed to the nines" in their wonderful outfits.

What time travel through photographs cannot do, of course, is take the viewer back to the era before the camera was invented. There is a very early photo in this volume of the 1852 Bourbon Agricultural Fair, but that is as far back as the camera's eye can reach. It would be wonderful to have photos of the Native Americans hunting the buffalo and other animals who roamed the uncut forests and cane brakes.

The first Europeans in the area included Daniel Boone and his companions who hunted here and later claimed homesteads along the area's many creeks as early as 1774. Stories that have come down from the early years of the European settlement of the area are full of harrowing tales of raids, massacres, and ambushes between the settlers and the Indians and their allies, the British.

Kentucky was at first a part of Virginia, and in 1785 the Virginia legislature created Bourbon County, naming it for the French royal family that supported the new nation, and making it the fifth county organized in Kentucky. In 1789, the Virginia legislature chartered the city of Paris at the confluence of Stoner and Houston Creeks as the county seat. There are wonderful pictures in this book of the town decorated with flags and banners to commemorate the anniversary of these events, but no photos of the events themselves.

Paris and Bourbon County began to grow and thrive with an agrarian economy that was based on hemp, corn, sheep, horses, tobacco, bluegrass seed, and whiskey. Many believe that Jacob Spears of Bourbon County was the first to make the whiskey that became known as bourbon. A photo of that event would go far in quieting the claims of other counties that bourbon was first made there.

Regardless of where bourbon was first made, whiskey distilling was one of the county's major industries right up to the Civil War. Distilleries and whiskey warehouses were found throughout the county up until Prohibition and there are photos of two distilleries and some of the men involved in making bourbon in this book. None of Bourbon County's distilleries reopened after Prohibition was repealed.

Bourbon Countians reacted to the Civil War much as the rest of Kentucky did. At first, residents were pro-Union in sentiment, while many were sympathetic to Southern culture. As the conflict intensified, the community, churches, and many families split over the war. Brother fought against brother, father fought against son, creating wounds that have taken generations to heal. This book includes photos of four Confederate soldiers, but we were unable to obtain a photo of any of the numerous Union soldiers from Bourbon County to include.

Toward the end of the war, many Union supporters in Bourbon County and across Kentucky chafed at the real and imagined abuses of the "occupying Federal forces," and opposed the idea of freeing the slaves without compensation for their Kentucky owners who had remained loyal during the conflict. This did bring about political unification that kept the county and state largely Democratic for more than a century. Photos of some of the county's politicians can be found in this volume. Especially interesting is a photo of a Democratic rally in Ruddles Mills in 1892 found in the chapter titled "Small Towns and Country Living."

Some of the freed slaves left the county after emancipation, but most remained, settling in communities on the outskirts of the county's towns including Paris, Millersburg, North Middletown, and Little Rock. There, as from almost the beginning of pioneer days, they were an integral part of the economy and the county's society. Bourbon County's African-American population had to fight for voting, working rights, equal education, and against racial bigotry as other blacks have, and they have continued to survive, thrive, and contribute to the community at large. There are numerous photos in this book of African-American life in Bourbon County.

The expansion of the railroad after the Civil War made Paris a hub with major repair shops and well-paying jobs for hundreds of new families. The expansion also meant bitter political disputes on financing new rail lines. The post-war economy saw the flourishing of a number of the county's smaller towns and villages like Millersburg, North Middletown, Ruddles Mills, Hutchison, Little Rock, Centerville, and Clintonville. Photos of some of these communities were impossible to find, but most are represented in this book.

Institutions like Millersburg Military Institute, North Middletown Classical and Business College, Millersburg Female College, Bourbon Female College, and Kentucky Wesleyan College helped build a reputation for Bourbon County as excelling in education.

The beginning of the 20th century saw a shift in the agricultural economy with the demise of the sheep and bluegrass seed industries and an increase in growing tobacco and raising Thoroughbred horses. It also witnessed the metamorphosis of Paris into a booming and important mercantile and banking town. Many of the Victorian-era buildings in the town's noted downtown were built in the decades surrounding the turn of the century.

The new century also saw dramatic changes in transportation and communication. Being able to catch the Interurban to Joyland Park in Lexington or a train to the "big city" of Cincinnati broadened the horizons of many Bourbon Countians. The electrification of first the towns and then the rural areas lightened the workload and lengthened the days. This era is the most completely photographed. A wide range of images of rural and urban life are the focus of this book.

So, sit back and open your own personal time machine. We hope you enjoy the "trip" and that the images you see in this book provide a meaningful look back at a time and place worth remembering.

One

City Scenes

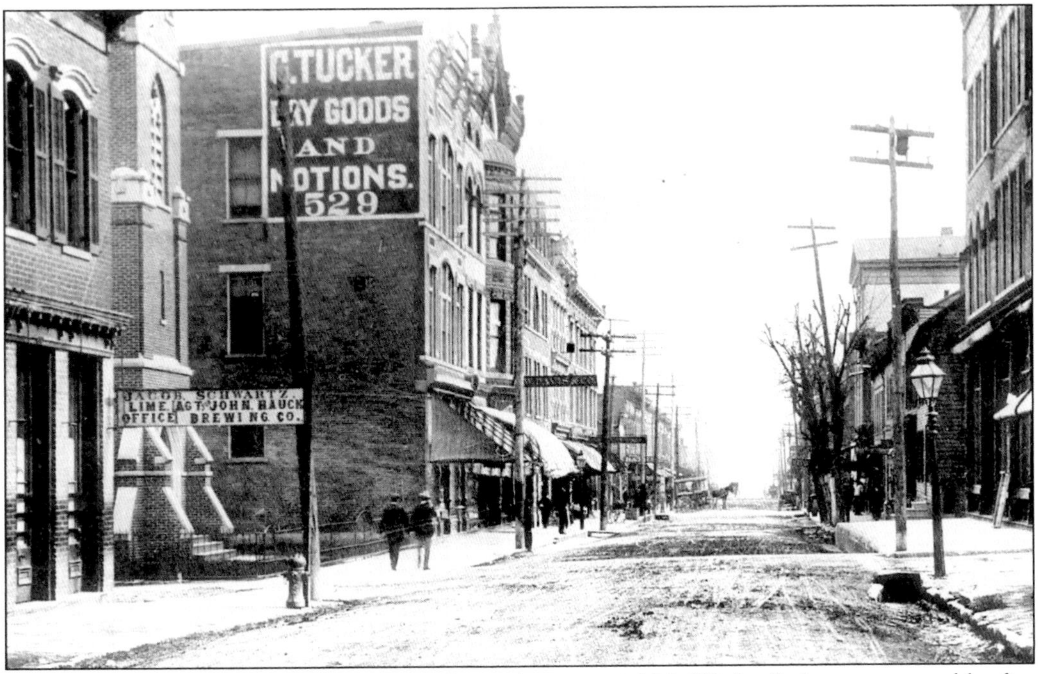

Take a Walk Down Main Street in Paris Around 1898. With all the gaps caused by fire in today's downtown streetscape filled in, the 500 block of Main Street looks very different than it does today. The two-story brick building on the corner of Fifth and Main, opposite the Hinton Building, which is still standing today, housed "Jacob Schwartz, agent for John Hauck Brewing Company," as well as the "Lime Office" according to the sign stretching across the sidewalk. Next to that, with a neat front yard enclosed by a wrought iron fence, is the First Baptist Church. Signs for other long-gone businesses can be seen further down the street as well as horses pulling buggies and wagons.

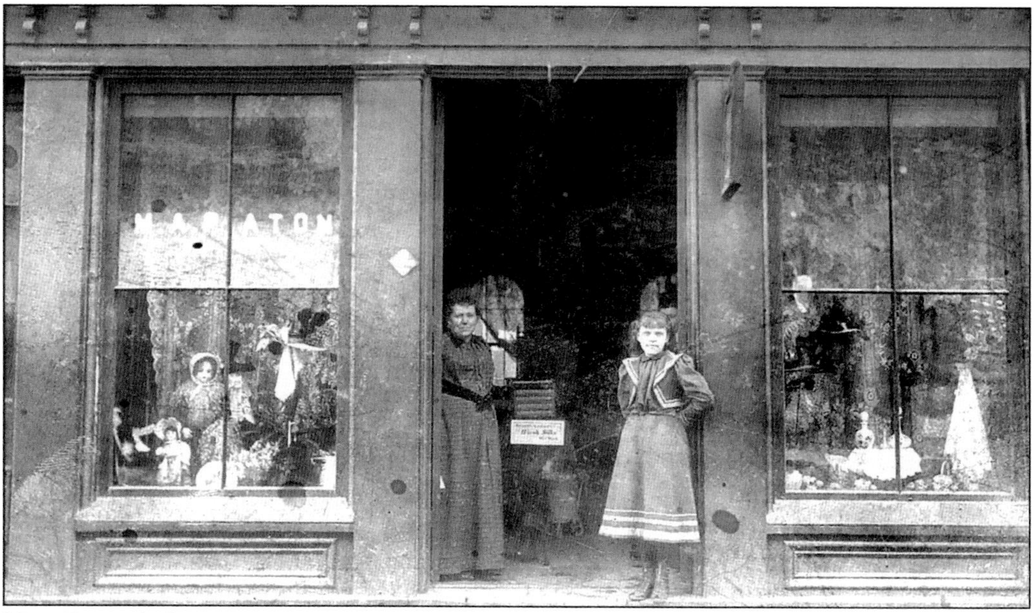

Mrs. Paton's Store,1893. Mrs. M.A. Paton and her daughter Effie can be see in front of Mrs. Paton's store located at 514 Main Street. The store looks like it would have been a fun place to shop for women and girls. The window on the right contains vanity sets and lace curtains and items for girls can be seen in the window on the left, including several dolls.

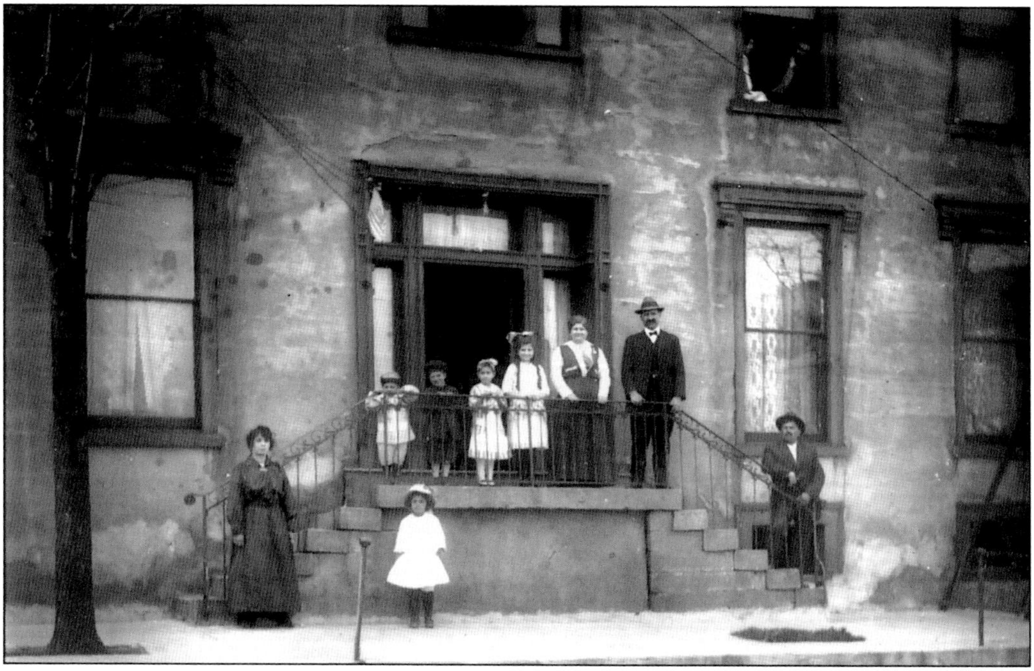

Proud Families in Front of Duncan Tavern. This 1890s photo shows Duncan Tavern, built in 1788 on the courthouse square, during the period when it was a boardinghouse known as Burr House. According to one local historian, Mr. Burr, who owned the boardinghouse, "went up in a balloon and never came down." After admiring Mama, Papa, and the children on the steps, notice the couple in the second-story window.

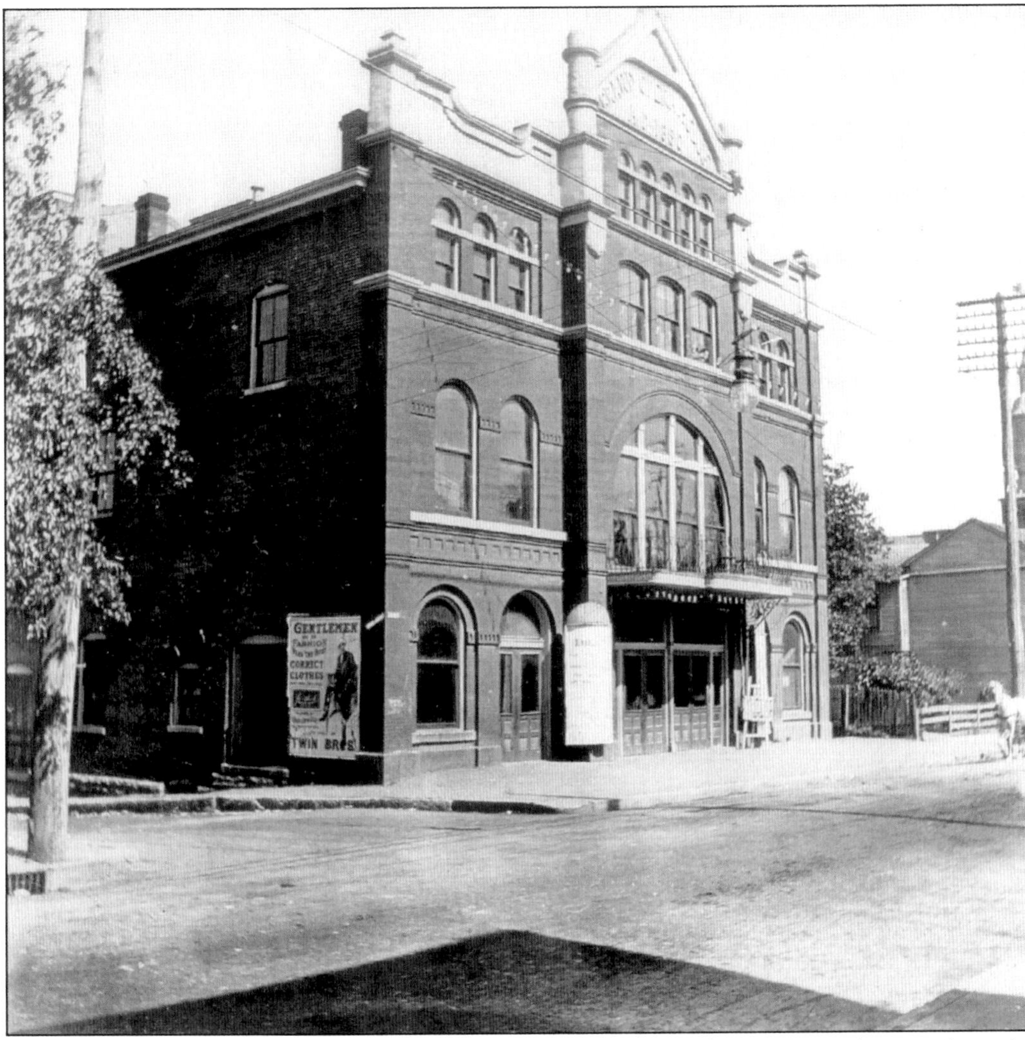

THE PARIS OPERA HOUSE, THE JEWEL OF MAIN STREET. More than 600 people turned out for the first performance held in the Paris Opera House in late December, 1890. That was the first of many live performances that took place in the imposing brick building located in the 800 block of Main. In 1893, an article in the *Louisville Courier-Journal* said: "Paris is a good show town with a $30,000 opera house and the leading road attractions come to it. A feature worthy of emulation everywhere is the ladies' cloakroom and here the offending hat is laid away until the opera is over and nobody is plagued into profanity by dodging around trying to see what is on the stage. This is worth the price of admission." When the building was converted for use as a "picture palace," the name was changed to the Paris Grand and then to the Bourbon Theatre. Later generations enjoyed movies, live wrestling matches, and an annual minstrel show. The Opera House was torn down in 1961. (U.K. Collection.)

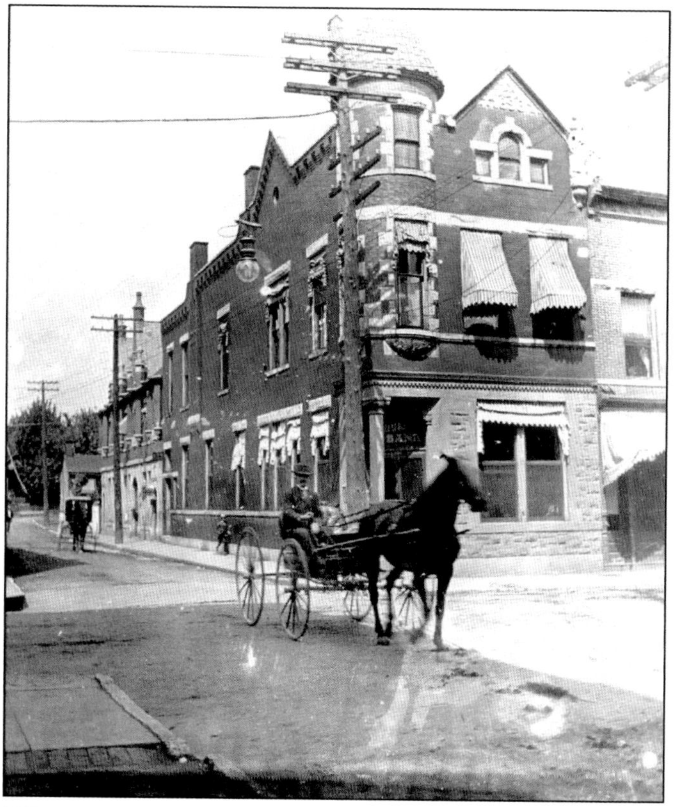

SURREY WITHOUT THE FRINGE ON TOP. The man driving through the intersection of Fifth and Main was possibly on his way home from a visit to the post office or the bank. The Bourbon Bank building can be seen on the corner behind him and the post office was located on the other end of Fifth where the parked buggy can be seen. City mail delivery was established in 1905 with three carriers. (U.K. Collection.)

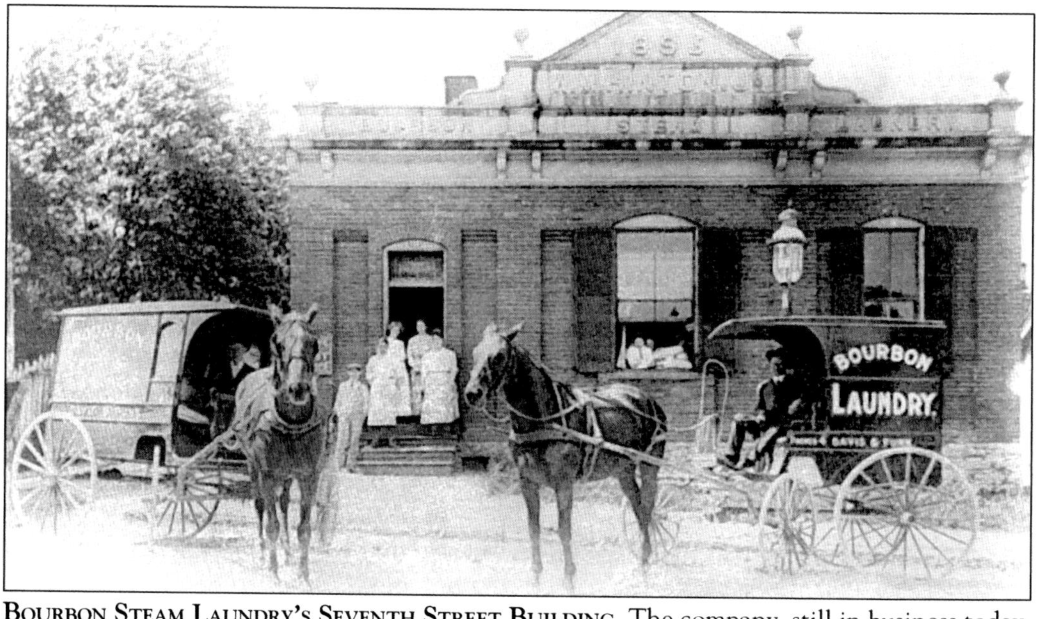

BOURBON STEAM LAUNDRY'S SEVENTH STREET BUILDING. The company, still in business today, was owned by M.H.H. Davis and T.M. Funk at the time this photo was taken (between 1900 and 1910). The other laundry listed in the 1908 Business Directory belonged to Hop Lee (Chinese). The delivery wagons made daily rounds throughout Paris picking up and delivering laundry. One of the wagon drivers is identified as Homer Shy.

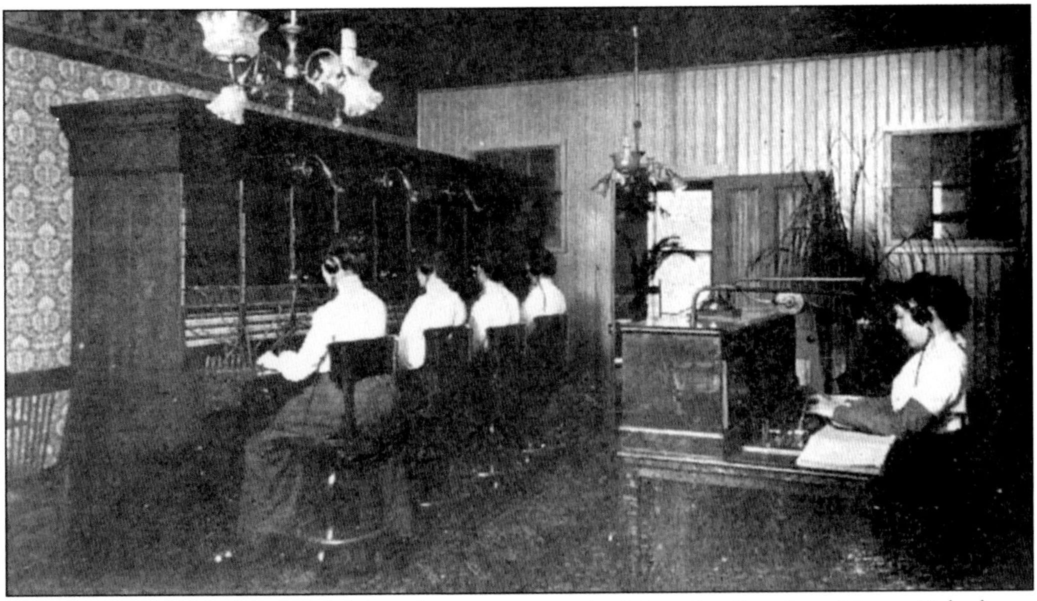

Number, Please. These switchboard operators worked for the Bourbon Home Telephone Company. The company began operations in 1902, with about 400 phones. Their advertising emphasized that they were owned "by our own home people, and we feel it is a duty that every progressive citizen owes to a home enterprise, to patronize a home industry." This emphasis pointed out the difference between the local company and their competition—the East Tennessee Telephone Company.

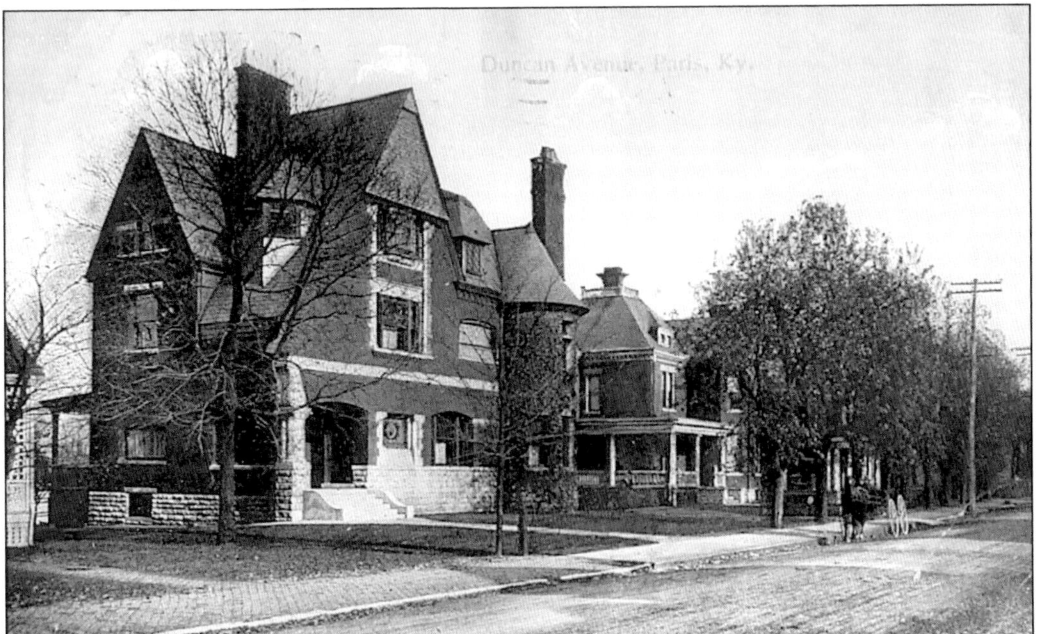

Early View of Duncan Avenue. This postcard view shows two of the substantial homes on Duncan Avenue. The 1911 postmark on the postcard places the photo around 1910. The shot looks like it was taken in the winter so the view of the houses was unobstructed, but leaves were added to some of the trees by the artists who "colorized" the black and white photo.

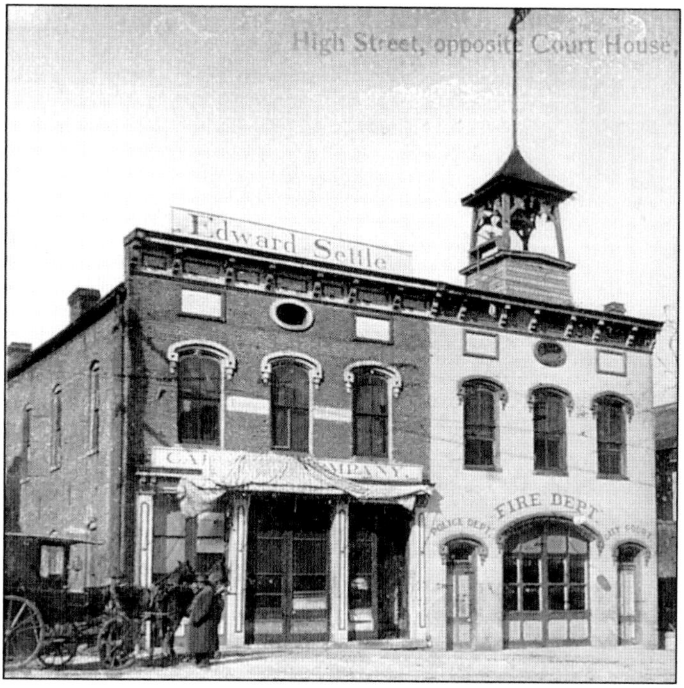

Fire Dept. Shared Double Building with Carriage Works. This photo was probably taken during the 1890s and shows the Edward Settle carriage works and the Paris fire department building. The fire department building also held the police department and the city court.The other photo on this page, taken about 1900 of the same building, does not show the lettering above the three doors on the city building seen here.

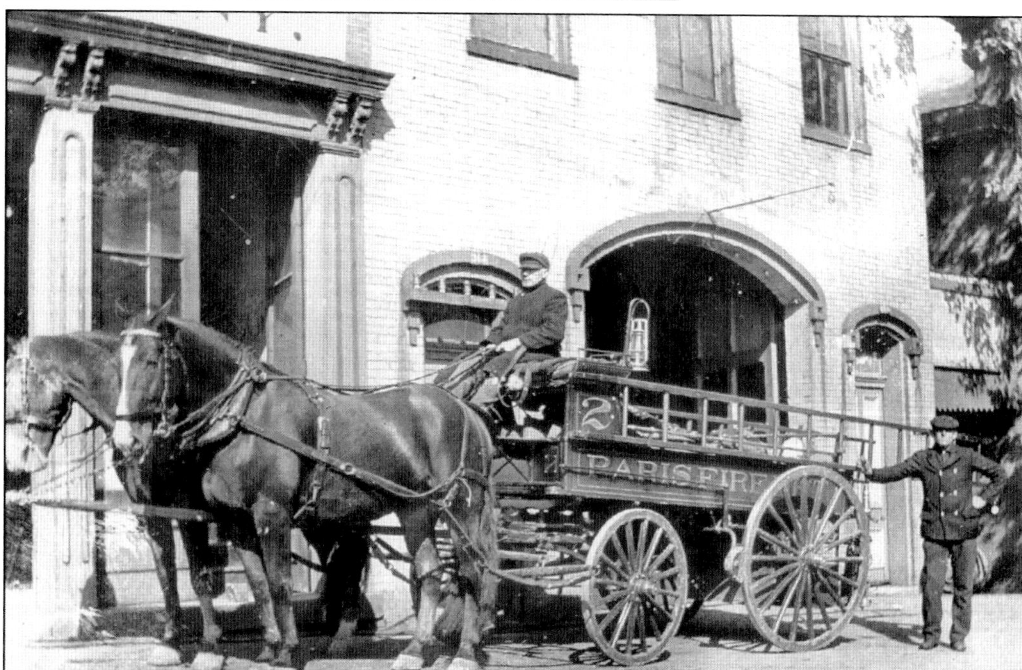

Paris Fire Company Number 2. In 1900, when this photo was taken, the Paris Fire Department had eight men and was ranked as a "part-paid" department. Their three vehicles included a horse-drawn, steam fire engine and a combination wagon that pulled a 50-gallon chemical pump. The wagon pictured would probably have been used to carry fire-fighting tools including hoses, nozzles, lanterns, wall ladders, and a roof ladder with folding hooks. (U.K. Collection.)

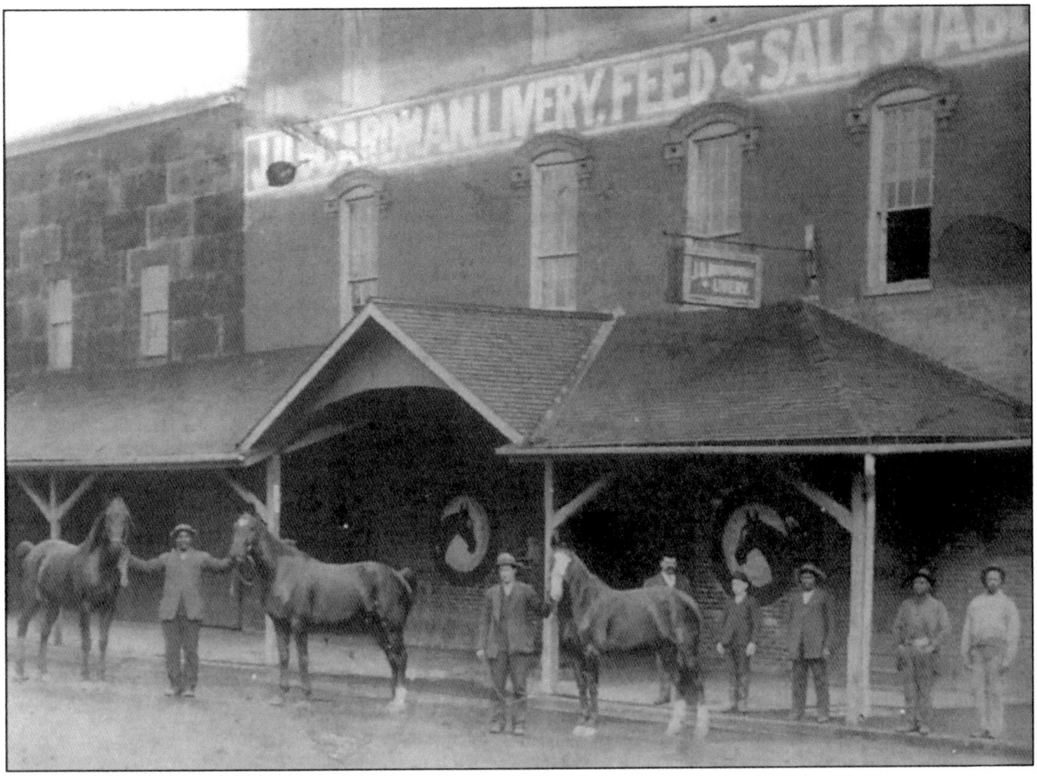

BOARDMAN'S LIVERY STABLE WAS ONE OF SEVERAL IN PARIS. This impressive building is often seen on the far side of the courthouse square in postcard views. James Uriah "Rye" Boardman was the proprietor of the establishment that advertised "Special attention given to commercial men." He is fifth from the right in this photo. It is obvious from period advertisements that commercial men (traveling salesmen) were important customers for hotels and livery stables.

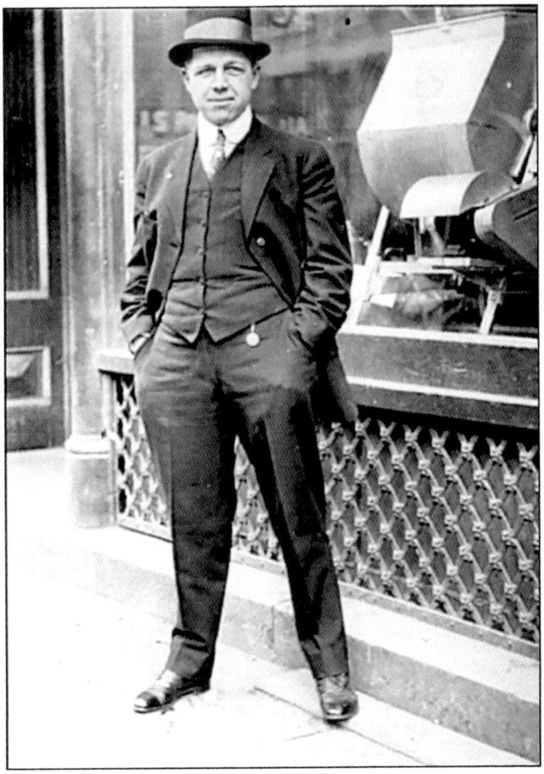

WELL-DRESSED MAN ABOUT TOWN. This photo shows C.E. Wehrung, possibly a traveling salesman in 1915, in front of the Paris Gas and Electric Company at 408 Main Street. In 1908, before electricity became more common, the business was known as the Paris Gas Light Company. In the 1908 Paris City Directory, Luke Connelly was listed under city officials as "Lamp Lighter," and was the last to hold that position.

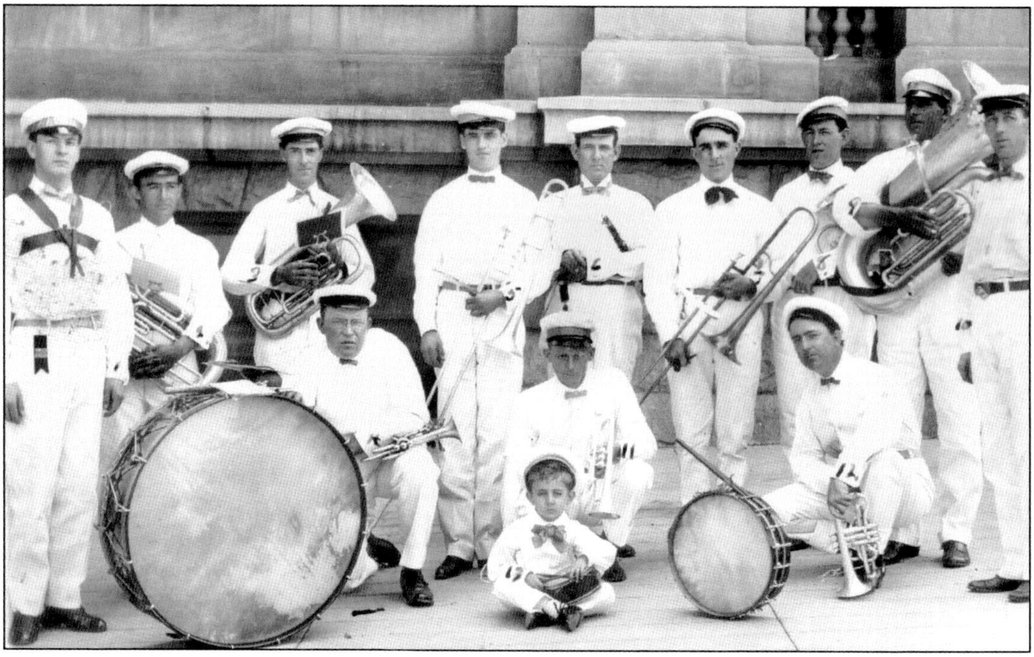

Early Paris Brass Band. This local band probably played at community events including some of the baseball games between Paris's semi-pro team, the Bourbonites, and teams from surrounding towns. Band member Dr. Ussery was a baseball expert who wrote the copy on the local team for the 1911 Spalding's Official Base Ball Guide. Those identified (not in order) are Harry Linville, Elmer Foote, Bruce Monson, Julian Howe, Dr. W.C. Ussery, and Pearce Paton (with cornet by drum). (U.K. Collection.)

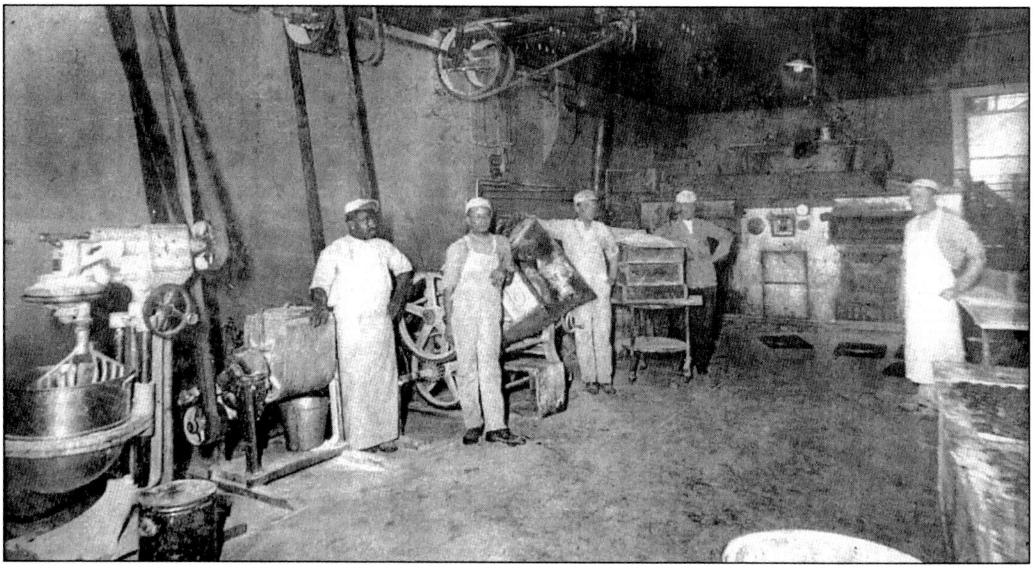

Modern Equipment Made Life Easier. This interior photo of a Paris bakery shows some of their "newfangled" equipment including huge mixers driven by belts probably run by electricity. Along the back wall are the giant ovens where the dough was magically transformed into bread—what many call "the staff of life." Although this photo was probably taken around 1905, even by 1922, there were still two bakeries in Paris.

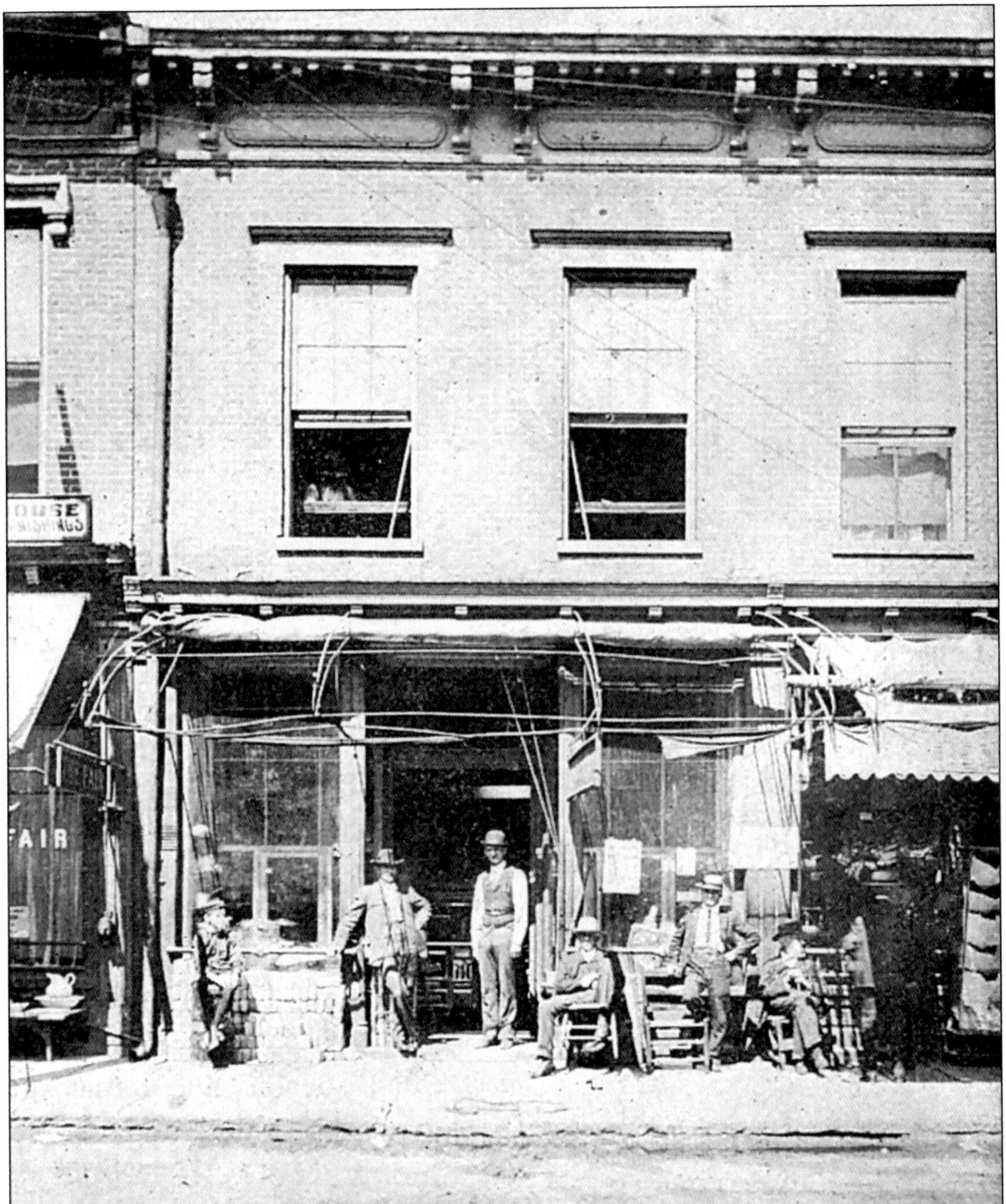

JANUARY & CONNELL SPECIALIZED IN TIN WORK OF ALL KINDS. E.B. January and Nicolas Connell established this business at 421 Main Street in 1890 and by the time this photo was taken 15 years later, had built up a prosperous establishment. They were the exclusive dealers for the Miller cooking range in Bourbon County and claimed to have sold 305 of them by July 1907. According to their billheads, the firm specialized in "tinwarc, stoves, mantles, pumps, house furnishing goods, sewer pipe, etc." and they were the largest handlers of steel ceilings in Paris. Besides selling hardware supplies, the firm worked on steel, galvanized iron and tin roofs, cornices, ceilings, and gutters. January was apprenticed to John J. Shaw at the age of 10 to learn the tinsmith's trade after both his parents died by the time he was seven. He later served as police judge for eight years before being elected mayor in 1917, a position he held for ten years.

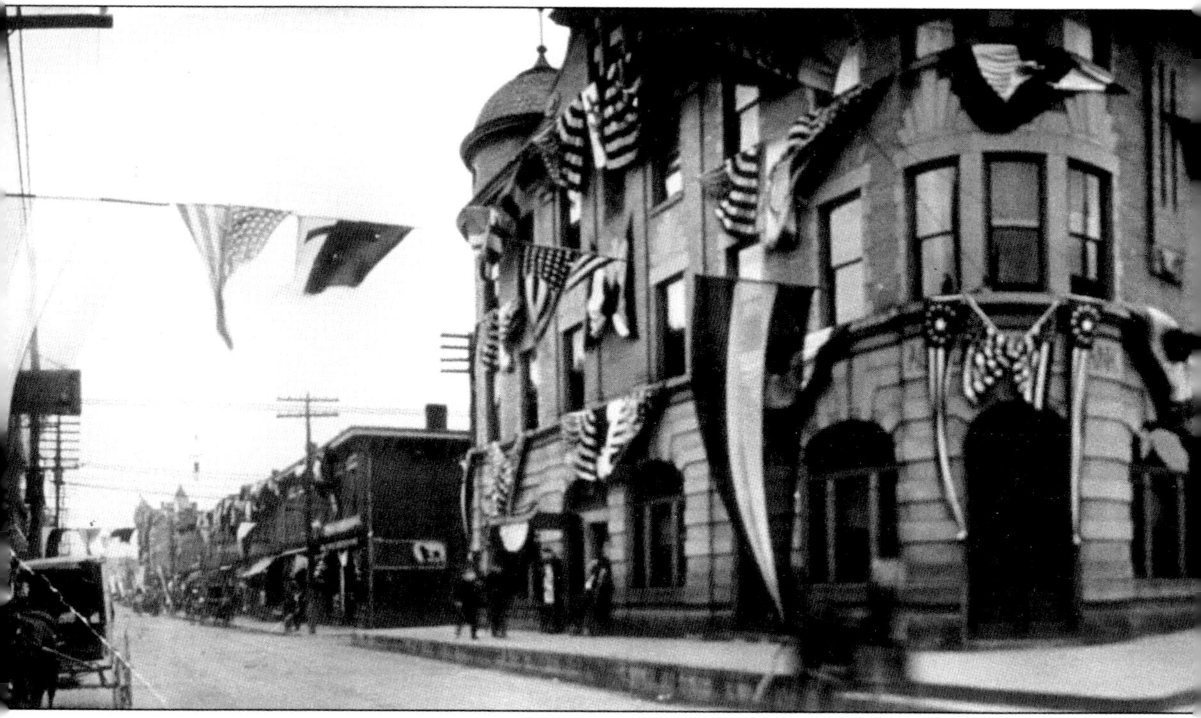

ALL DECKED OUT FOR A BIRTHDAY CELEBRATION? This wonderful shot of the Agricultural Bank building and a portion of Main Street must have been taken between 1905 and 1915. Using deductive reasoning, the authors decided that the occasion calling for all the flags was probably the county's 125th birthday, which would have been in 1910.

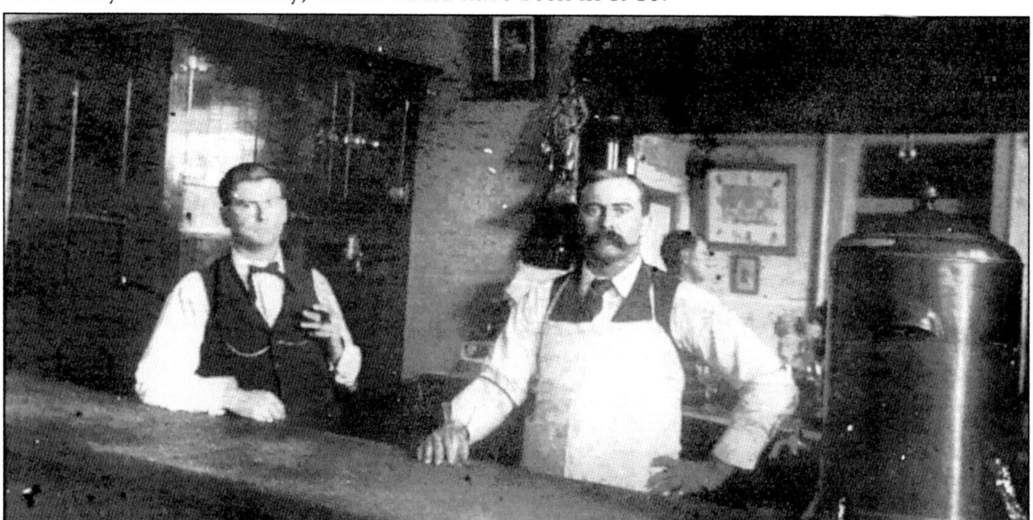

SALOONS COMMON IN PRE-PROHIBITION PARIS. There were 16 saloons in 1908 Paris, including Connelly's Saloon at 727 Main, pictured here with owner James Connelly on the right. Most saloons were like European pubs—somewhere to catch a meal, a drink, and the news of the day. Other saloon proprietors in 1908 included Malachi Flanagan, Louis Saloshin, and French Thompson, an African-American man who owned a saloon located on Main Street.

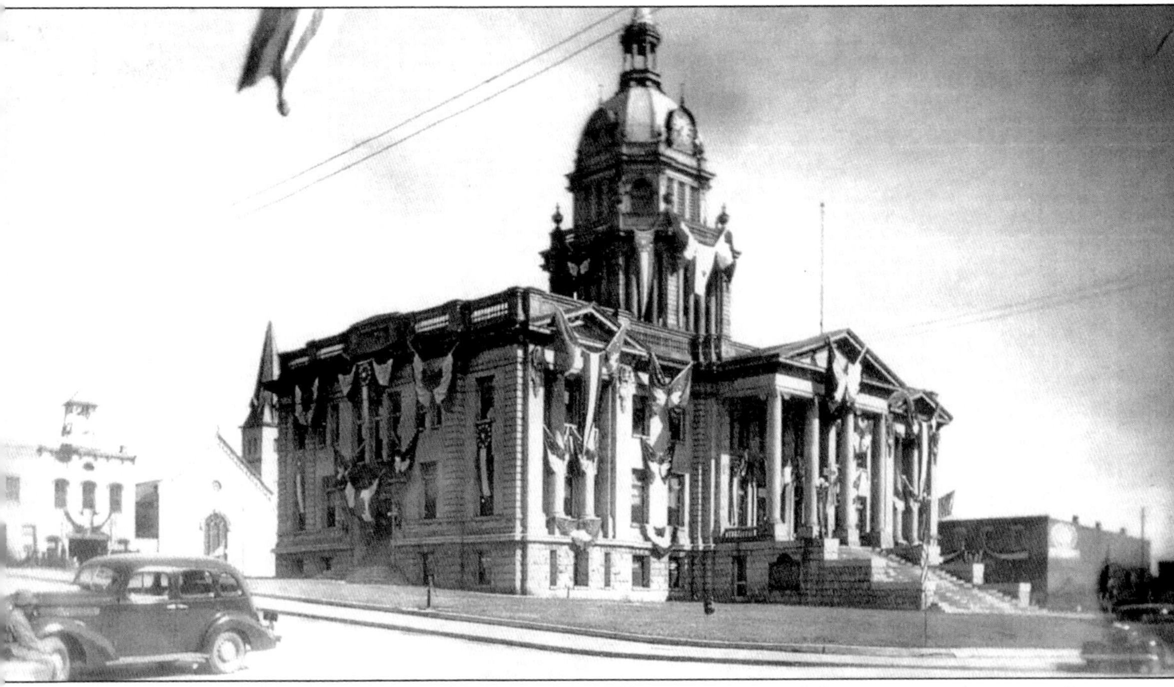

COURTHOUSE DECKED OUT IN FLAGS AND BUNTING. We are not sure of the occasion that caused the decoration of the Bourbon County Courthouse, but it may have been connected to the renovation and repaving of Main Street in 1936. Built in 1905, it has been carefully maintained and renovated and maintains most of its interior design.

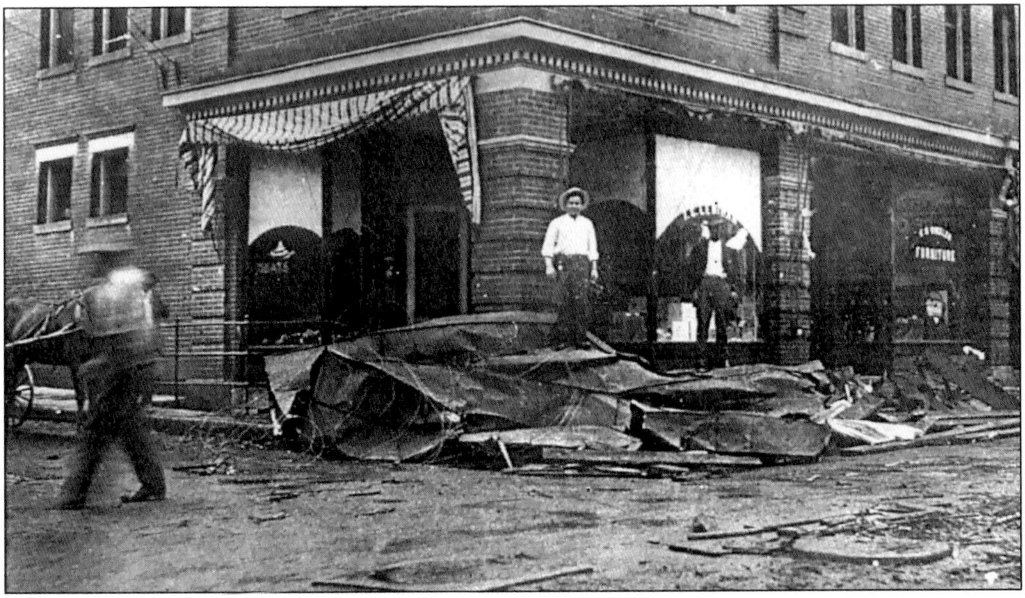

WATCH OUT FOR FLYING ROOFS! The destructive tornado that hit Paris on July 19, 1913, sent the roofs of several large buildings flying. It also changed the face of the commercial area, as many of the damaged buildings were not reconstructed. This photo shows the corner of Eighth and Main, which was then Baldwin Bros. Grocery. The debris is the roof of the original First Christian Church building, which stood opposite the grocery.

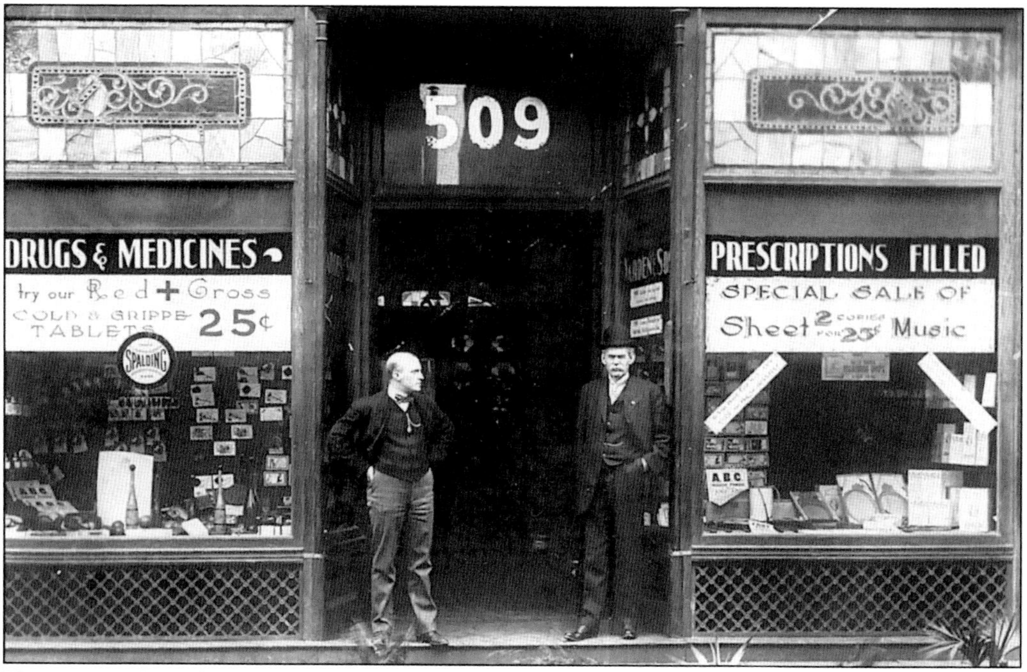

VARDEN & SON OFFERED A WIDE SELECTION OF GOODS. Jo S. Varden (left) and Dr. George Varden are shown in front of their Main Street store in the 1920s. As seen in the window displays, the main business of the store was "Drugs and Medicines" and "Prescriptions Filled." However, much more was available including paint, varnish, snuff, fly paper, rock candy, sheet music, guitar strings, and a myriad of other items.

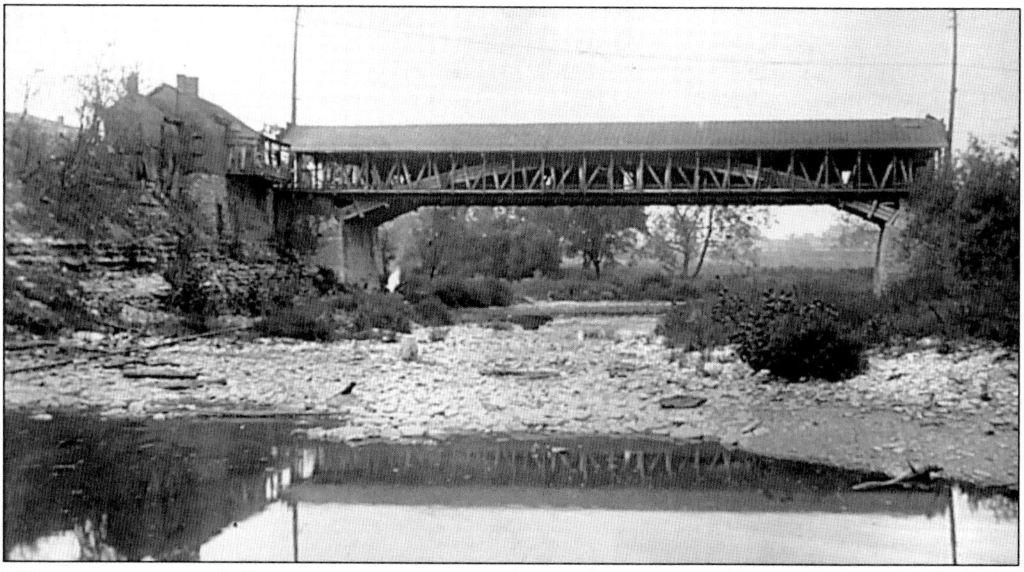

"DOUBLE-BARRELED" COTTONTOWN COVERED BRIDGE LASTED 100 YEARS. Serving to link the Main Street business district and the "Cottontown" section off east Main where several mills and other industries were located, this bridge carried vehicular traffic in two separated lanes and featured a pedestrian footbridge. This 1890 photo shows the bridge when the siding had been removed to allow repairs. The bridge, built in 1833, was torn down in 1933.

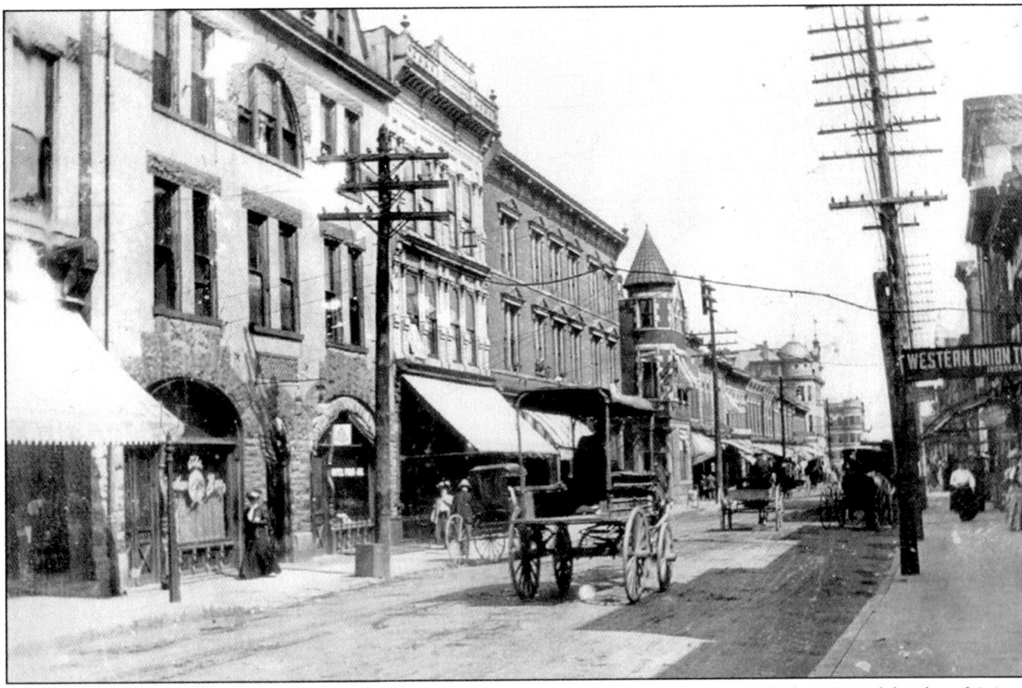

Delivery Wagon Driving by the Fordham Hotel. This photo of the 500 block of Main Street taken in 1909, shows a very busy thoroughfare, including an interesting-looking delivery wagon in the foreground. The wagon is passing between the Fordham Hotel on the left and the Western Union Telegraph office. In the days before telephones were common, sending a telegram was often the only way to reach someone quickly. (U.K. Collection.)

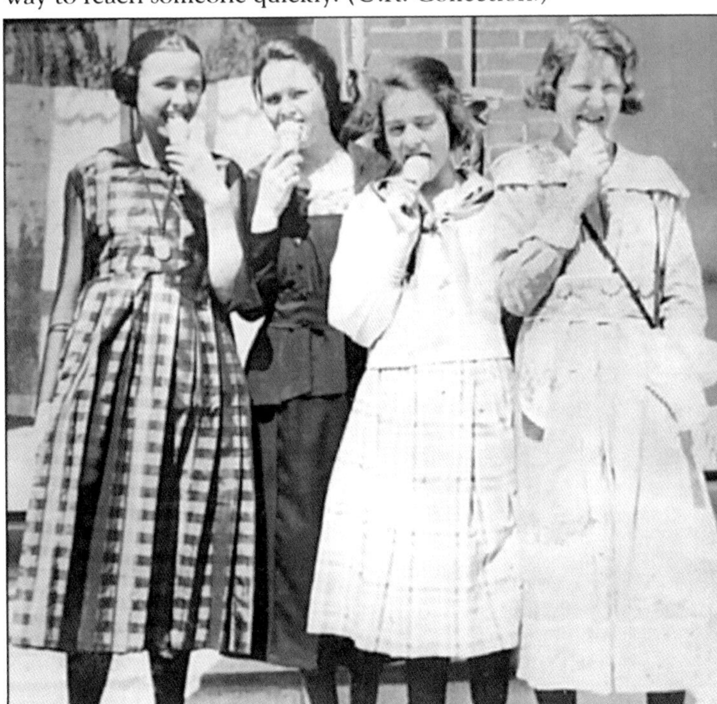

Ice Cream Cone or a Fancy Ice? Whichever it was, the four girls seem to be enjoying them and each other's company. There were "confectionery" stores on Main Street for many decades, including Spikes Confectionery, Alex's Place that offered "excellent soda fountain service," and Benedetti & Co. Confectionery which featured "pure, wholesome and delicious ices and drinks."

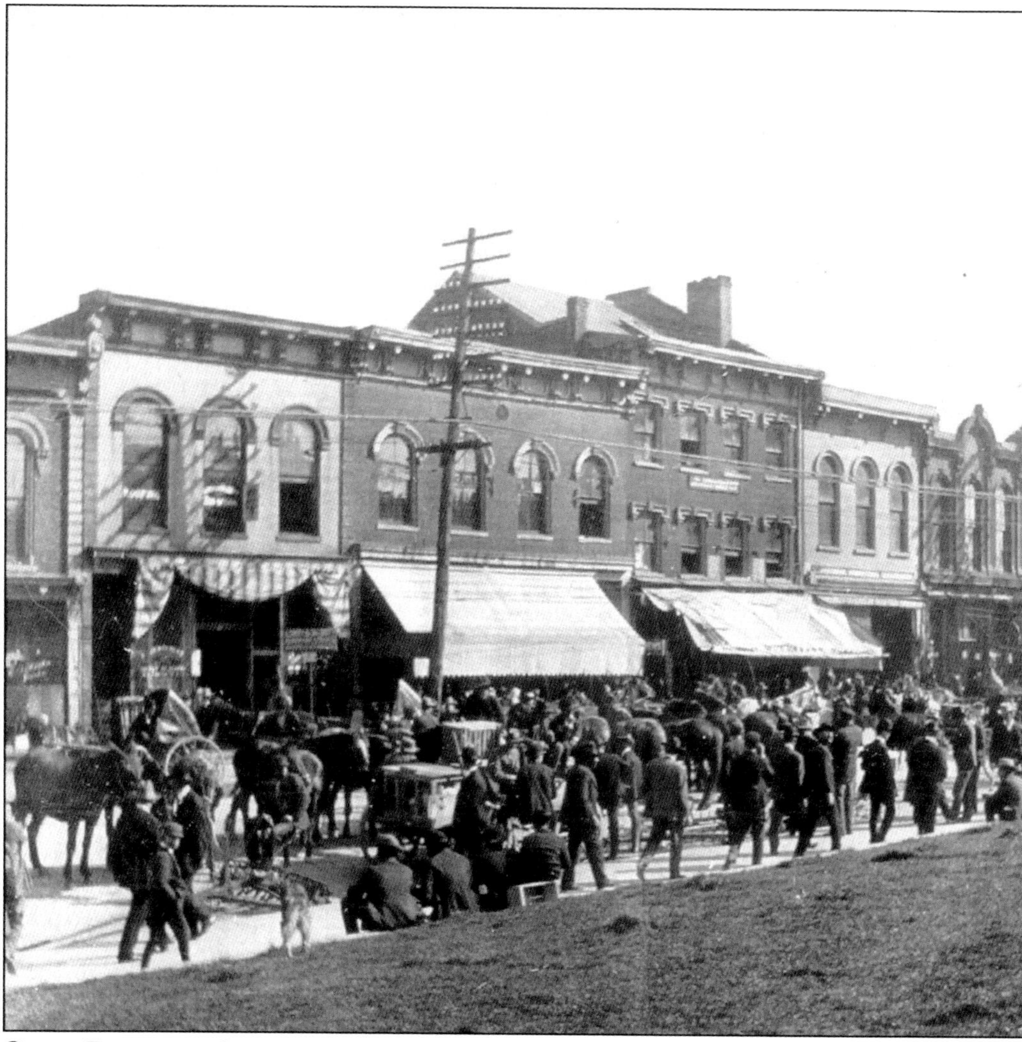

Court Days were Opportunities for Local Farmers. This court day photo was taken from the vantage point of the front lawn of the courthouse. It shows a part of the busy scene that would have taken place when local farmers and livestock producers brought horses, mules, and other livestock for sale. As can be seen from this photo, the crowd was almost exclusively male—of all ages and skin colors. Even those who did not have anything to buy or sell could gossip with their neighbors and trade tips on what crops were doing best and who had the fastest horses. One would imagine that local shopkeepers also took advantage of the crowds of men to sell their wares. (U.K. Collection.)

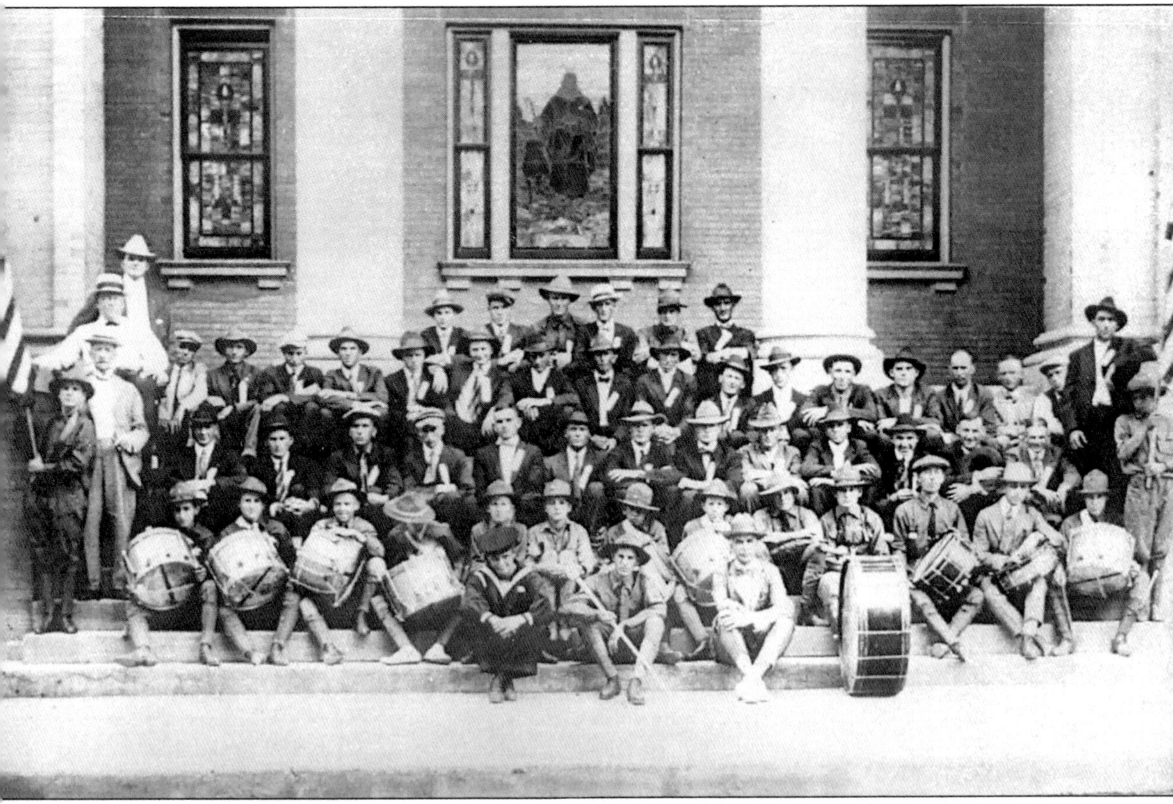

Bourbon Countians Going Off to War in 1918. World War I stirred up a great deal of patriotic zeal in Bourbon County and more than 1,500 men, black, and white volunteered to help defeat the "Huns." Almost 800 Bourbon Countians served in some branch of the military during this period and 22 men died. The group pictured above on July 17, 1918 was a group of 46 volunteers on their way to Fort Knox for training and were probably one of the last groups of local volunteers as the war ended just four months later. A large group of citizens, community leaders and the Roxie David Drum and Bugle Corps reportedly gave this group a rousing send off. The men are shown sitting on the steps of the First Baptist Church on Main Street.

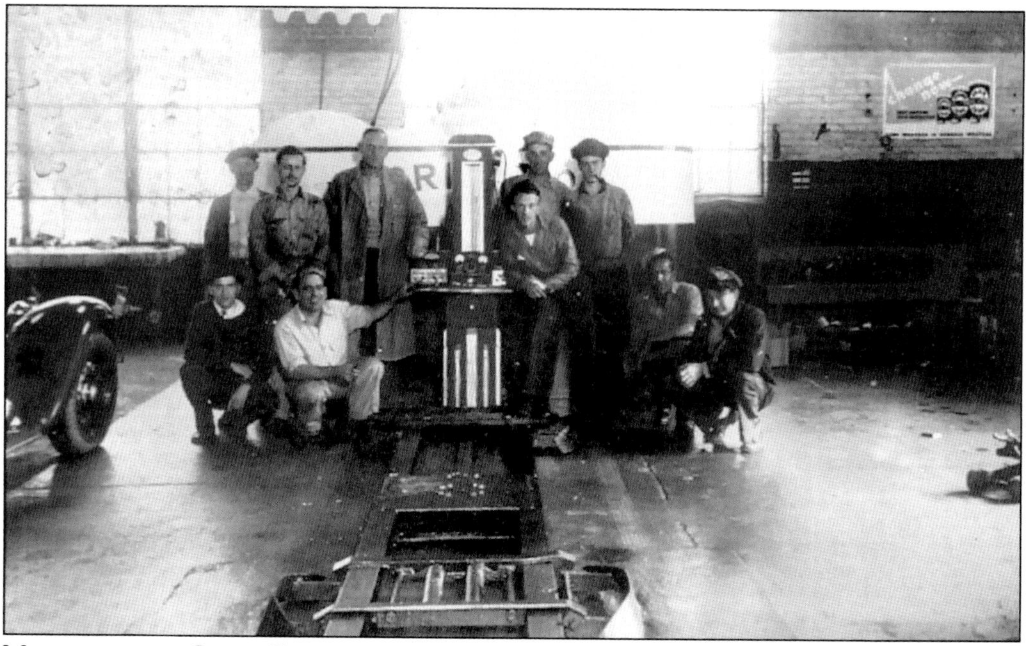

MECHANICS AND OTHER EMPLOYEES OF WORICK BROS. GARAGE. This photo was taken in 1939 and shows the interior of a portion of the Worick Bros. Garage, which used to stand at one corner of Main and Second. Worick Bros. was also the official Dodge dealer in Paris from 1924 to 1948. The Worick Bros. building was constructed in 1922 and was known for the built-in swastika decorations along the front, obviously chosen well before World War II.

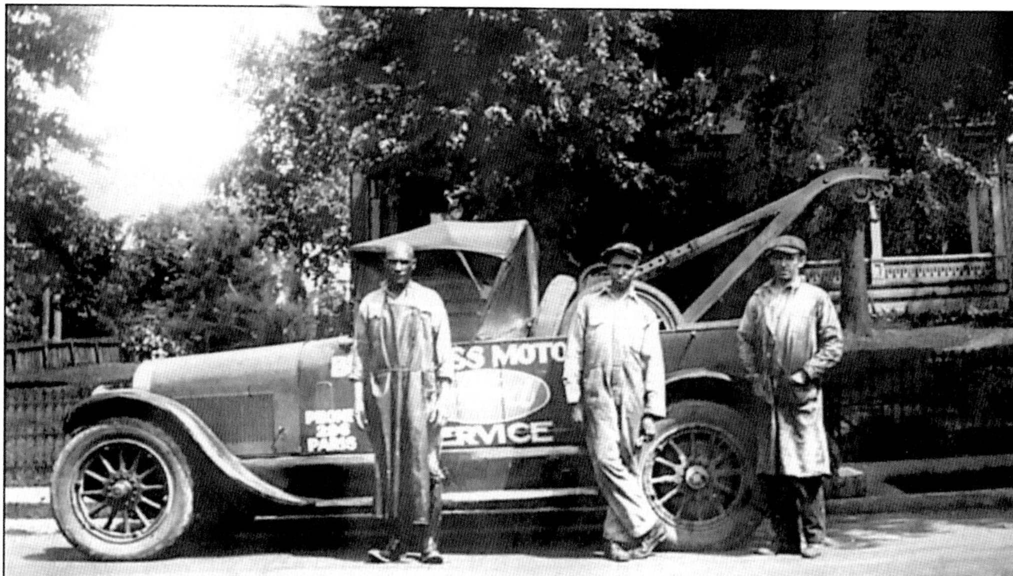

1920S FORD GARAGE TOW TRUCK AND CREW. When your Ford broke down in the 1920s, you would call the Ford Garage, also known as Bluegrass Motor Service. The crew, which consisted of Mitch (last name unknown), Marion Owens, and Rollie Mains, would show up to tow your car in for service. This tow truck is a modified early Ford that would be worth a pretty penny today. Note the three digit phone number—Paris 296.

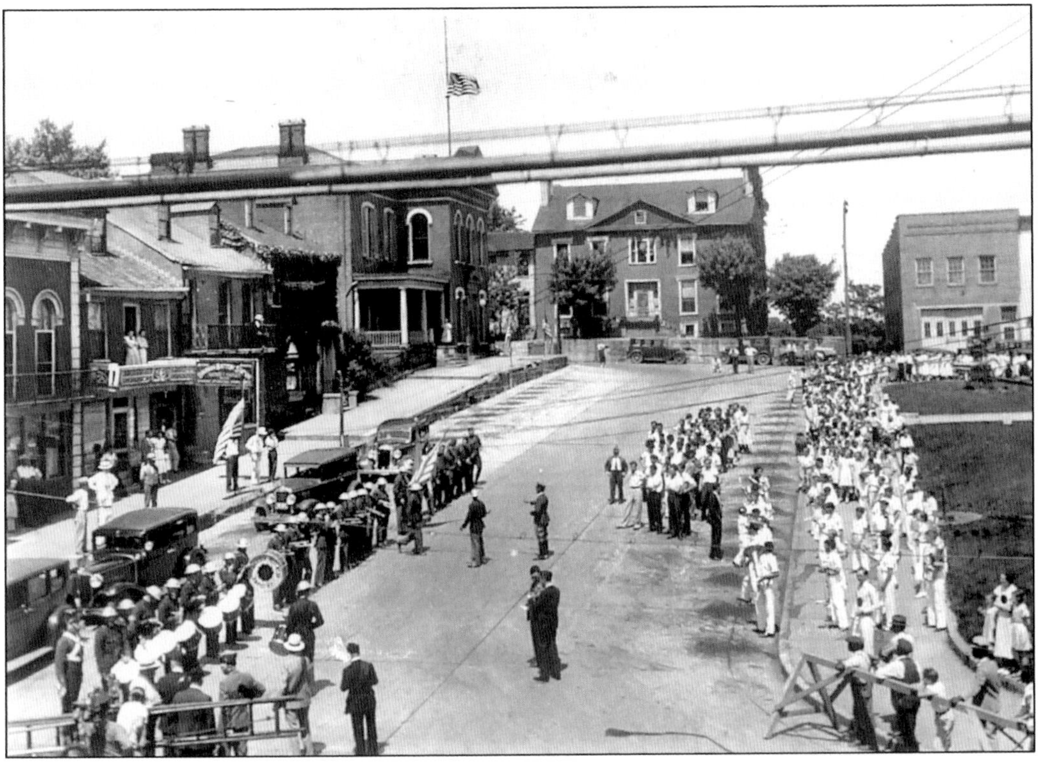

Marching to Remember Veterans. This Memorial Day parade held on May 30, 1933 formed up along Broadway (now known as Ardery Place)—scene of countless other parades and gatherings. The American Legion band from the Paris post can be seen lining up in the street while what looks like a high school band (in white) waits on the sidewalk.

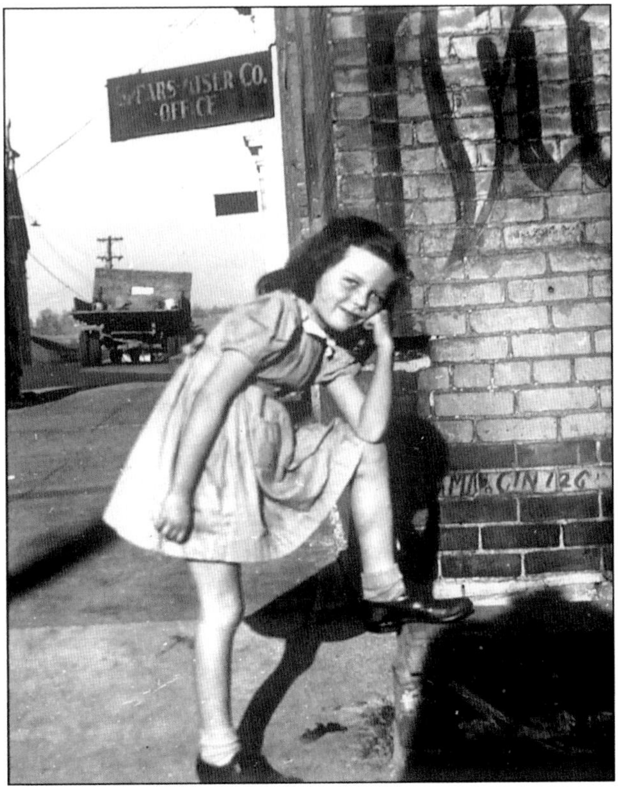

"Cutie-Pie" on High Street. Young V.G. Royce struck a pose in the late 1930s in front of a feed store and the Spears-Kiser Co. office located on the corner of Fourth and High Streets. High Street and other commercial areas like Main and Pleasant Streets were denser before the 1940s because buildings destroyed by fire or other disasters were replaced by another building and not a parking lot, as is usually the case today.

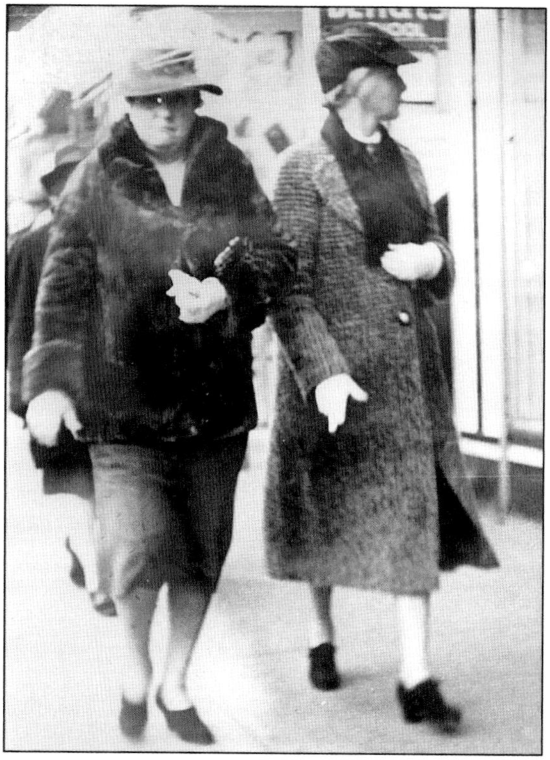

DRESSED TO SHOP. Going out for a day of shopping downtown was once an occasion for getting dressed up. Adorned in hats and white gloves are Mrs. Julian Frank Sr. (left) and Mrs. Dave C. Parrish Sr. seen in this photograph taken around 1940. Nowadays, shopping at Wal-Mart is just not a dressy event and finding white gloves would be a difficult task.

WOMEN'S EXCHANGE OFFERED HOME-BAKED FOODS. This photo shows a portion of the interior of the Women's Exchange, which was located at 719 Main Street. The business was famous for the home-baked treats like cakes, pies, and bread that were featured in the shop's window. The business also carried country cottage cheese, cream, and butter furnished by local women as well as a wide variety of gift items, many of which are pictured here.

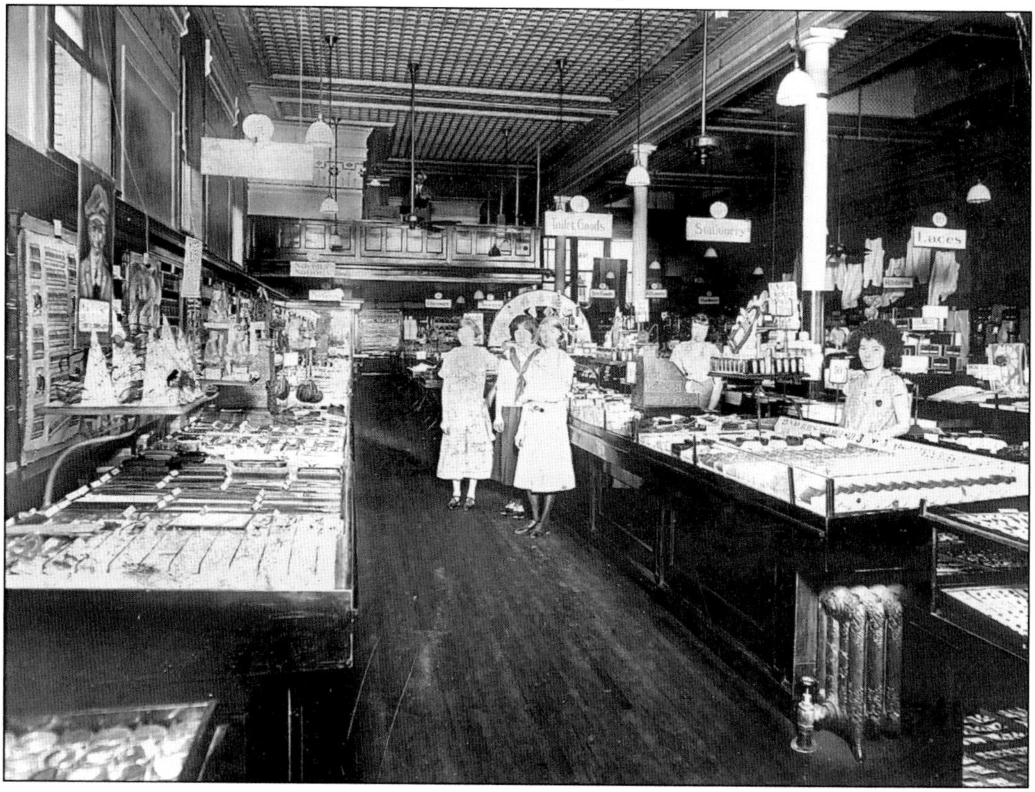

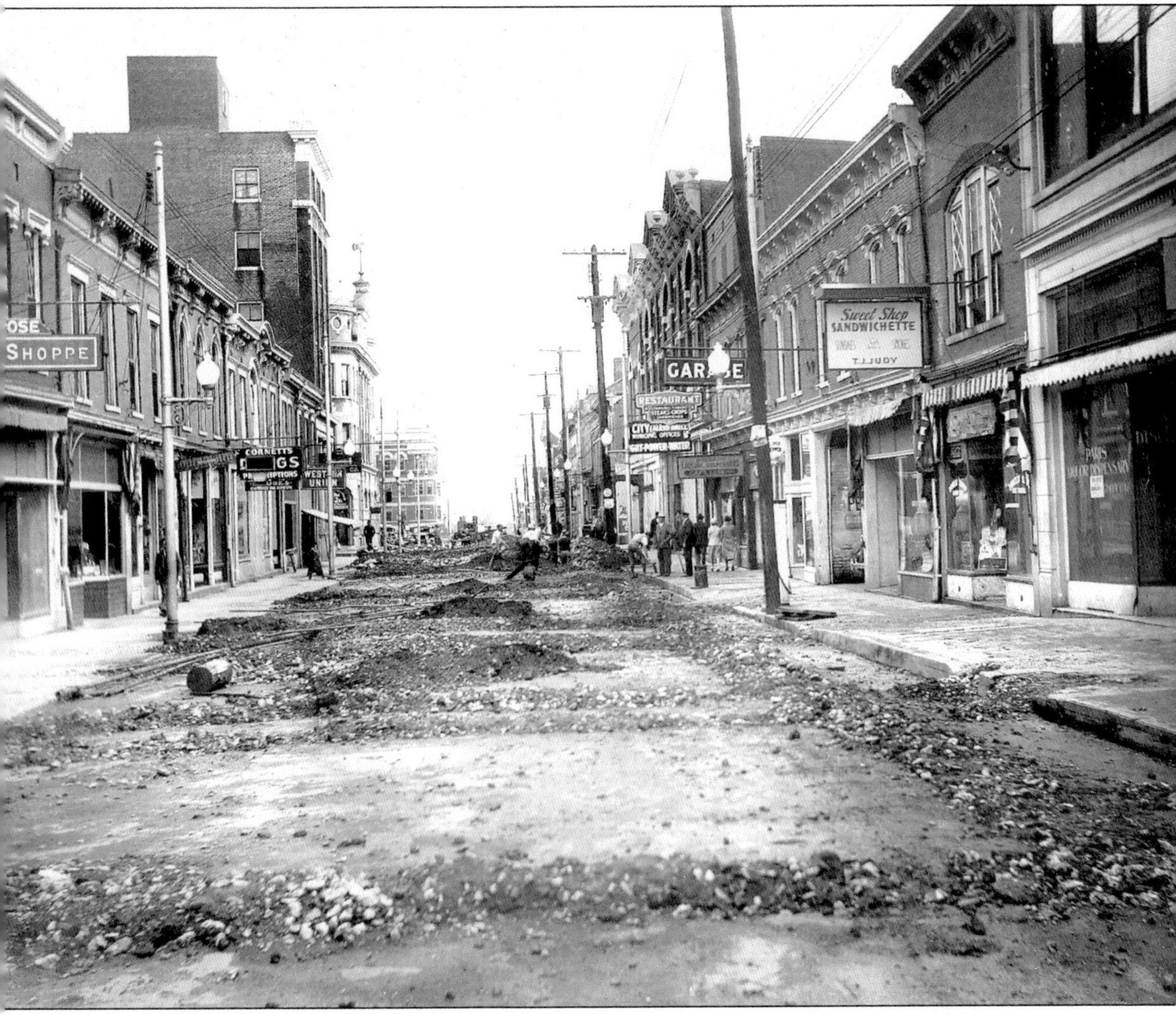

1936 Main Street Mess. Even though the street itself looks awful as the old blacktop is removed so that smooth new concrete can be laid down, the commercial vitality is unmistakable with no empty stores to be seen on the 400 block in this photo taken in 1936. The businesses with visible signs include the Sweet Shop Sandwichette featuring shakes and smokes; a garage with a drive-through from Main Street to Pleasant Street; the Liquor Dispensary; the Municipal Light, Power and Water office; Western Union; Cornetts Drug Store (also selling domestic and imported liquors) and Alex's Grill offering steaks and chops. Gov. A.B. "Happy" Chandler came to Paris that November to lead the annual Armistice Day parade down the newly repaired Main Street.

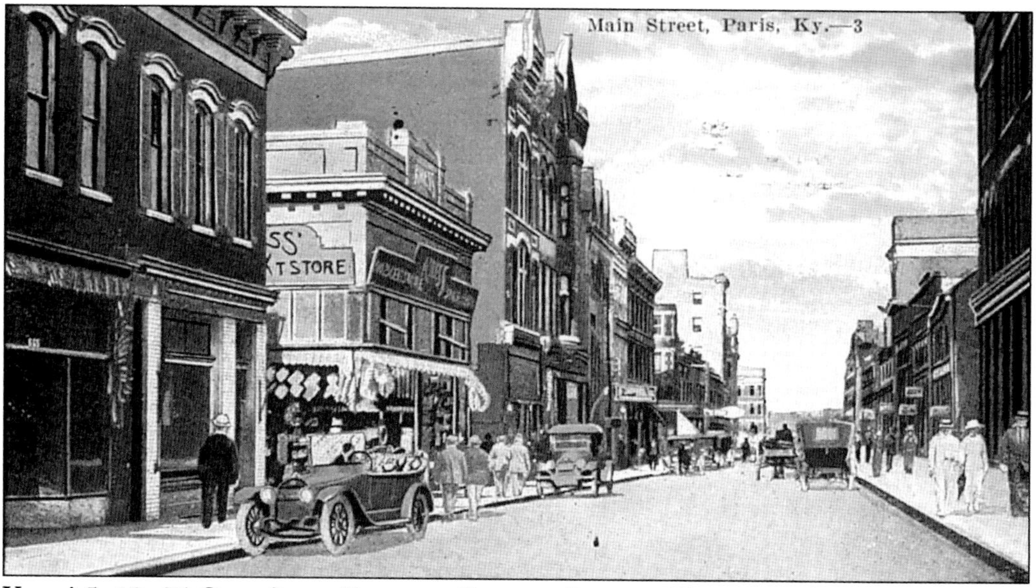

KRESS' 5, 10, 25 CENT STORE REPLACED BAPTIST CHURCH. The store, which offered a wider price range than the "five and dimes," replaced the Baptist Church near the corner of Sixth and Main that can be seen in the photo that opens this chapter. The building was destroyed by fire and was replaced by a gas station—another sign that the reign of the horse was over and the automobile was king.

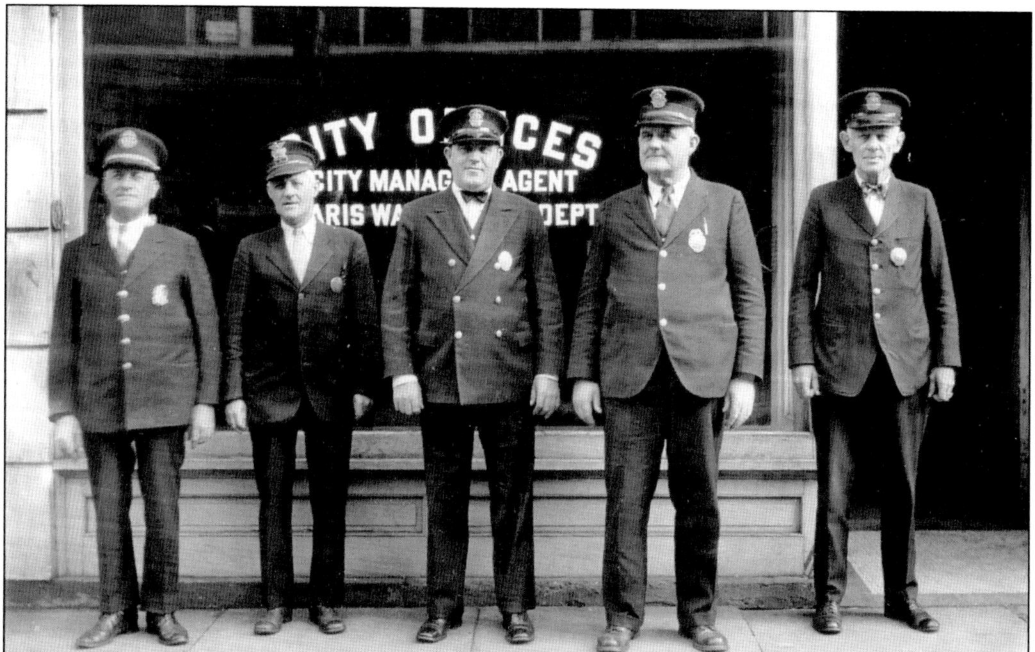

FIVE FIREMEN IN FRONT OF CITY OFFICE. This 1933 photo was taken in front of the city office located in the 400 block of Main Street. The men from left to right are Jonny Neal, Bud Lancaster, Pat "Cokie" Quinlan, Cannon Williams, and unidentified. The city manager or managing agent, whose title is shown on the window behind the firemen, was Boone Baldwin. He served in that position for more than 20 years. (U.K. Collection.)

Two

Country Living and Small Towns

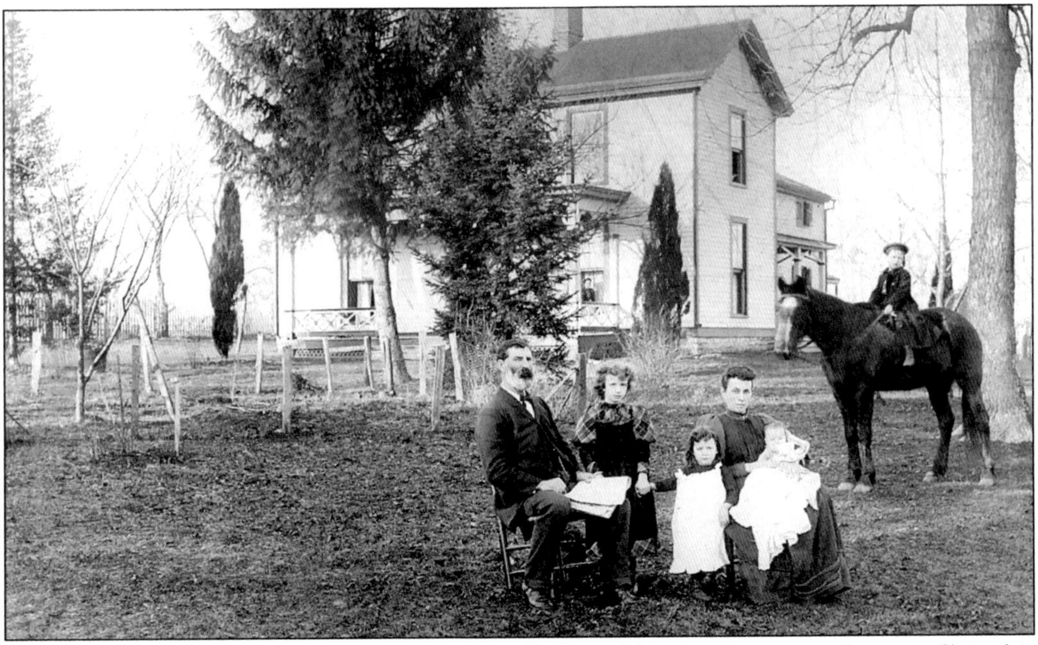

County Living Idealized. George Wyatt Sr. (left) and his family seem to have it all in this photo taken in 1893–1894. Their home was a large country dwelling with plenty of room for trees, horses, and a growing family. Pictured with Mr. Wyatt are (from left to right) Martha Wyatt, Louise Wyatt, Mrs. George Wyatt holding Mary Belle Wyatt, and George Jr. on the horse. We do not have any information on the older lady seen in the window behind the children. The house, located near Shawhan in the northern part of the county, is known as the Fleming R. Wyatt House. The earliest part of the structure was built in 1830 while the Italianate central section was added in 1880. George Sr. was a successful farmer and part owner of a distillery near Shawhan.

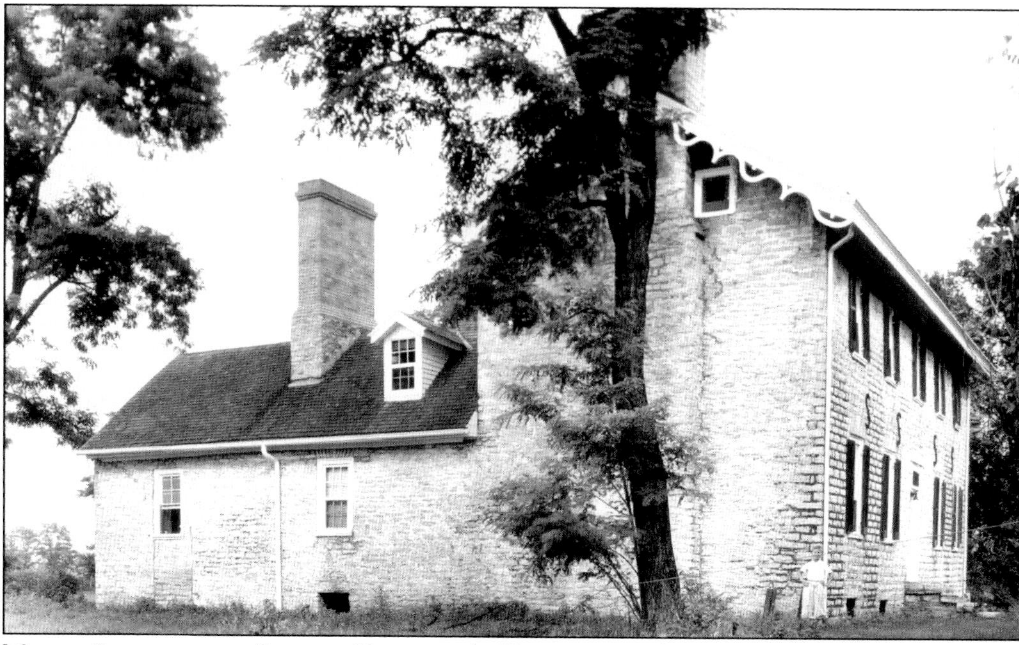

Mount Lebanon was Second Governor's Home. Located about three miles north of Paris on Peacock Road is this historic stone home known as Mount Lebanon. It was built in 1785–1786 by Thomas Metcalf for James Garrard, who was Kentucky's second governor. Garrard was elected in 1796 and 1800, the only governor to serve successive terms until Paul Patton. Bourbon County's first county court was held here on May 16, 1786. (U.K. Collection.)

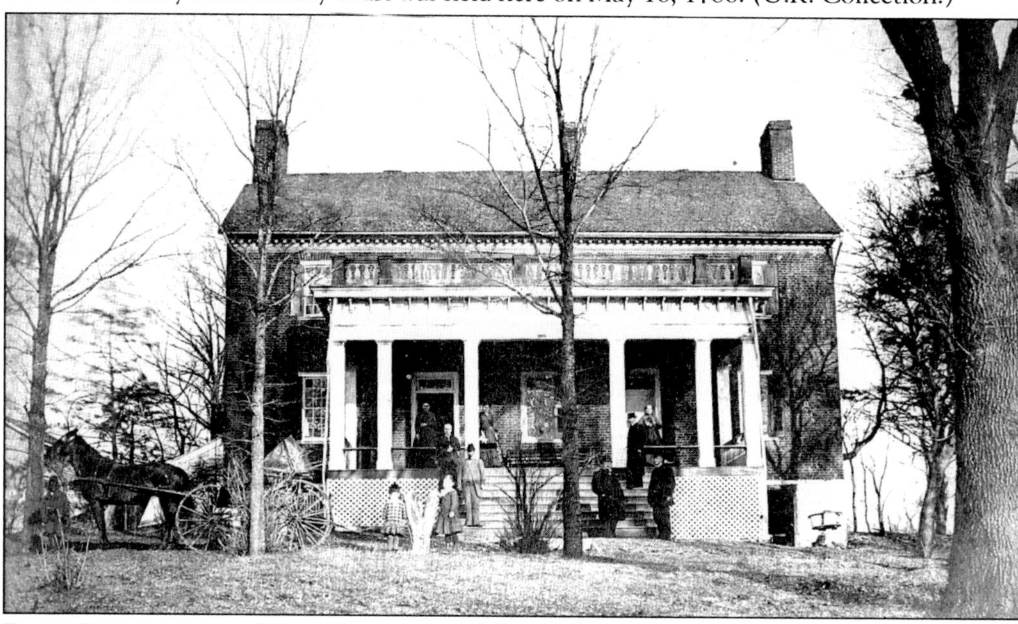

Early Photo of the Reed-Hutchcraft House. This photo, probably taken in the early 1870s, shows members of the James Hutchcraft family at their home on the Paris-Winchester Road. The impressive brick house was built in the early 1780s for John Reed, one of the early millers in the area. James Hutchcraft acquired the house about 1830. One of his 13 children was the well-known artist Hattie Hutchcraft Hill (1847–1921).

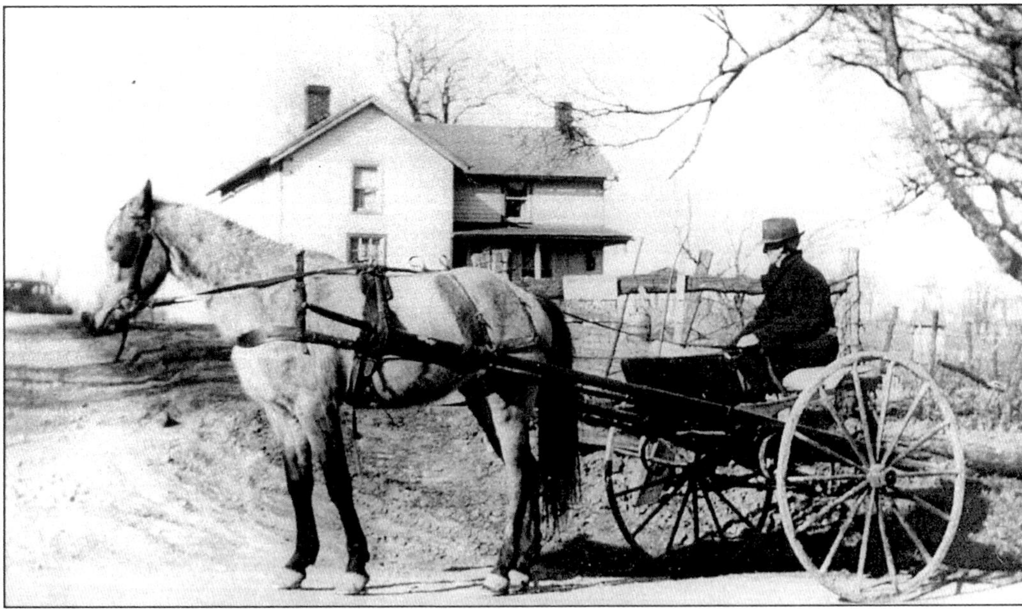

Not Exactly the Pony Express. Larry Buchanan delivered mail in the Clintonville area for 28 years, beginning in 1930. Buchanan never missed a delivery in 28 years. Buchanan took over the route from his father, who delivered mail on the same rural route for 40 years. The free delivery of mail began in the rural areas in 1896 and mail was delivered six days a week, including holidays.

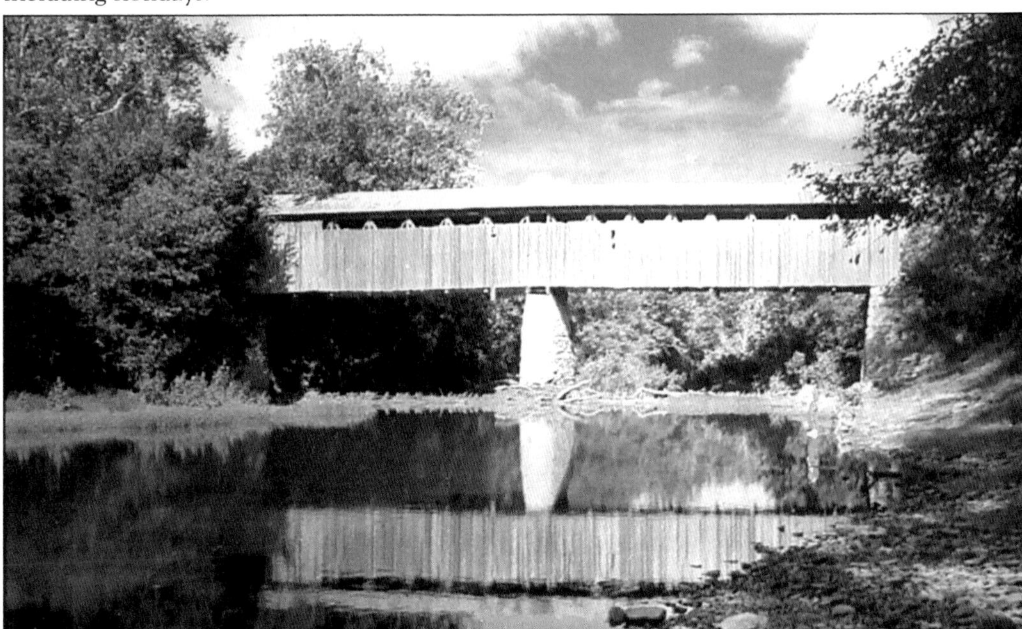

Covered Bridge at Ruddles Mills. This bridge, known as Skinner Bridge, crossed Stoner Creek at Ruddles Mills near Shawhan. At one time more than 400 covered wooden bridges could be found in Kentucky, but most have been destroyed by fire (as this one was in 1964) or left to rot, leaving 13 still standing in 1990. The bridges were covered to protect the complex wooden trusses from the weather.

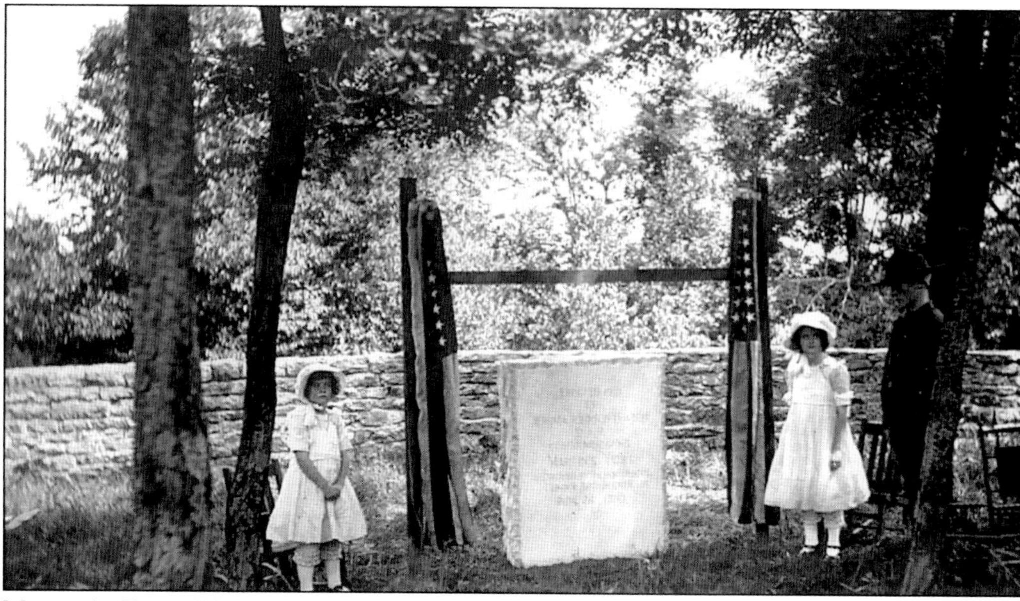

MARTIN'S FORT MARKER DEDICATED IN 1921. John Martin, one of Kentucky's earliest settlers, established a stockade on Stoner Creek in 1779 that attracted a number of pioneer families who settled nearby. In the spring of 1780, a force of British soldiers and their Native American allies threatened the fort with artillery and took the inhabitants captive. Pictured at the 1921 monument dedication are Mary and Ann Clay, daughters of Mr. and Mrs. Brutus Clay.

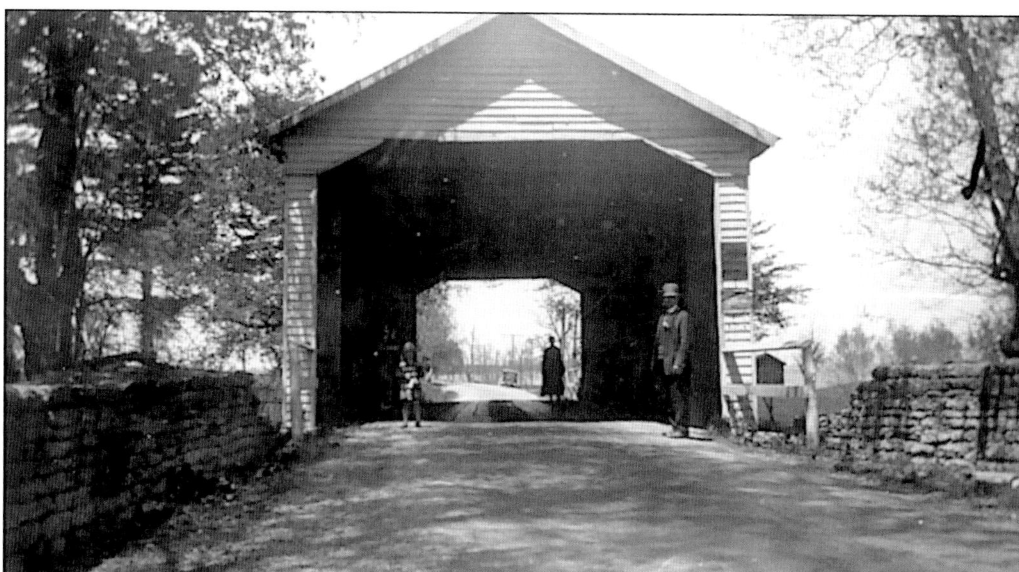

COVERED BRIDGE OVER STRODES CREEK. In 1902, this bridge was one of 15 covered bridges in the county and one of three on Thatcher's Mill Road. At the same time, Bourbon County listed 40 iron bridges. The Colville covered bridge, built in 1877 in the northern part of the county, was the only remaining covered span in the county by 1970. Notice the three figures in the photo, most likely a family group.

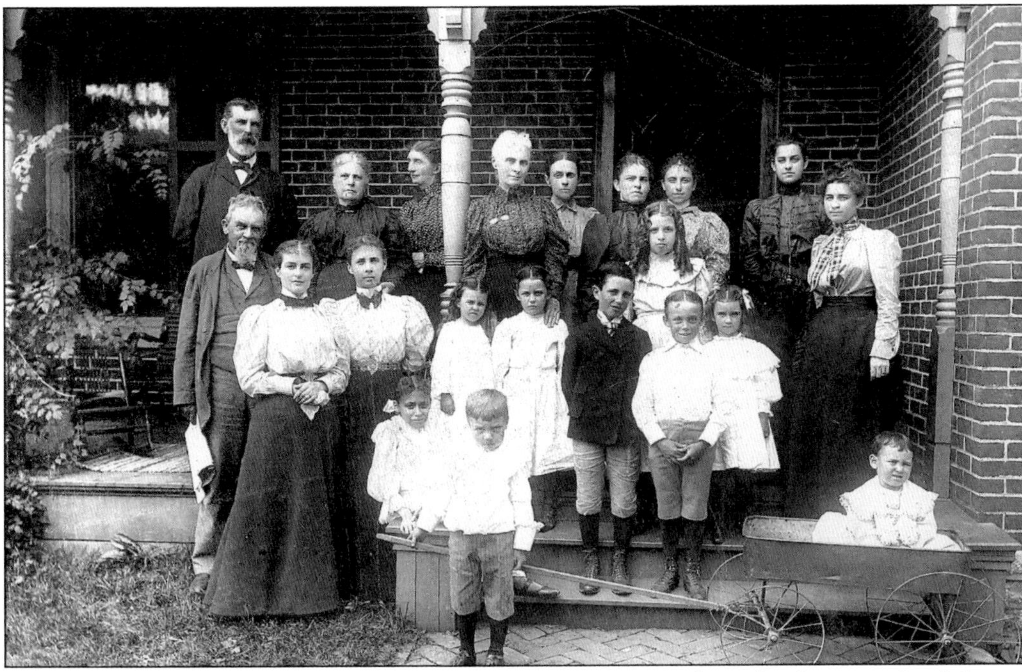

PORTRAIT OF EXTENDED FAMILY TAKEN ABOUT 1900. Pictured on the front porch of George Wyatt's home on North Middletown Road are, from left to right, (first row) Belle Palmer McClintock, Edgar Dodge and Bryan Davis in wagon; (second row) Lula Honaker Hedges, Kate McClintock, Mary Belle Wright, Louise Wyatt, George Wyatt Jr., Irvin Keller, and Margaret Davis; (third row) David Dodge, Martha Fleming Wyatt, and Carrie Davis; (fourth row) George Wyatt, Lucy Bowen, Rebekka Dodge, Lou Palmer, Mary Wyatt, Callie Keller, Lucy Dodge, and Lucy Keller Frank.

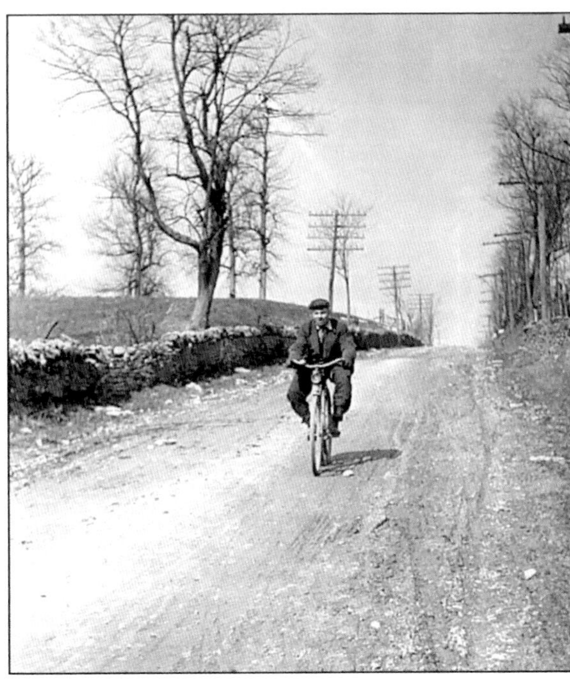

BICYCLIST ON THE NORTH MIDDLETOWN ROAD. Just 10 years after posing for the other picture on this page, the teenaged Edgar "Smiley" Dodge is seen riding on the dusty North Middletown Road. In 1910 he did not have to worry too much about speeding vehicles as he could probably travel faster than anyone else on the road that day—especially going downhill.

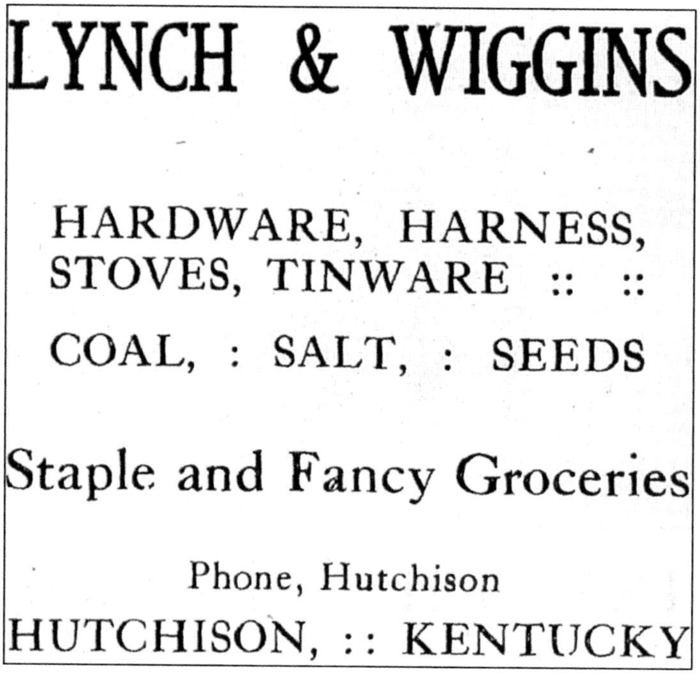

HUTCHISON—ONCE A BUSTLING VILLAGE. Nestled around the Hutchison train station, which served the Cincinnati and Frankfort Railroad, was a village that included at least two businesses by 1908—M.R. Jacoby's, selling all types of grain as well as wheat, corn, and grass seed, and Lynch & Wiggins (ad seen here). Local residents could ride the train into Paris or Lexington and ship their goods with ease before the C&F closed down.

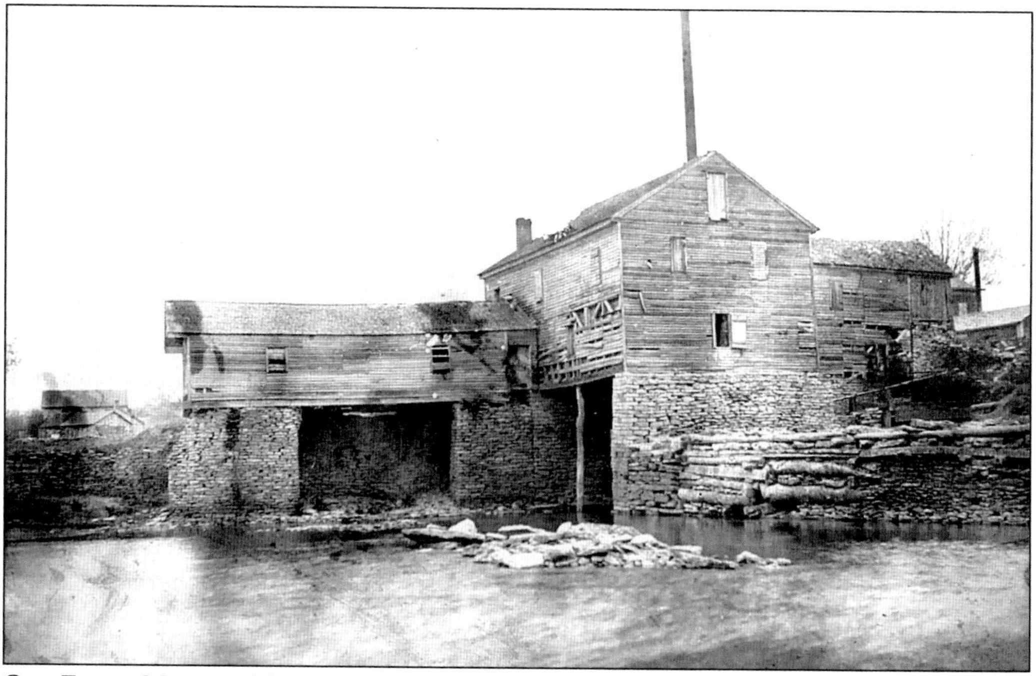

OLD FLOUR MILL AT MILLERSBURG. This flour mill on Hinkston Creek in Millersburg was already beginning to deteriorate around 1902 when this photo was taken. Mills located along the county's many watercourses played a major role in the growth of Bourbon County. As early as 1798, they provided a way to utilize wheat, corn, and other products produced on local farms. In the mid-19th century, Millersburg had several prosperous mills on Hinkston Creek.

CHAS. M. MASON, SUCCESSFUL GROCER. Mr. Mason (seated) owned a successful grocery store near the post office on Fifth Street in Millersburg in 1905. He advertised "Keeps on hand at all times a varied assortment of Staple, Fancy and Green Groceries. Fish and Oysters in Season." He also boasted that he had Paris Milling Co.'s flour "always in stock." Upon close inspection of this photograph, the authors saw that Mr. Mason had only one leg.

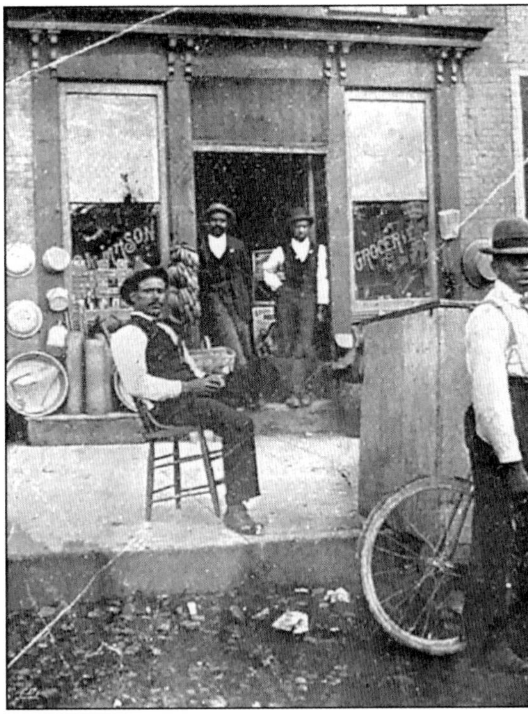

MAPLEWOOD, BUILT IN 1850. This grand antebellum house is found on the northern side of Millersburg and was built for John Clark Miller, grandson of Maj. John Miller, the founder of Millersburg. An early and prominent family in the area, the Millers accumulated much of their wealth by operating mills and distilleries along Hinkston Creek. A later descendant, William M. Layson, named the house "Maplewood."

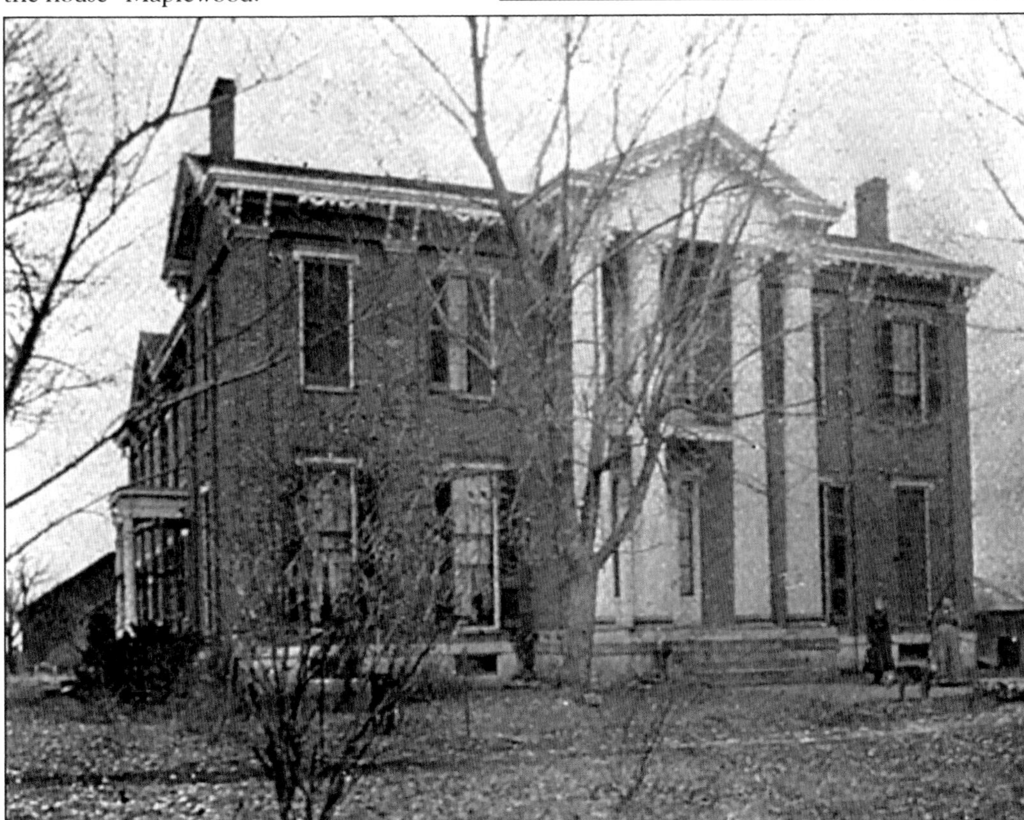

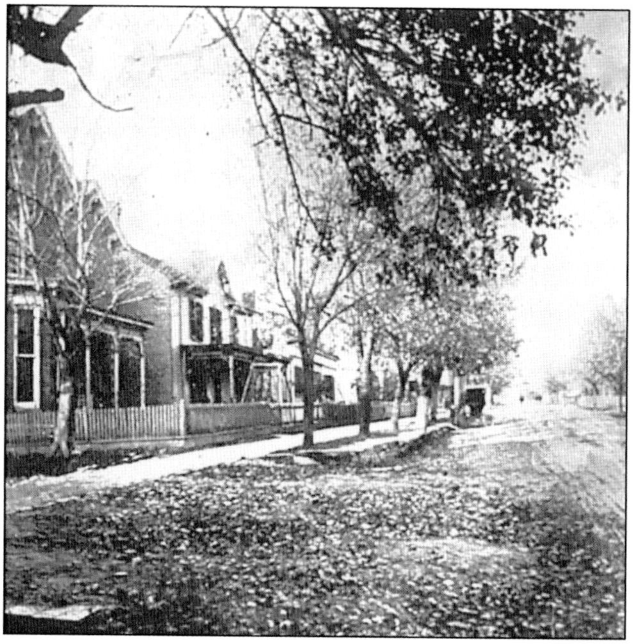

Tree-lined Downtown Millersburg. At the beginning of the 20th century, when transportation was slower and time away from the family farm was limited, small towns like Millersburg were commercial and social hubs for people a carriage ride away. The stores along the tree-lined Main Street were busy throughout the week. No one imagined going to a single "super store" or traveling all the way to Lexington to shop for groceries, and everyday needs.

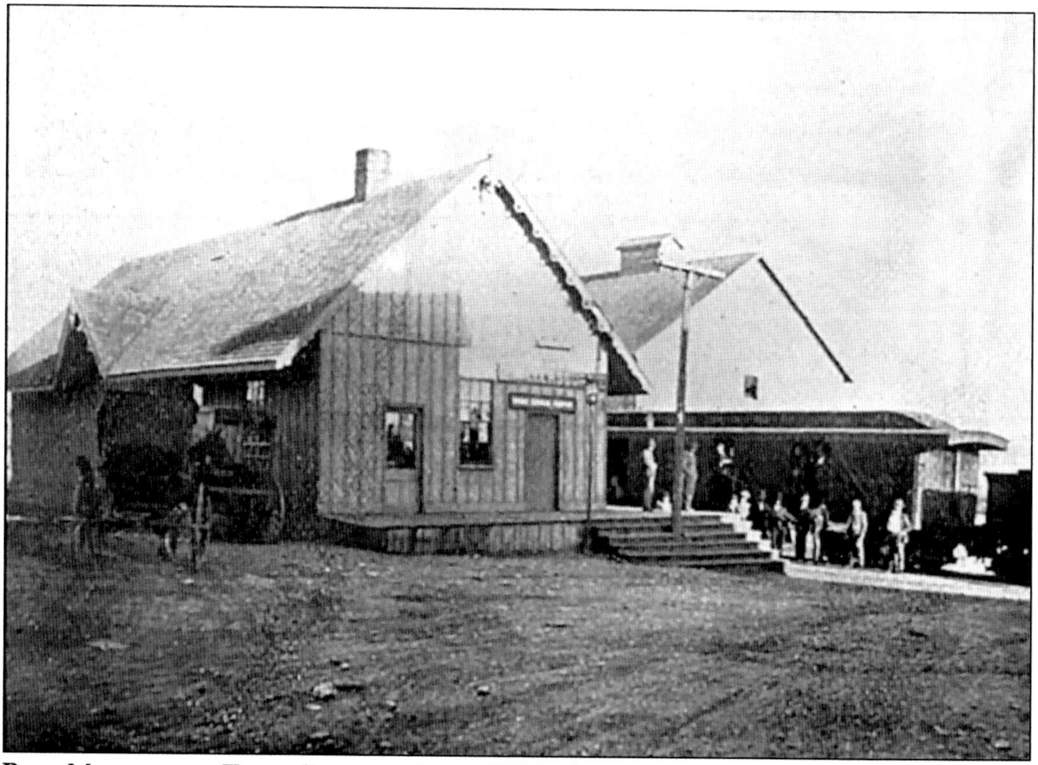

Busy Millersburg Train Station. Agent W.V. Shaw ran the Louisville & Nashville depot station in Millersburg in 1905. Both freight and passengers used the trains that passed through here for many years. Countless young people arrived and departed from this station—students at the town's boarding schools and colleges. In addition, around the turn of the century, as many as 20,000 turkeys were shipped from this depot annually.

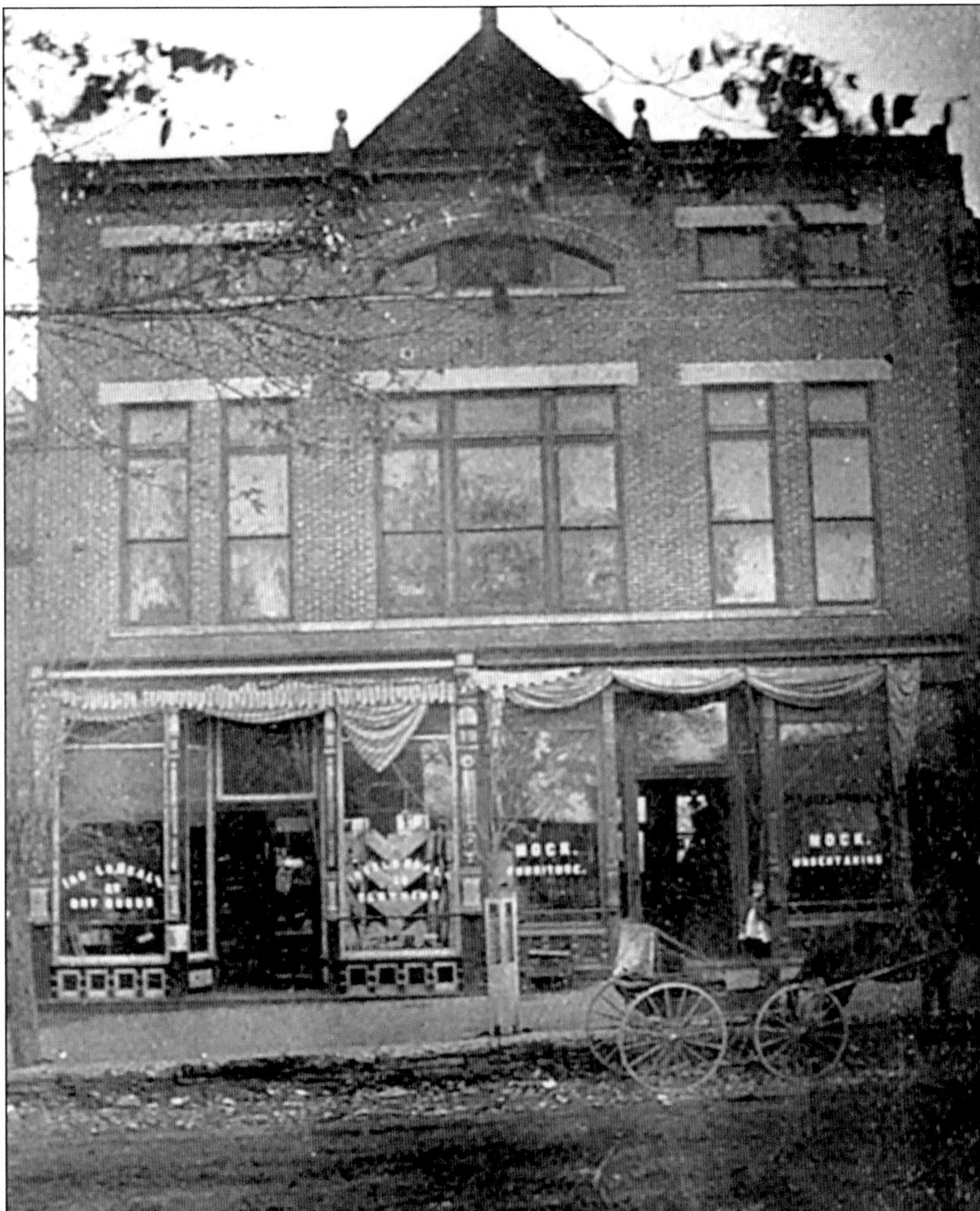

IMPRESSIVE MILLERSBURG OPERA HOUSE. Built sometime between 1885 and 1890, this stalwart landmark on Millersburg's Main Street housed commercial establishments at street level and a large theater on the second level. According to a booklet on Millersburg produced in 1901, "An opera house, well-seated and supplied with scenery, is owned and managed by the Oddfellows." The Oddfellows are one of the two "secret" societies for white Millersburg residents listed in the booklet. The Masons were the second "secret" society. African-American "secret" societies listed were: the Oddfellows, Knights of the Wise Men, and Benevolents. Although it is doubtful that *Aida* was ever staged there, the Millersburg Opera House provided a venue for plays and ceremonies for the community for many years.

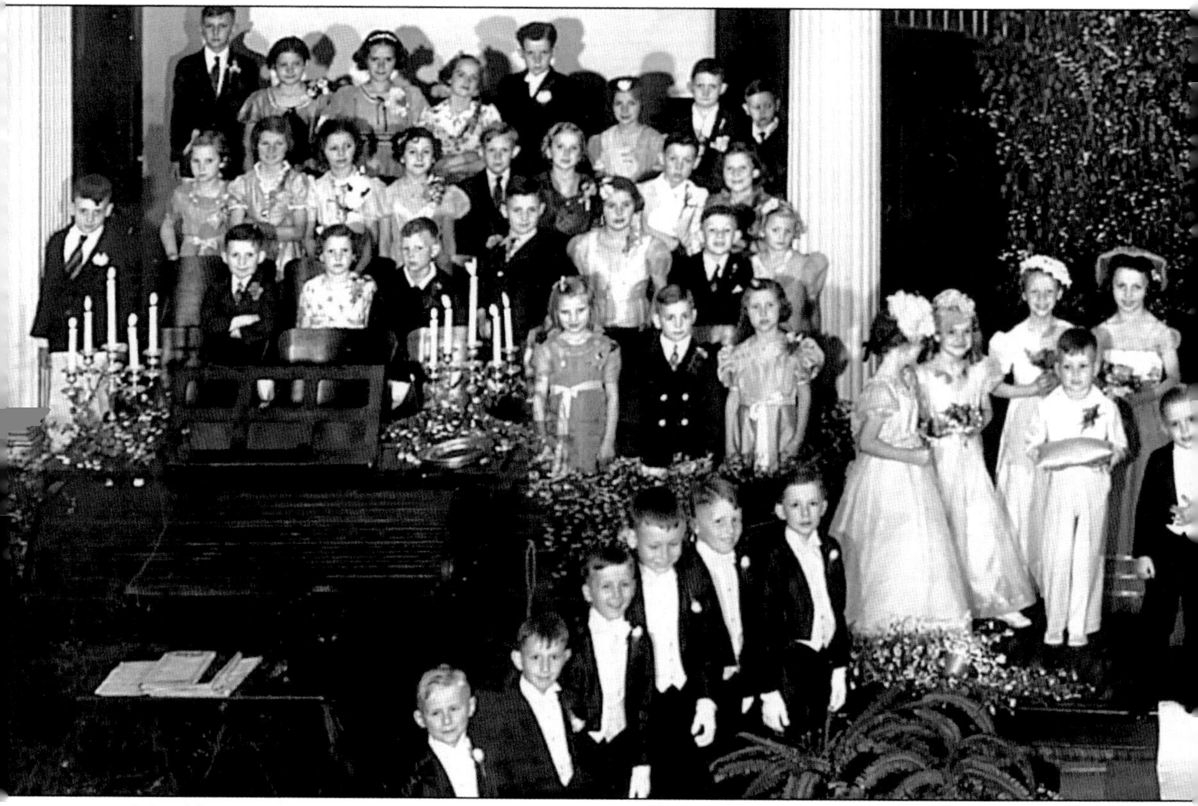

1940 North Middletown "Tom Thumb Wedding." Weddings, both real and pretend, provided immense entertainment to area residents for a number of generations beginning in Victorian times. Events included public weddings, "womanless" weddings, and in the case of this photo "Tom Thumb" weddings that involved children playing at nuptials. This elaborate,

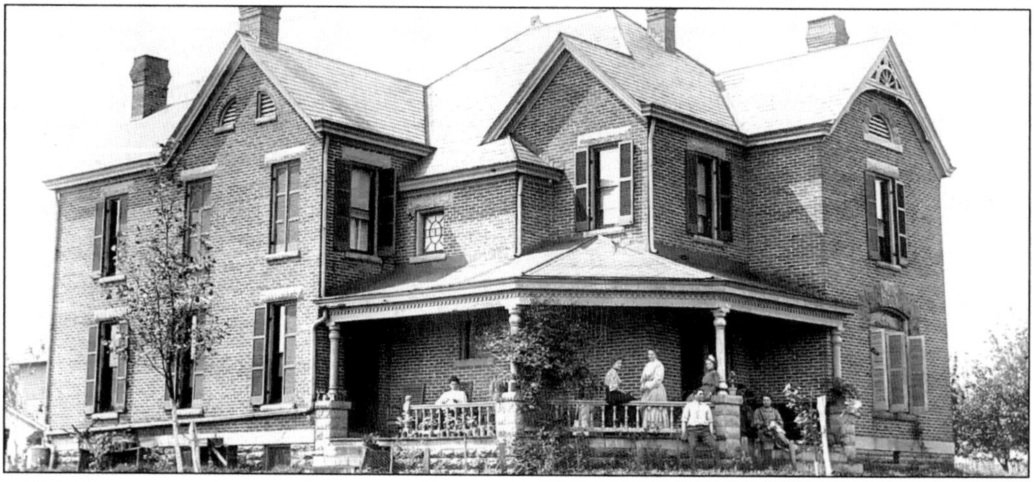

1908 Photo of Lovely Country Home. Found on Thatcher's Mill Road near North Middletown, this large brick residence was built in the late 1890s. Its many fireplaces and thick brick walls provided warmth in the winter, while its shuttered windows and wide shady porch insured respite from the heat of summer. Pictured here in 1908 are (left to right on porch) Mrs. J.N. Mason, Lillian Mason, Eliza Mason, two unidentified, and John Mason is in front.

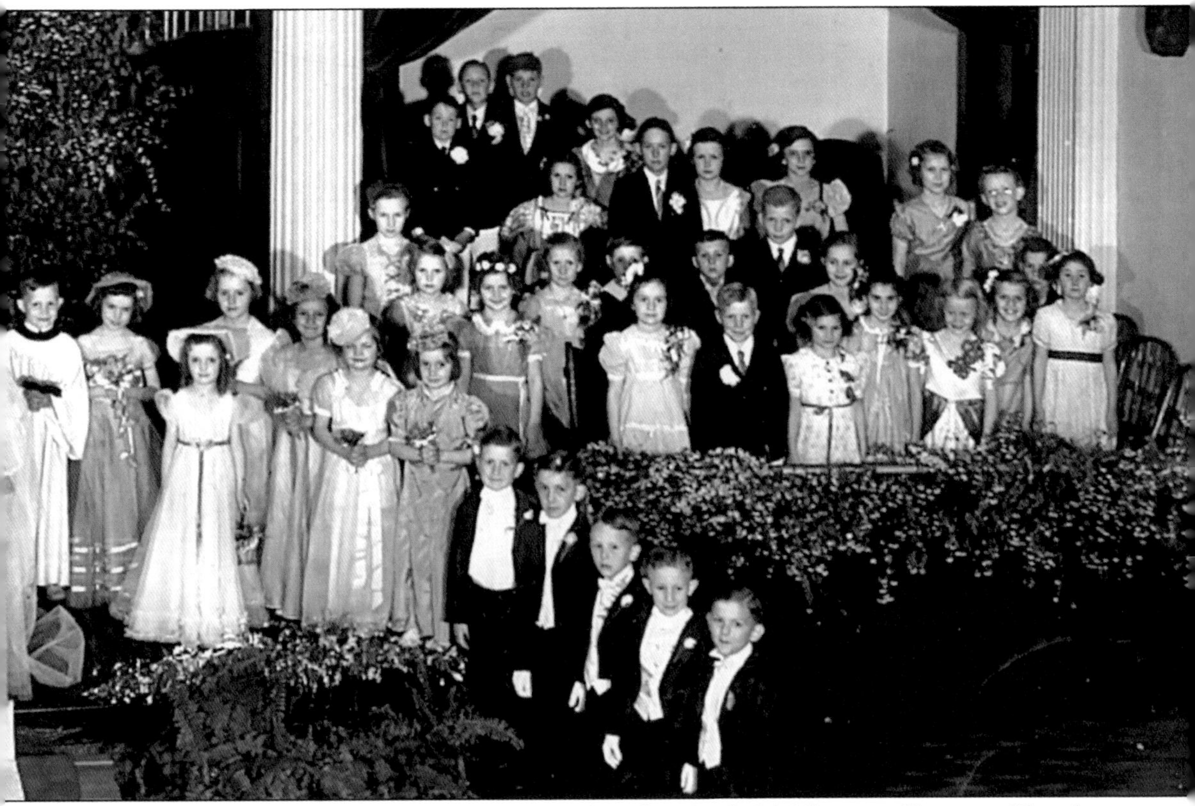

and no doubt expensive, charade was performed at the North Middletown Christian Church in May of 1940. There are 79 children in this photo. Betty Catesby Woodford played the bride and Russell Summay Jr. was the groom. One hopes that the "make believe" father of the bride, Henry Prewitt, did not have to pick up the tab.

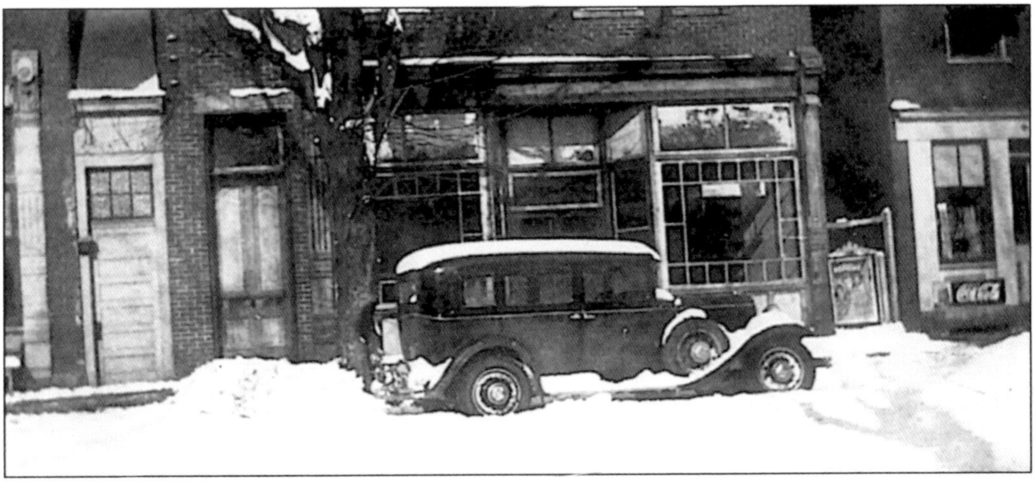

RECORD COLD AND LOTS OF SNOW IN NORTH MIDDLETOWN. In January of 1936, record cold temperatures ranging from 16 to 20 below zero were recorded in Bourbon County for several days. This touring car in front of Skidmore Grocery in North Middletown probably took awhile to start that week. It is parked in front of G.W. Rash's building, which was constructed in 1900 as a dry goods store.

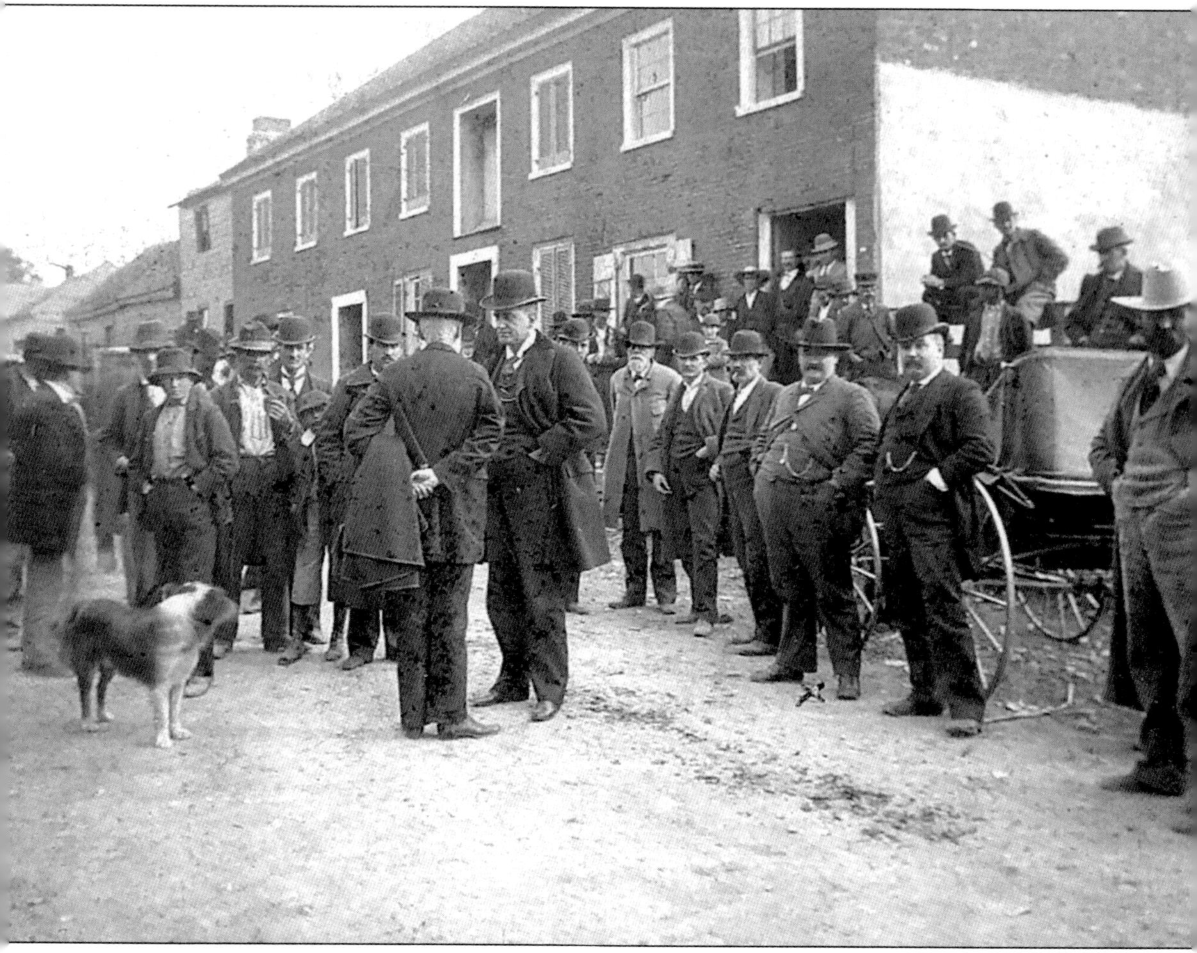

A Gathering of Democratic Faithful in Ruddles Mills. Ed D. Paton is the man standing next to the vehicle, fourth from the right, at a Democratic meeting held at Ruddles Mills in 1892. Paton was elected county clerk for four successive terms beginning in 1895. Since women's suffrage was still only a dream for local women, the Ruddles Mills gathering was for men only and more than 40 men, along with a couple of boys and one curious dog, turned out for this meeting. The building in the background was probably a boarding house or hotel. In 1879, T.T. Thornton was listed as the hotel owner in Ruddles Mills. A member of the Paton family held office as circuit clerk or county clerk for decades. Ed D. Paton's father James was elected circuit clerk for several terms and his son Pearce and grandson Ed Drane followed Ed D. in the office of county clerk.

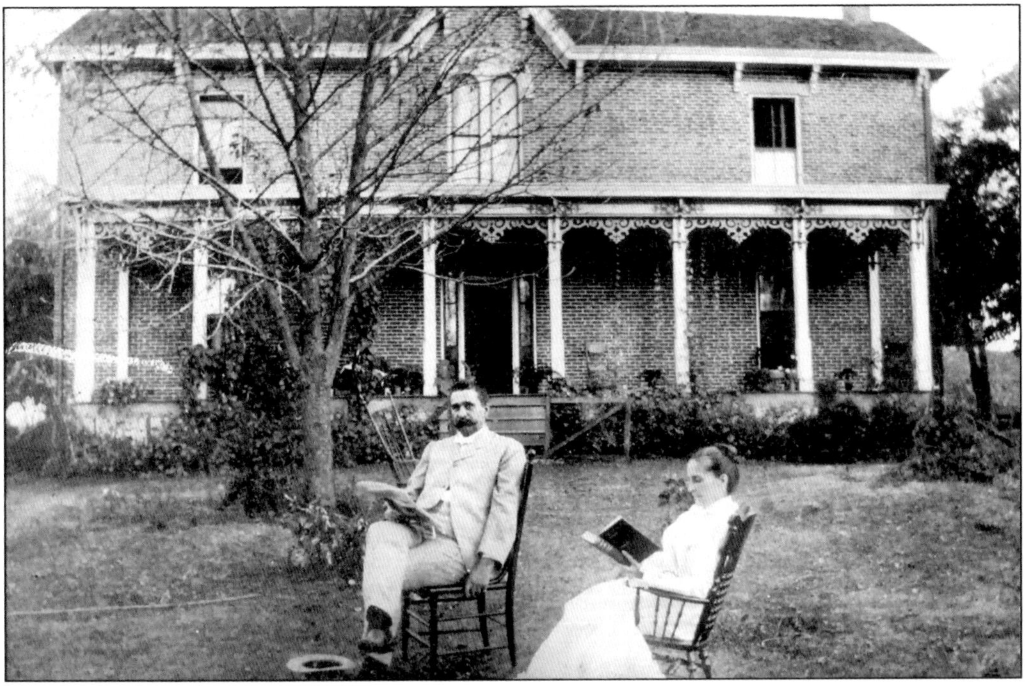

A Quiet Afternoon in the Country. William Porter Ardery and his wife Ellen Adair Ardery are seen outside their home on Brentsville Road. The photo was probably taken before their only child, William, was born in 1887. That son would become a leader in the community and circuit court judge. Photographic portraits of families and their country homes were quite popular at this time. (U.K. Collection.)

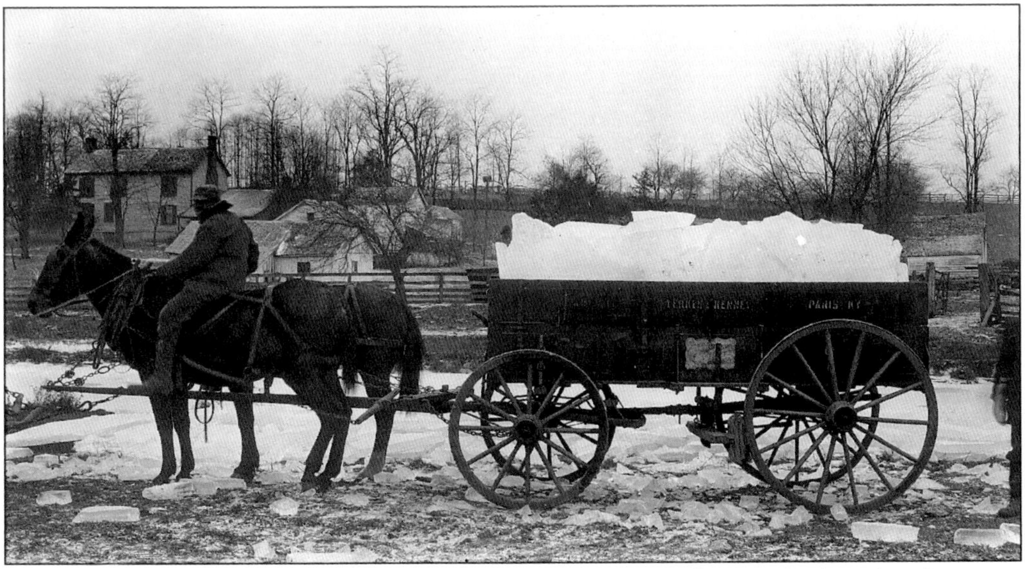

Ice Came from Ponds and Streams, Not Refrigerators. Back in 1912 when this photo was taken, people cut blocks of ice from ponds during winter and hauled them to ice houses where they were packed in hay. This wagon has "Yerkes & Kenney-Paris, KY" painted on the side of it. Yerkes & Kenney was a business located at the corner of Fourth and Pleasant Streets that sold carriages, wagons, and farm machinery.

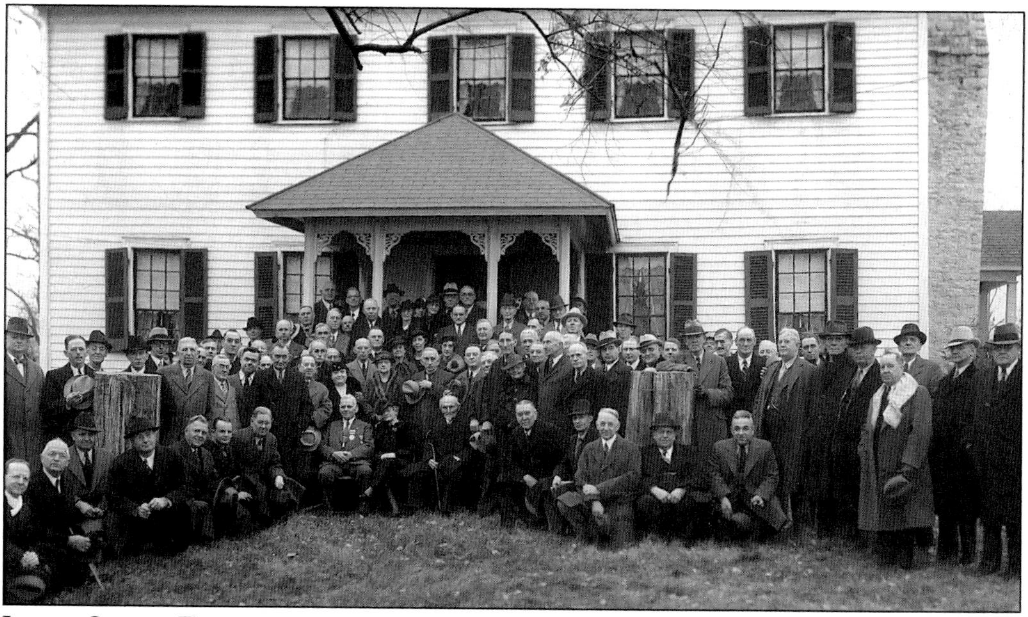

LARGE CROWD TURNED OUT FOR EWALT'S CROSSROADS RECEPTION. In November of 1936, Grand Masons from around the region gathered at Ewalt's Crossroads in honor of Joseph H. Ewalt's 50th anniversary of being made a Master Mason. The central part of the home was built by Henry Ewalt, a Revolutionary War veteran, around 1788 when he purchased the parcel of 200 acres. An Ewalt descendant has lived on the property ever since.

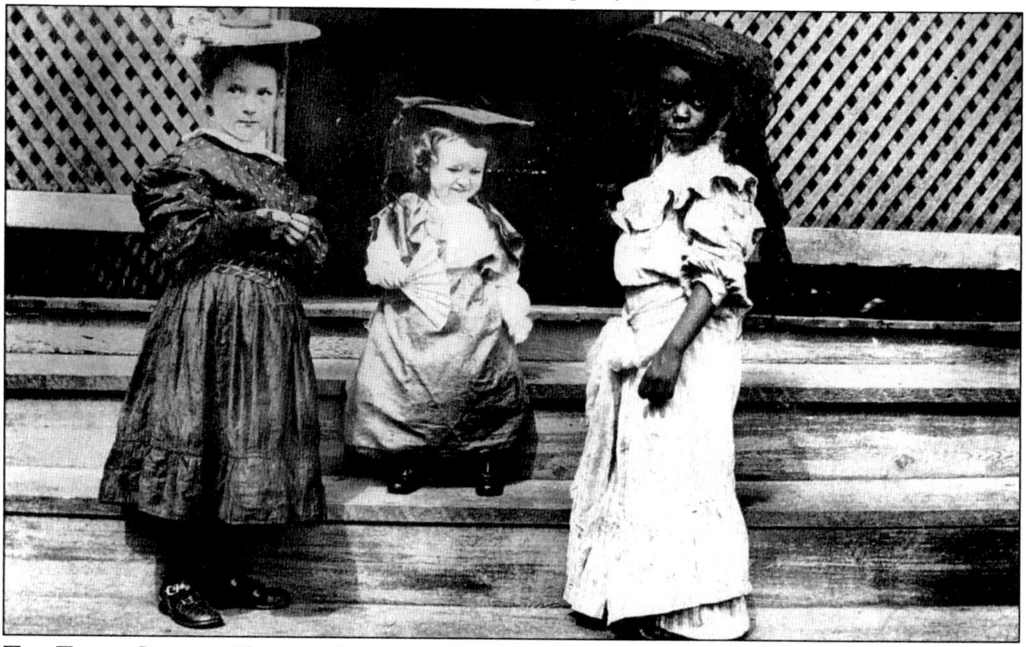

THE THREE GRACES. That was the title under this photo in a wonderful Ewalt family scrapbook. The Ewalt sisters, Anne Thomas and Josephine, and their unidentified friend are shown playing "dress up" in some very stylish clothes. The photo was taken about 1910 at Ewalt's Crossroads. Little girls have not changed much in the past century; they still enjoy dressing up in pretty, grown-up clothes.

Three

Religion and Churches

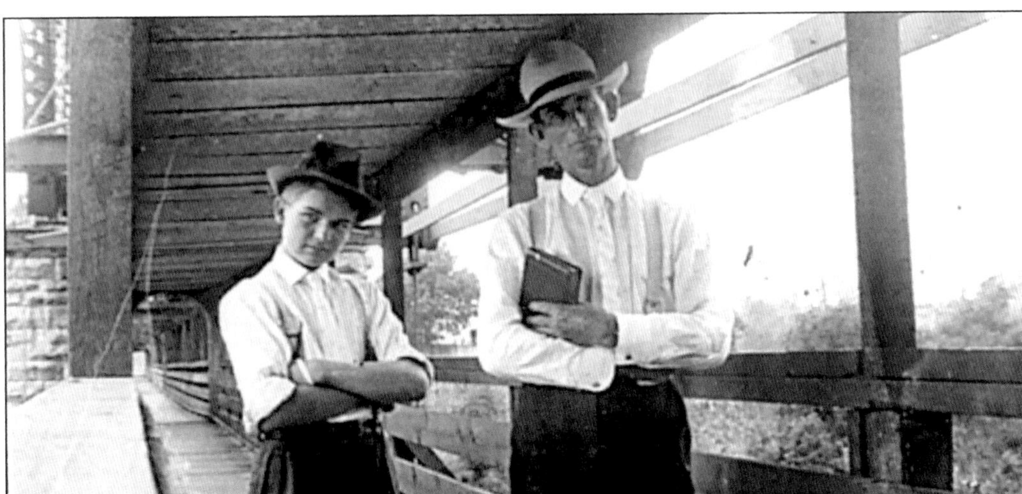

On Their Way to Church. It was about 1910 when this photo of John Henry Richard and his son Clyde Wilson Richard was taken on the footbridge beneath the L&N Railroad Bridge that crossed Stoner Creek. Their bright white shirts and stiff starched collars bespeak the respect and seriousness people of the time paid to their church services. Churches in Bourbon County to this day play an important role in the social and political life of the area. Clyde Richard began his career in the funeral director business in 1917 and for quite a few years was known as "Kentucky's oldest funeral director" before he died in 1995 at the age of 99.

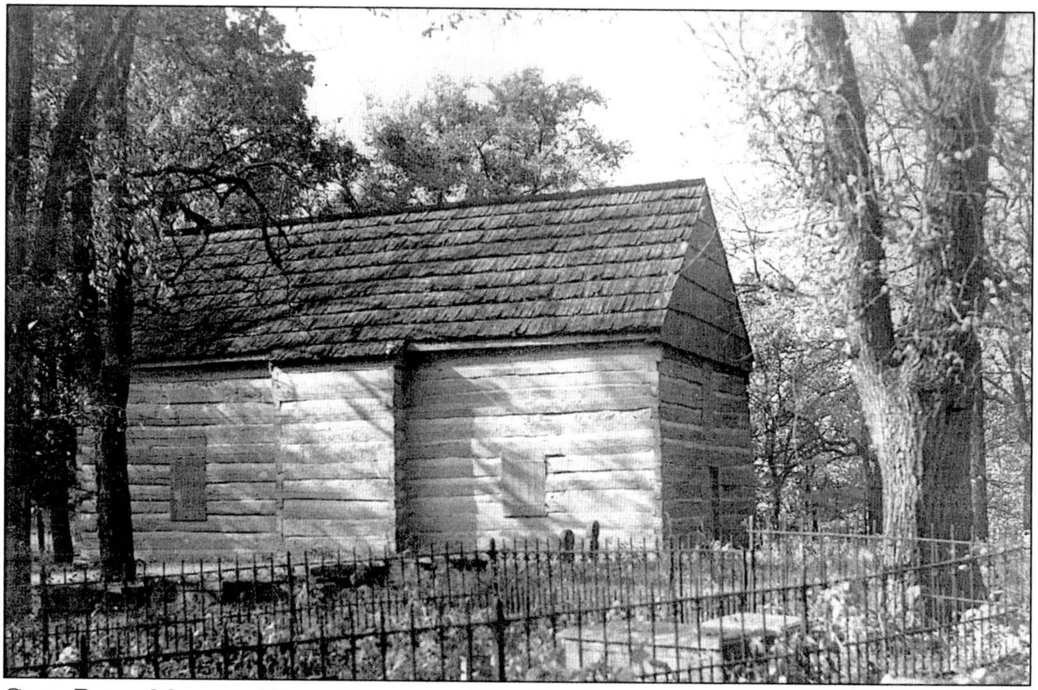

Cane Ridge Meeting House Built in 1791. This historic church is considered the largest one-room log structure in the United States. Built of blue ash logs in 1791, it is approximately 30 feet wide and 50 feet long and can accommodate more than 300 people. Originally built as a Presbyterian Church, it became the birthplace of the Christian Church in 1804. It was the site of the famous Cane Ridge Revival in 1801 that attracted more than 20,000 people.

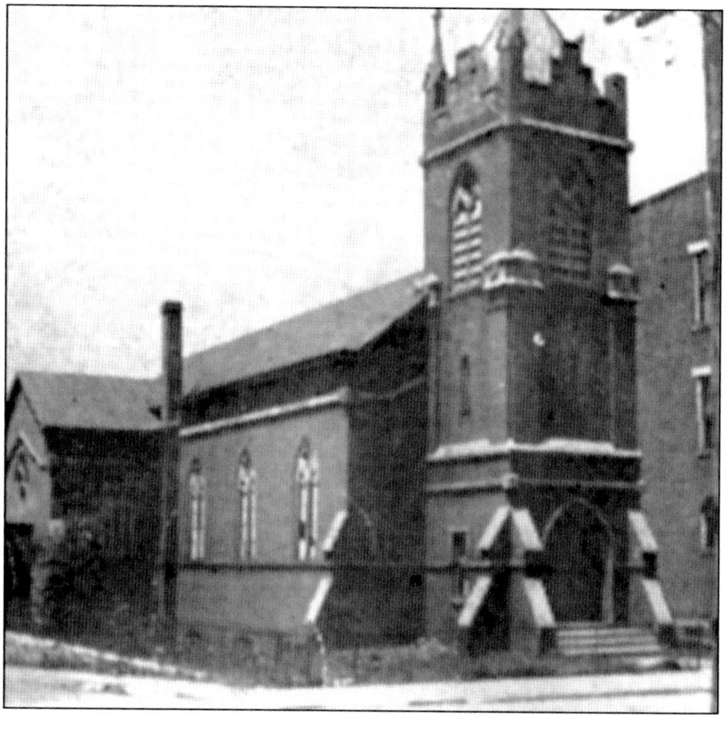

First Baptist Church on Main Street in Paris. This was the second church the Baptists built in Paris. The first "meeting house" was built in 1822 in a walnut grove at the corner of Pleasant and Winchester Pike (10th Street). This building was finished in 1868 under the direction of Rev. George Varden and was at the corner of Main and Locust (Sixth Street). It served the congregation until 1910 when they moved to the present location.

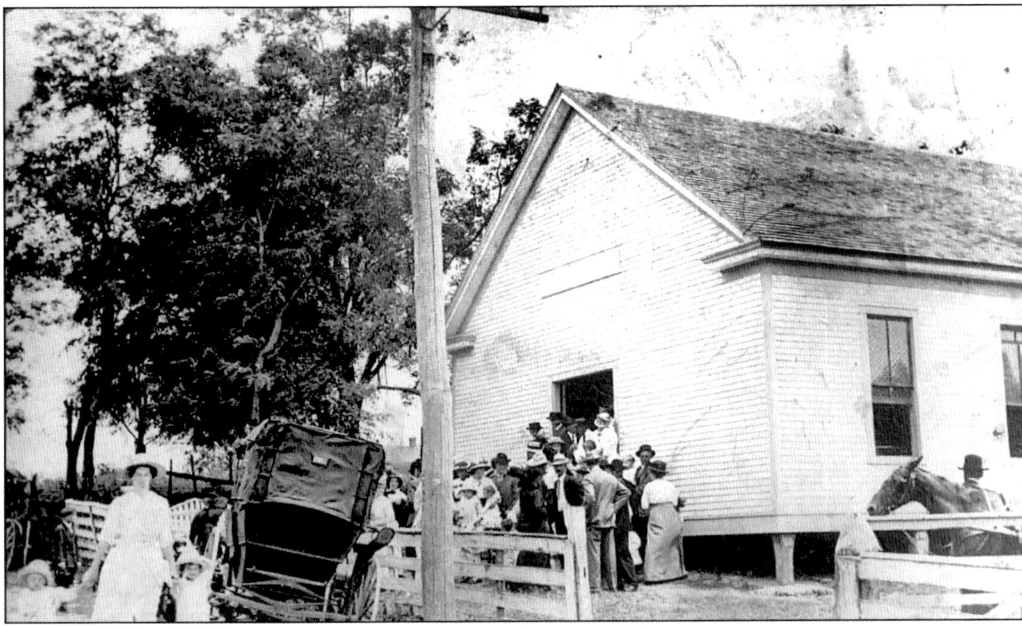

CENTERVILLE METHODIST CHURCH, 1915. Dressed in their "Sunday best," the Methodists of Centerville pour out of their neat frame church built in 1911 near the crossroads of Georgetown Pike (US 460) and Newtown Pike. The "parking lot" back then was filled with real horsepower. The church has had many names over the years, but today thrives as the Centerville United Methodist Church.

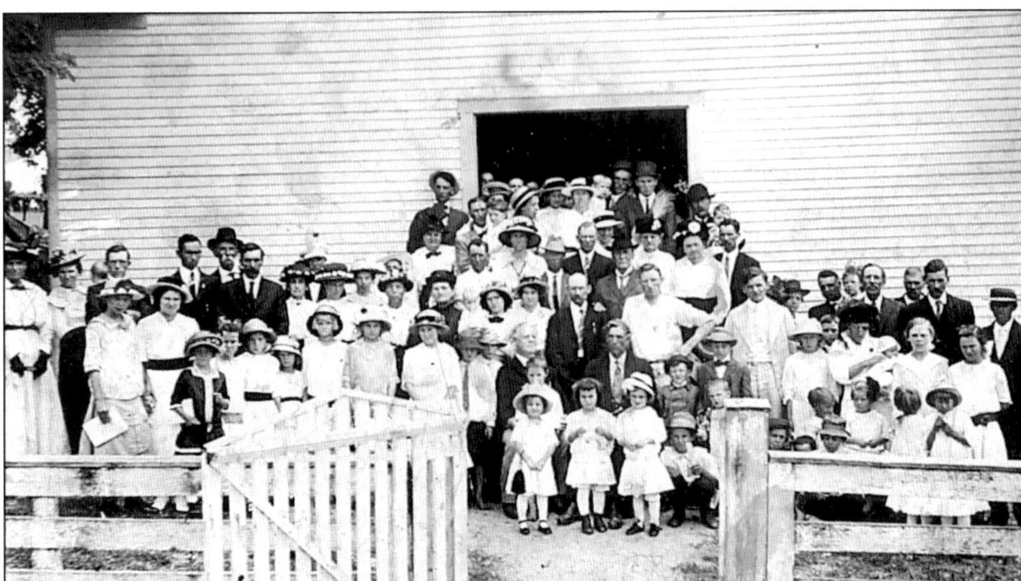

CONGREGATION OF CENTERVILLE METHODIST CHURCH. Around 1915, when this photo was taken, Centerville was a busy hamlet with churches, a school, stores, blacksmith shops, and a rail station where farmers could ship their produce to market or pick up the latest catalog merchandise ordered by their families. The two men seated in front of this well-dressed group (almost hidden by the bevy of small girls) are probably the minister and deacon or eldest member.

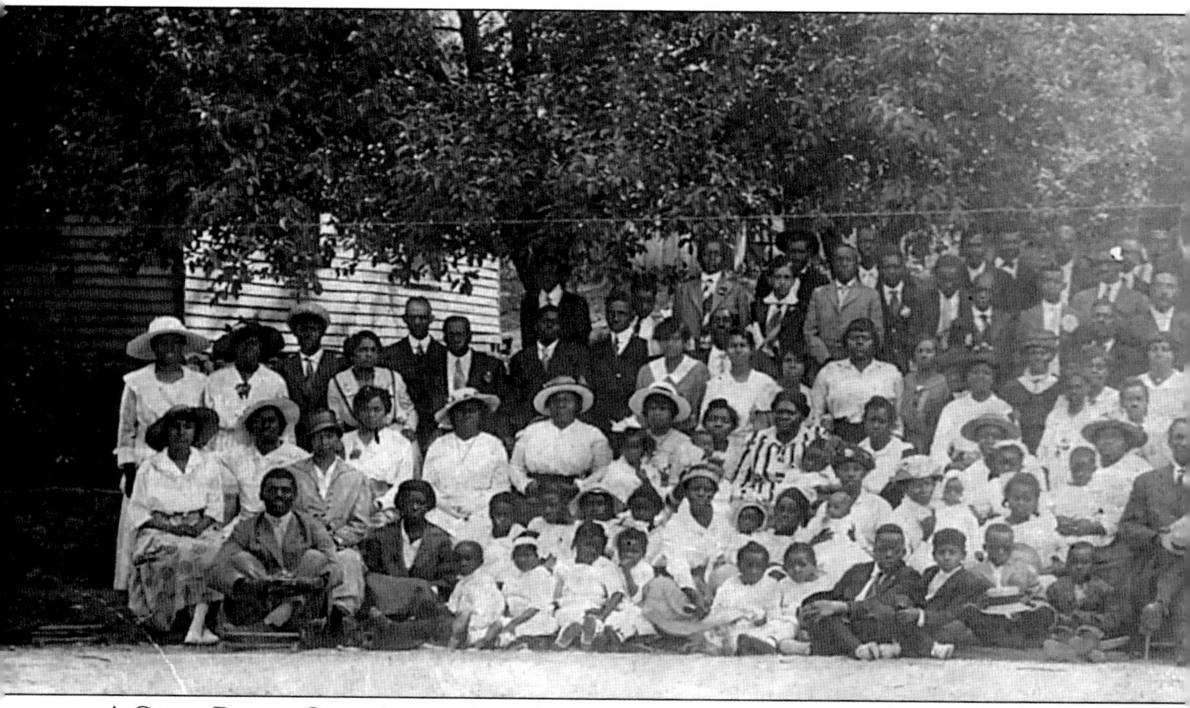

A Great Day to Go to Little Rock Christian Church. This photo, probably taken in the early 1900s, at the Little Rock Christian Church, shows the large congregation, minister, and deacons. The church, founded by Samuel Buckner in 1861, was said to have the largest African-American membership in the county. The church began under an elm tree and when the elm tree was cut down, a gavel and block was carved from the wood of that tree and is still

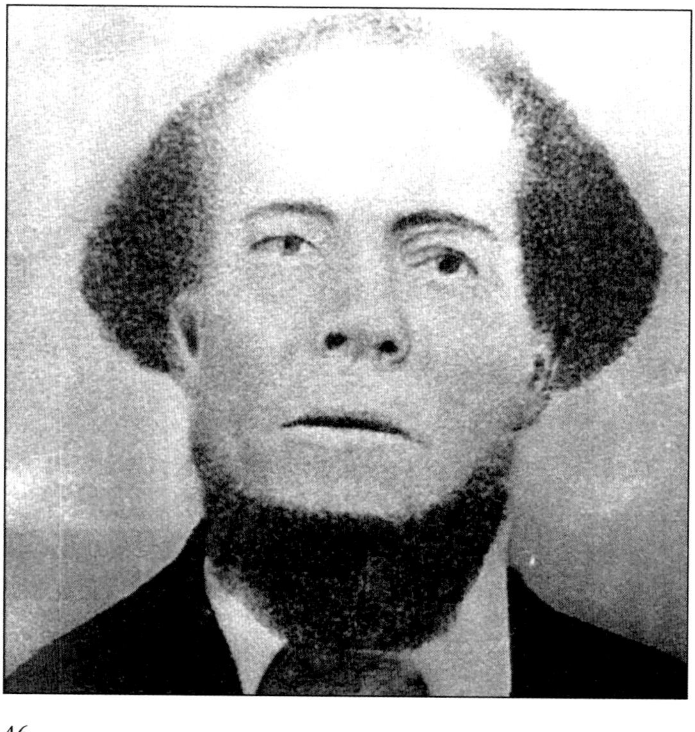

Samuel Buckner Ordained at Cane Ridge in 1855. Samuel Buckner excelled in public speaking and was trained to preach and teach other slaves before the Civil War. He was eventually set free so that he could spread the gospel and he established Little Rock Christian Church in 1861. His grandson, E.B. Toles, was also a minister at Little Rock as well as the principal at Western High School.

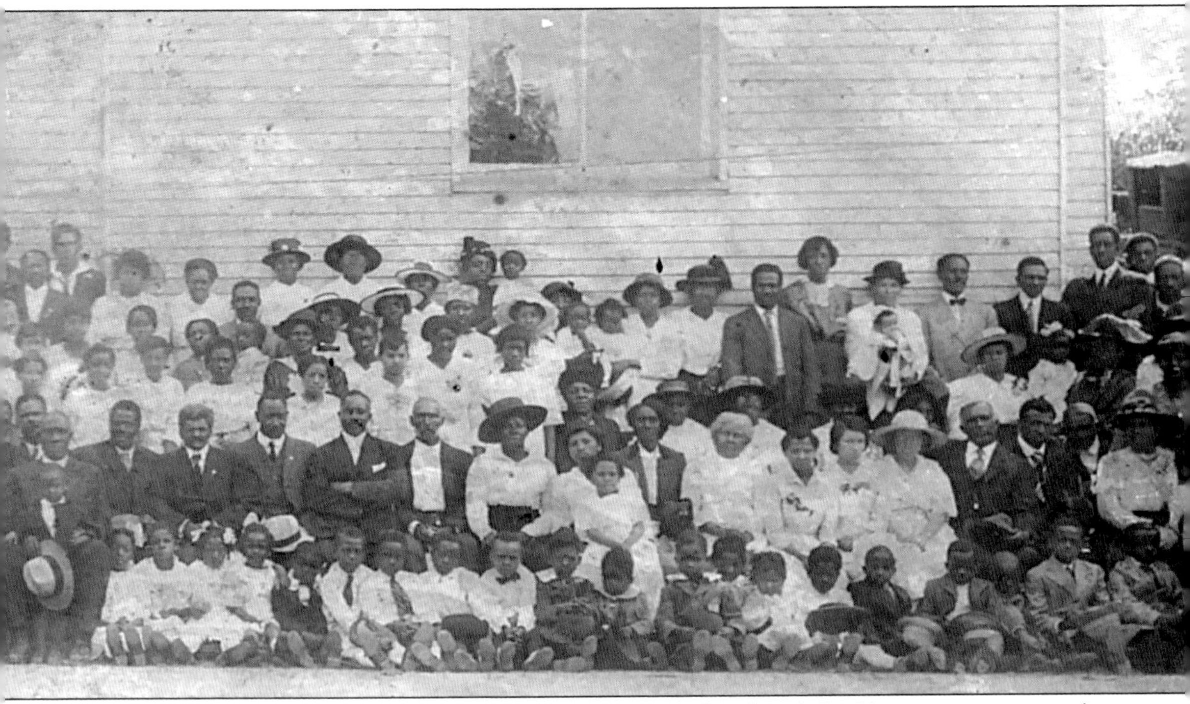

used by the Kentucky Christian Missionary Convention. The church building was constructed in 1877 and has been in use ever since. The church served an African-American community in the Little Rock area that thrived from the period after the Civil War until the 1930s and 1940s, when the younger generations began leaving for better jobs in cities and towns.

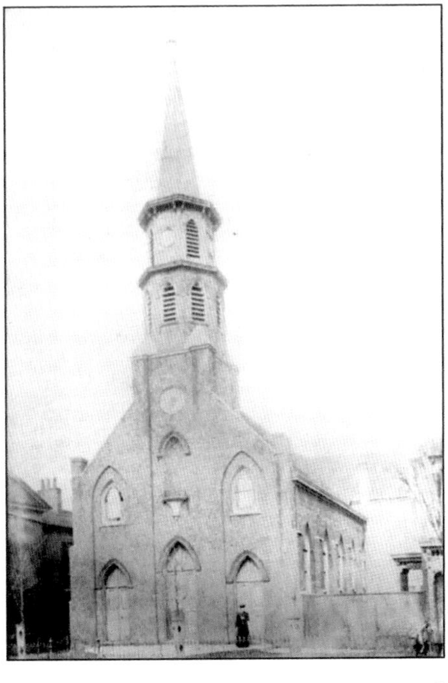

CHURCH OF THE ANNUNCIATION, 1890. The lot where this church stands on Main Street was purchased by the Catholic Diocese of Covington in 1855. The cornerstone was laid in 1858 and the completed church was dedicated in 1861. Two additions were added to the building since, but the exterior still appears much as it did in 1890 when this photo with Fr. John Redmond was taken.

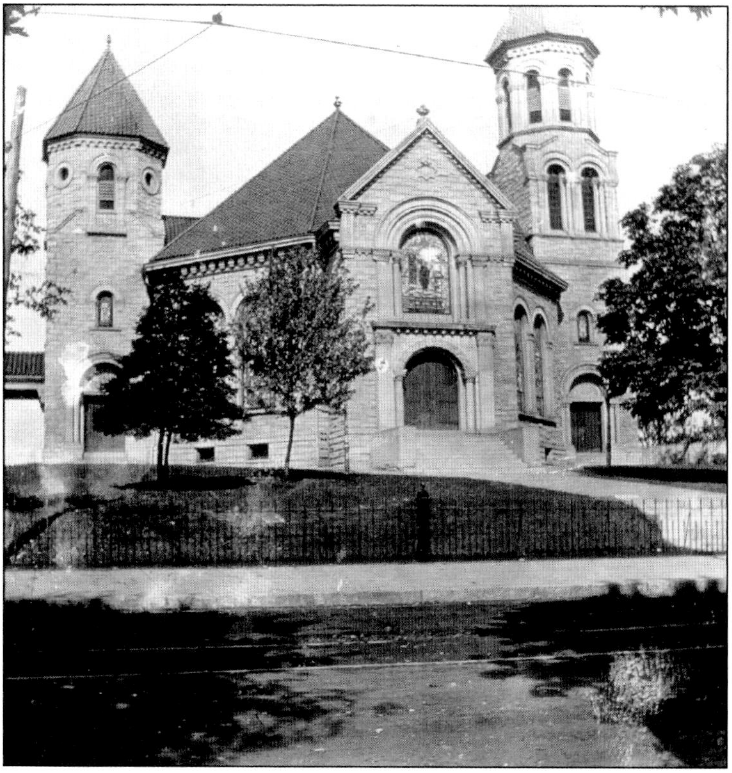

PARIS FIRST CHRISTIAN CHURCH, LARGEST IN COUNTY. The largest church structure in Bourbon County, this stone building on High Street was completed in 1902. It replaced a smaller church at the corner of Eighth and Main (later the site of the Schine movie theater, now a parking lot) that served the congregation for 44 years. The impressive structure is noted for its large art painted windows and red tile roof.

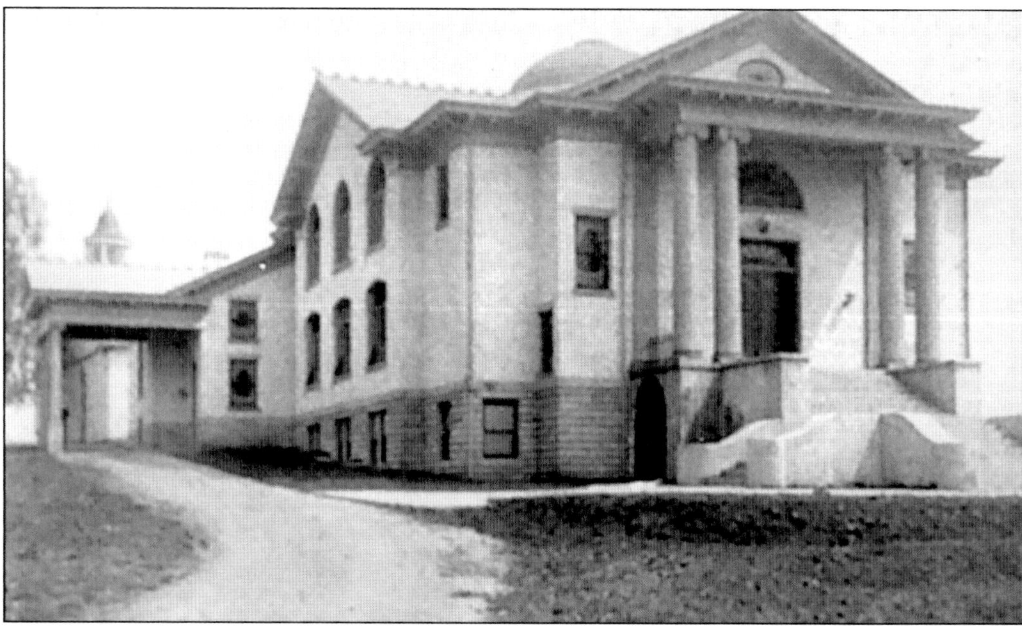

NORTH MIDDLETOWN CHRISTIAN CHURCH, COMPLETED IN 1913. Some of the most interesting buildings architecturally in the county are the churches. The North Middletown Christian Church building is one of the more unusual with its Roman dome. It was dedicated on October 19, 1913, and was built at a cost of $15,512.17. It replaced a frame church building on the same site that was built in 1840.

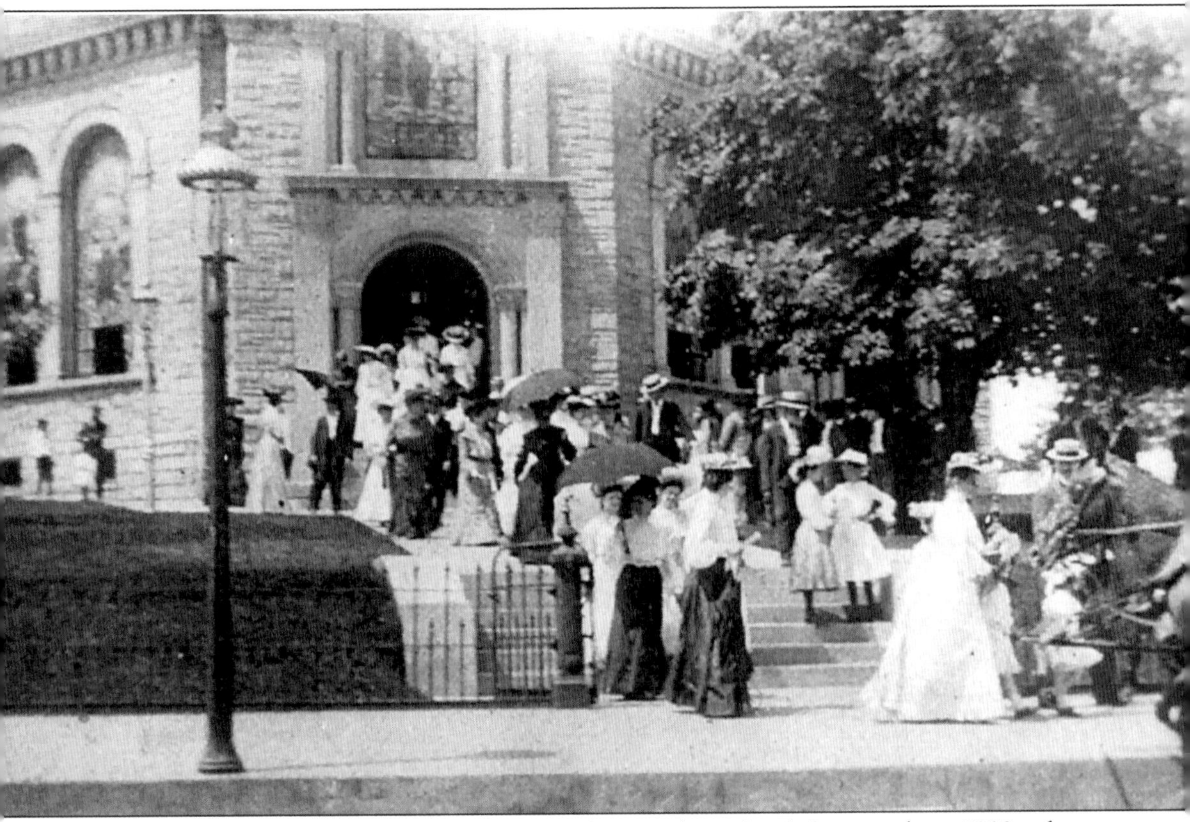

After the Dedication Ceremony in 1902. The sun shone brightly enough in 1902, when the massive First Christian Church was dedicated, to bring out the parasols for the well-dressed Paris ladies. Straw hats were all that protected the gentlemen from the sun. Notice the gas lamp, one of the hundreds that lit Paris streets back then. According to the history of the church, workmen were busy until midnight the night before the dedication finishing up the interior, but everything was ready the morning of the dedication. Special trains brought in visitors from across the state for the dedication and the women of the church served lunch for 400 at the old church.

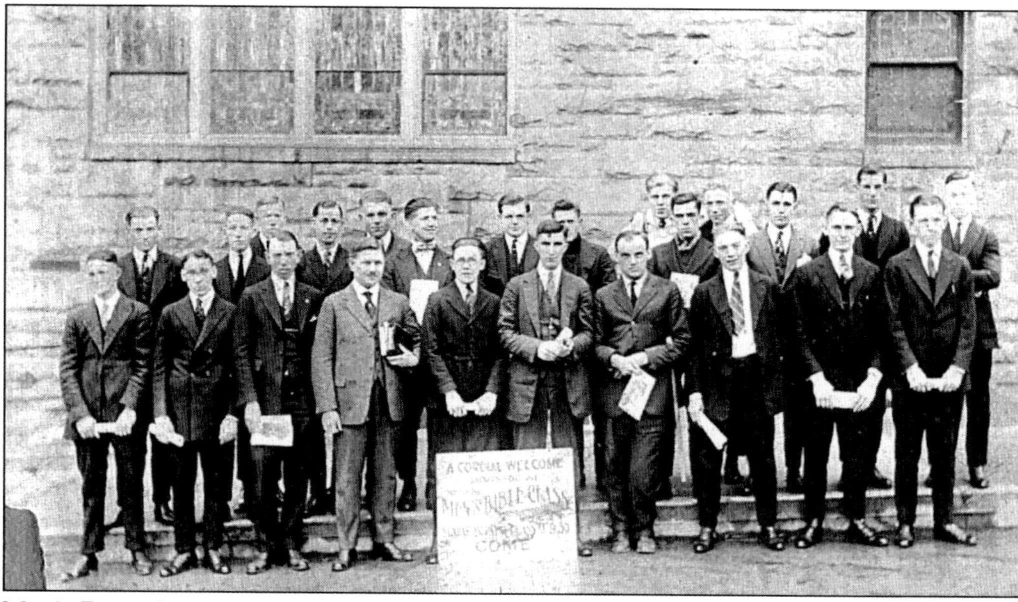

MEN'S BIBLE CLASS OFFERED "CORDIAL WELCOME." The 1922 Men's Bible Class at the First Methodist Church on Pleasant Street in Paris was a friendly group who believed it pays to advertise. The sign reads, "A Cordial Welcome Awaits You At Men's Bible Class, Sunday Morning Class At 9:30. COME." The first Methodist church near the corner of Seventh and Pleasant Streets was built in 1817.

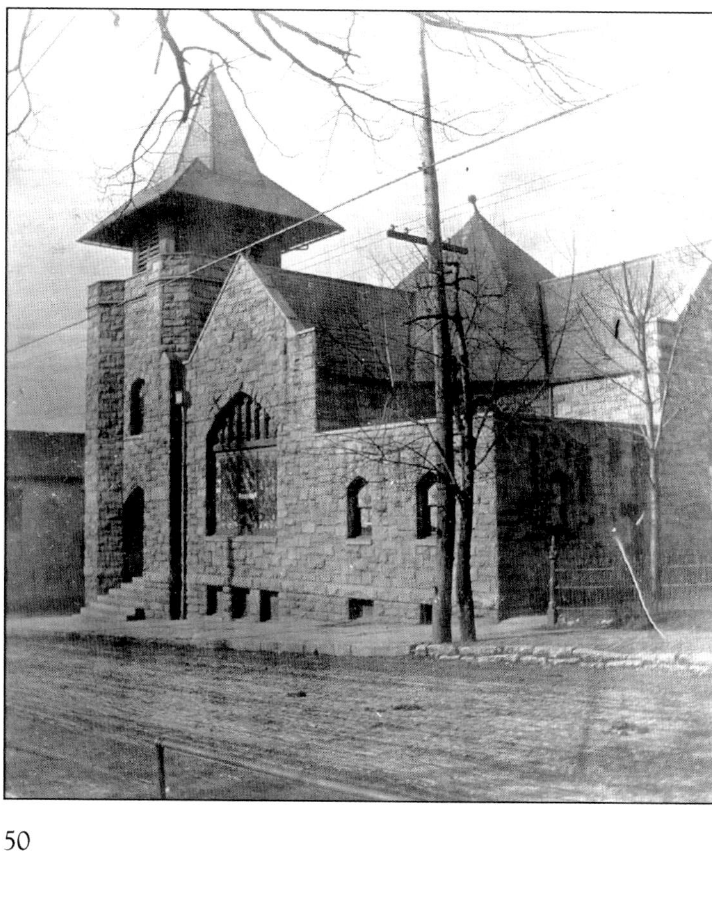

FIRST METHODIST CHURCH HAD UNUSUAL BELL TOWER. In 1897, the Methodists constructed this building at the corner of Seventh and Pleasant Streets in Paris. The unique wooden bell tower, an interior of antique finished oak, and a number of beautiful, stained glass windows were destroyed in a fire on December 29, 1909. With only the sturdy, stone walls left, the church was rebuilt, without the wooden tower, and was re-dedicated in June of 1911. (U.K. Collection.)

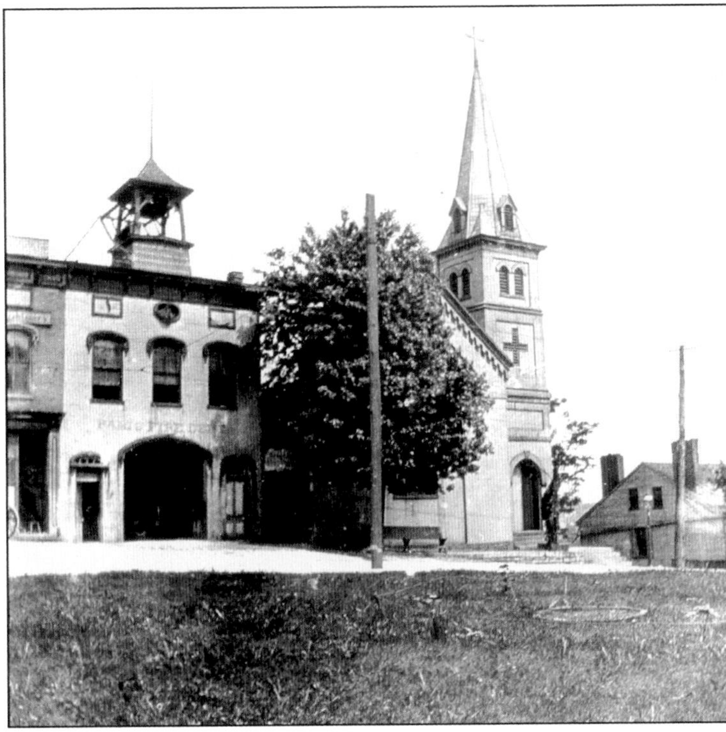

St. Peter's Episcopal Church on Busy Street. Pictured here in 1904, the church on Courthouse Square next to the firehouse has been there since 1833. The fourth Episcopal parish to be founded in Kentucky, St. Peter's was rebuilt and enlarged in 1870. It has faced four different courthouses located directly across the street and appears in as many, if not more, photographs than any other building in the city. (U.K. Collection.)

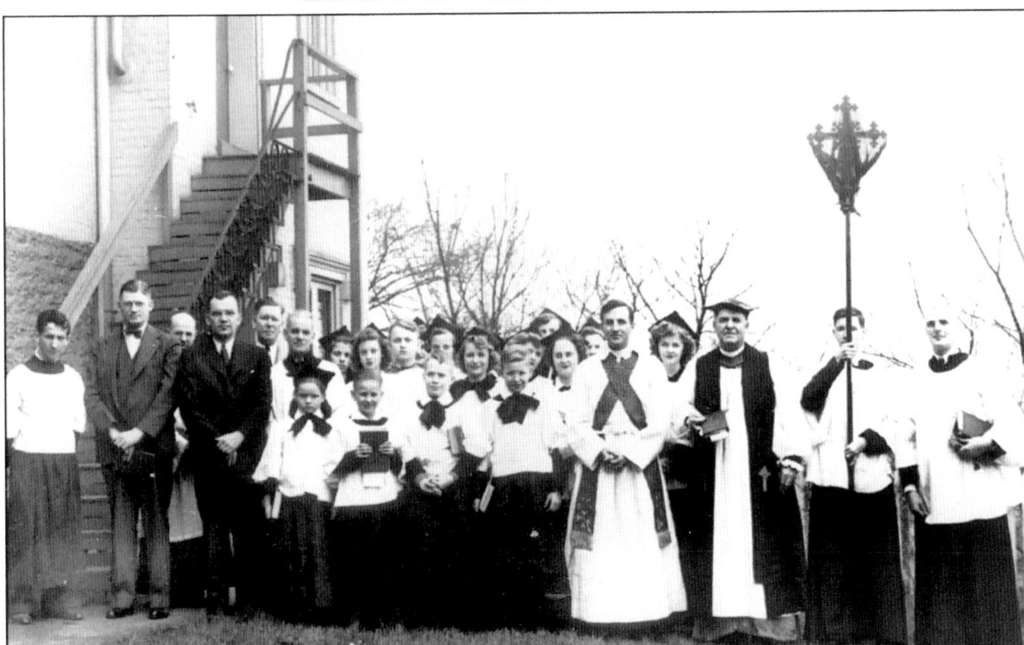

Bishop Visits St. Peter's. This picture, taken in 1940, shows Bishop Almon Abbott (in vestments and hat) with St. Peter's rector the Rev. Harold Williamson, members of the choir, servers, and members of the vestry. Famous football coach Blanton Collier (fourth from left) was coaching at Paris High in 1940 before leaving to serve in World War II. He later coached the University of Kentucky Wildcats and the Cleveland Browns.

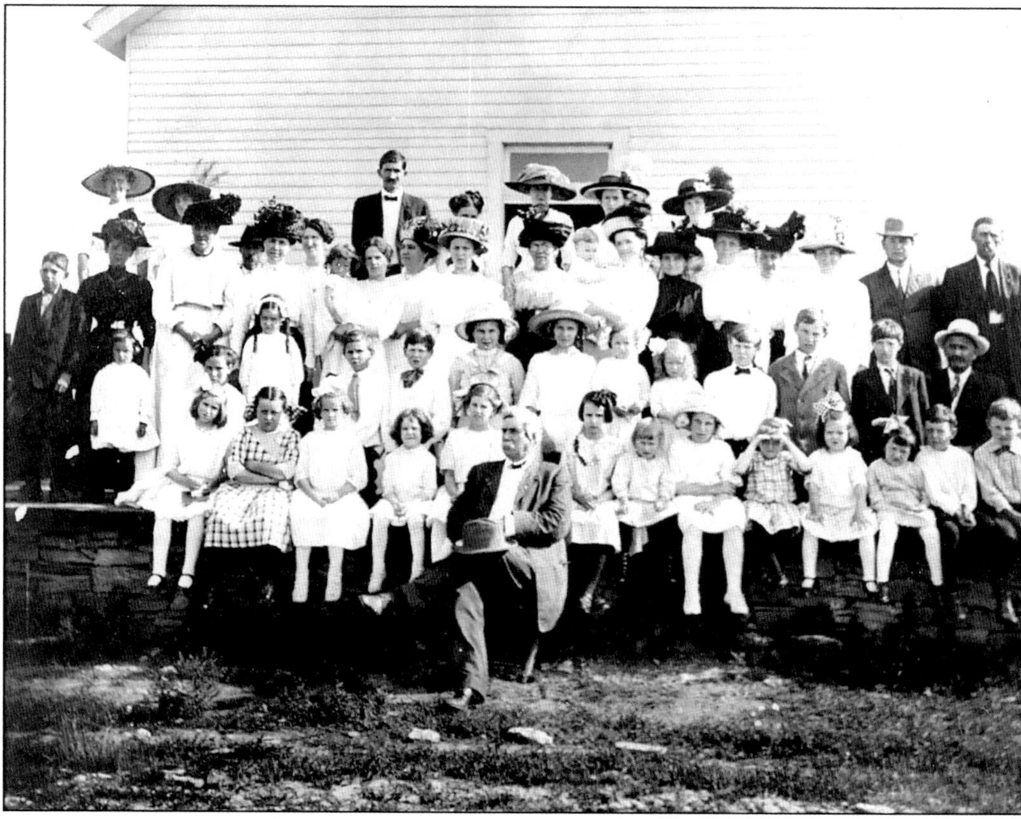

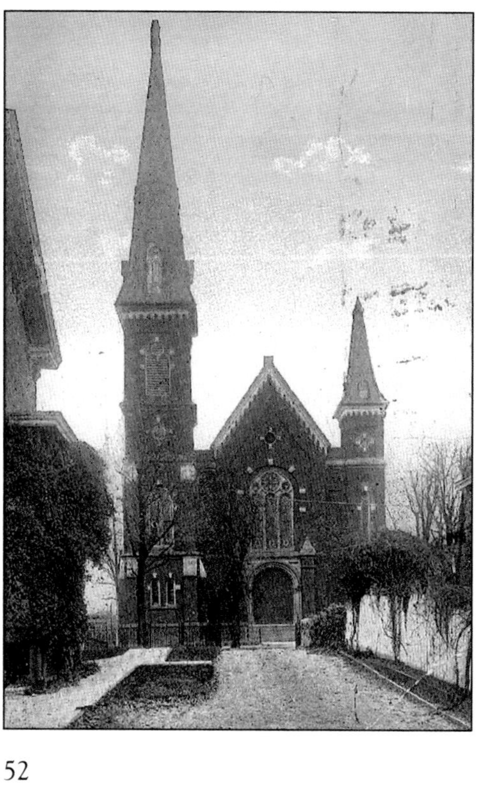

Hats Galore at Jackstown Christian Church. Because this group seems more than usually dressed-up and because of the women's elaborate hats, it is possible this photo was taken on Easter Sunday in 1912. The patriarchal pastor seated in front seems content with his flock, but some of the little girls behind him look like they are ready to go home and look for Easter eggs.

1870 Presbyterian Church in Paris. This impressive Victorian Gothic church, with two steeples that were landmarks in the Paris skyline for years, was erected on the corner of Pleasant and Sixth Streets in 1870. This image is from a postcard made in 1910. The structure was torn down and rebuilt after a windstorm toppled the steeples on March 26, 1916.

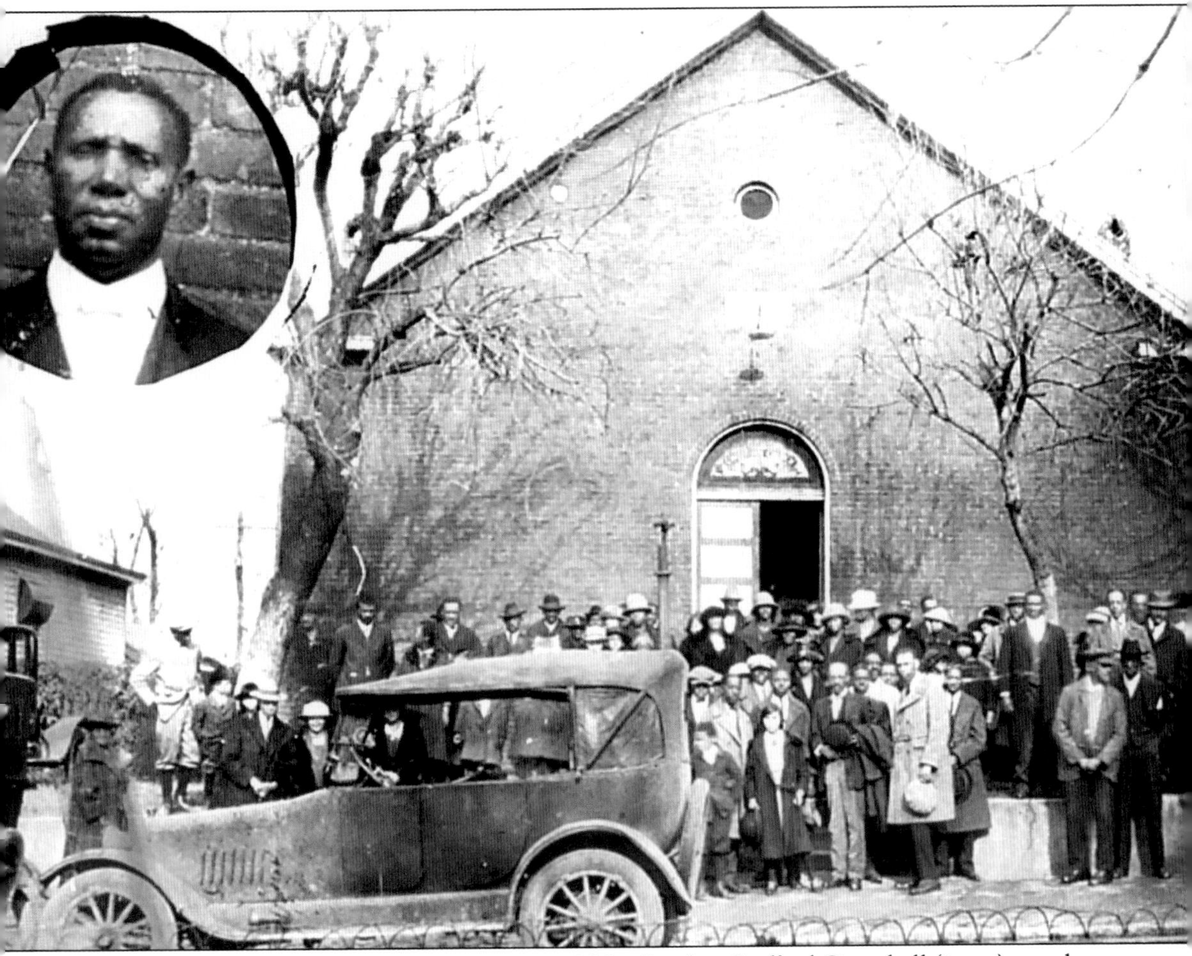

SEVENTH STREET CHRISTIAN CHURCH IN THE 1920S. Brother Stafford Campbell (inset) was the pastor of the Seventh Street Christian Church in Paris from 1899 until 1942. During his first years as pastor, according to a church history, many Sundays he would walk from Lexington to Paris to be with his congregation. Under his pastorage, the annex and vestibule were added to the original building and the building's exterior was stuccoed. The Seventh Street Christian Church was built in 1870 by a group of African-Americans who had been members of the First Christian Church. According to the church history, Brother J.C. Graves was one of the pastors of the church prior to 1899 and he also served as the principal of a school for African-American children in the "Cottontown" areas of Paris. The history continues: "After many years the school was brought to Paris and known as Western School."

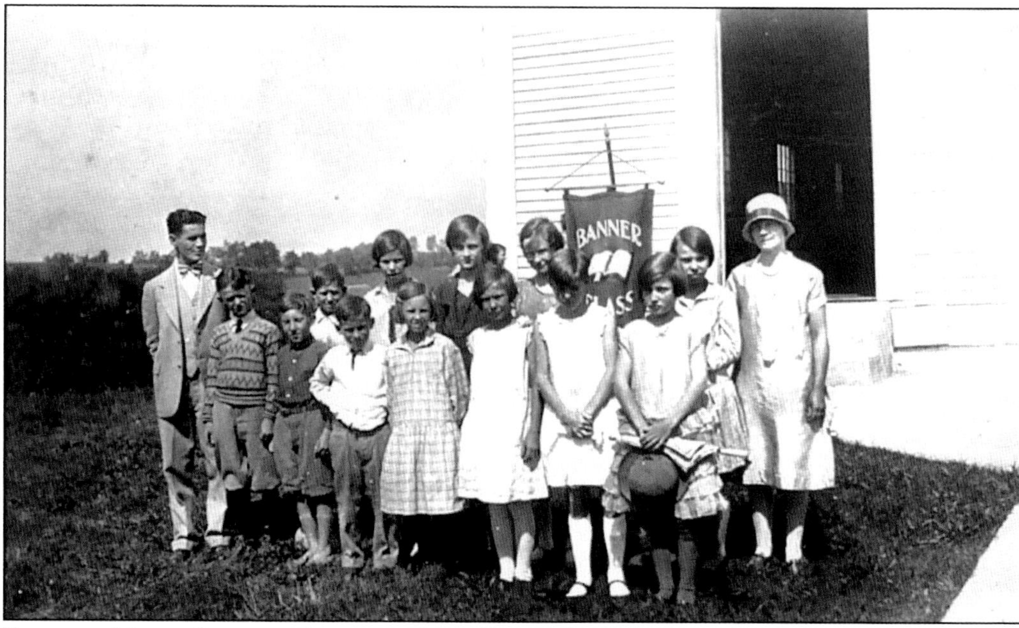

RUDDLES MILLS SUNDAY SCHOOL, 1926. Being the "Banner Class" at the Ruddles Mills Christian Church in 1926 was no doubt an honor. Mrs. William Linville (lady in hat) was a longtime Sunday school teacher there. Since 1841 when the church was first organized in the small town in northern Bourbon County, the Christian Church there has been a unifying and inspiring force in the community.

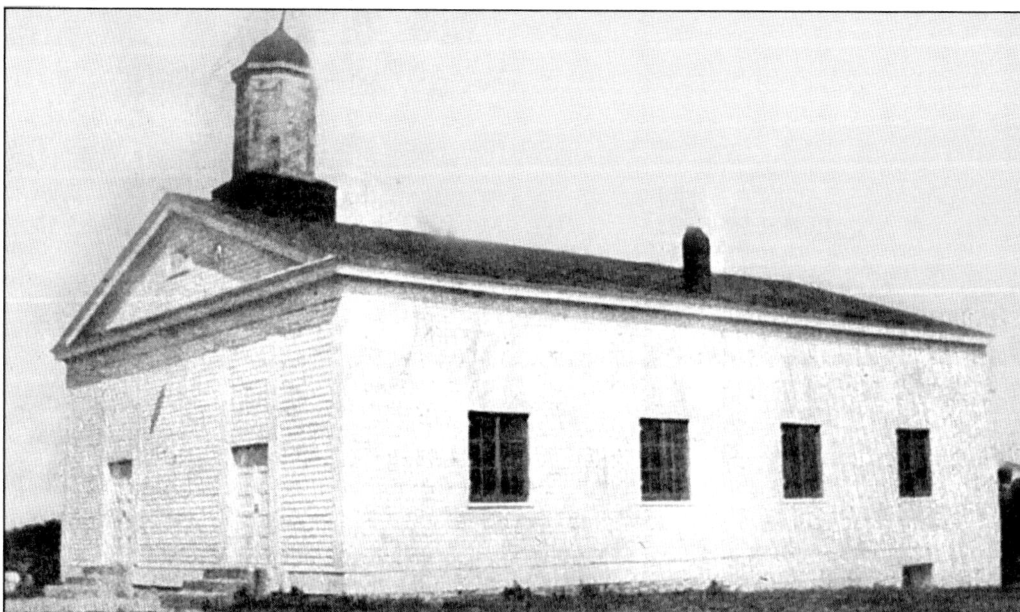

RUDDLES MILLS CHRISTIAN CHURCH, BUILT IN 1854–1855. Construction of this building began in 1854 and was completed in June of 1855. Through 1940 (when this photo was taken), the church had two entrances, traditionally one for men, and the other for women. In 1941, the church underwent renovations for the congregation's centennial. Before 1946, services were held only on the second and fourth Sundays. Since 1946, they have been held every Sunday.

Four

Fascinating Faces

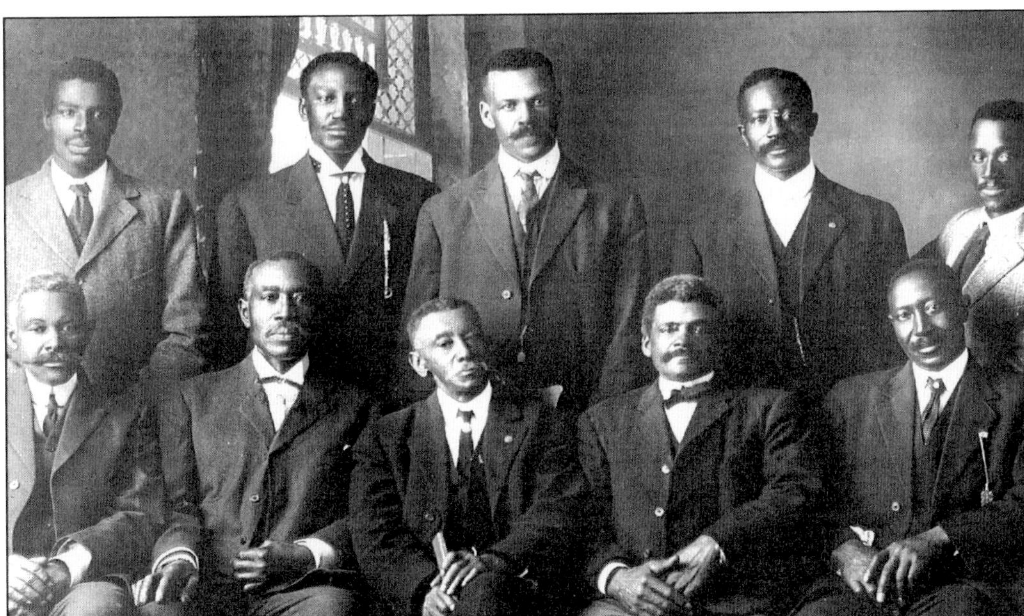

Church Elders and Minister of Little Rock Christian Church. Taken in the early 1900s, probably around the same time as the photo showing the large congregation included in the previous chapter, this photo is a close-up view of the men who were in charge of the Little Rock Christian Church during that era. Leaders in the church were usually leaders in the community and this group includes two generations of men who obviously felt pride in their accomplishments. From left to right are the following: (front row) ? Bristow, David January, the Rev. R.E. Hathaway, Sing Hall, and Jim Duncan; (back row) Cershaw Anderson, Clay Johnson, Green Cuningham, Charlie Duncan, and Benny Freeman.

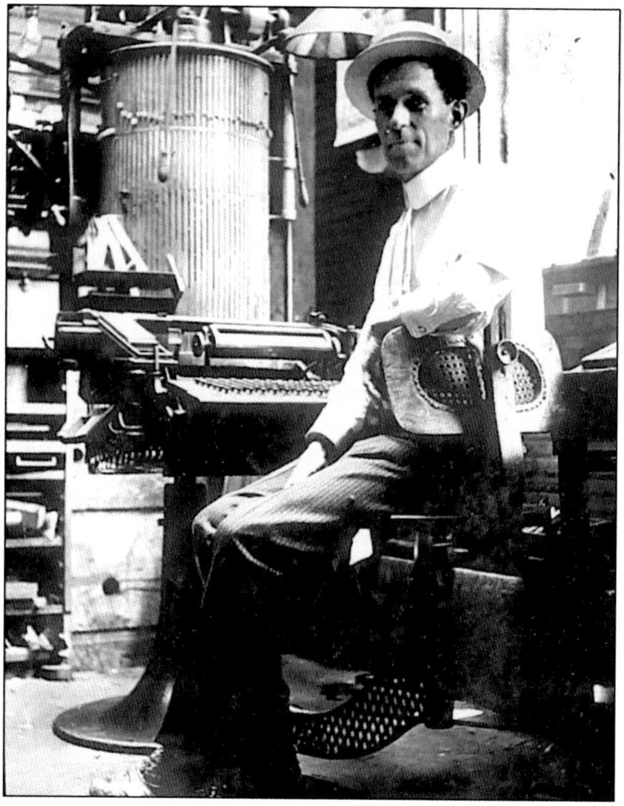

JAUNTY JOURNALIST SEATED AT EARLY TYPESETTING MACHINE. Will Hill Jr. was a special correspondent for the *Louisville Times* and other "metropolitan newspapers" according to a 1905 newspaper article. He also assisted his father, Will Hill Sr., in running the family business, the Bourbon Marble and Granite Works. The elder Hill had been the proprietor of that concern since 1855. It looks like the younger Hill is seated at an early typesetting machine.

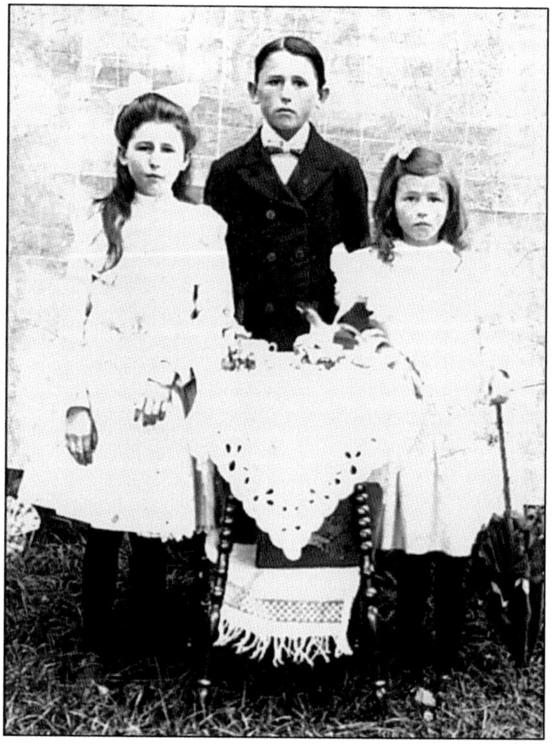

TEA TIME FOR THREE. It looks like big brother Chester Lee was drafted into accompanying his sisters Hallie and Cora to have their photo taken in this tea-party setting. This photo of the three Lee children is obviously a photographer's posed setting taken outdoors, since they are standing on grass. Perhaps it was taken at the Bourbon County Agricultural Fair or at Joyland.

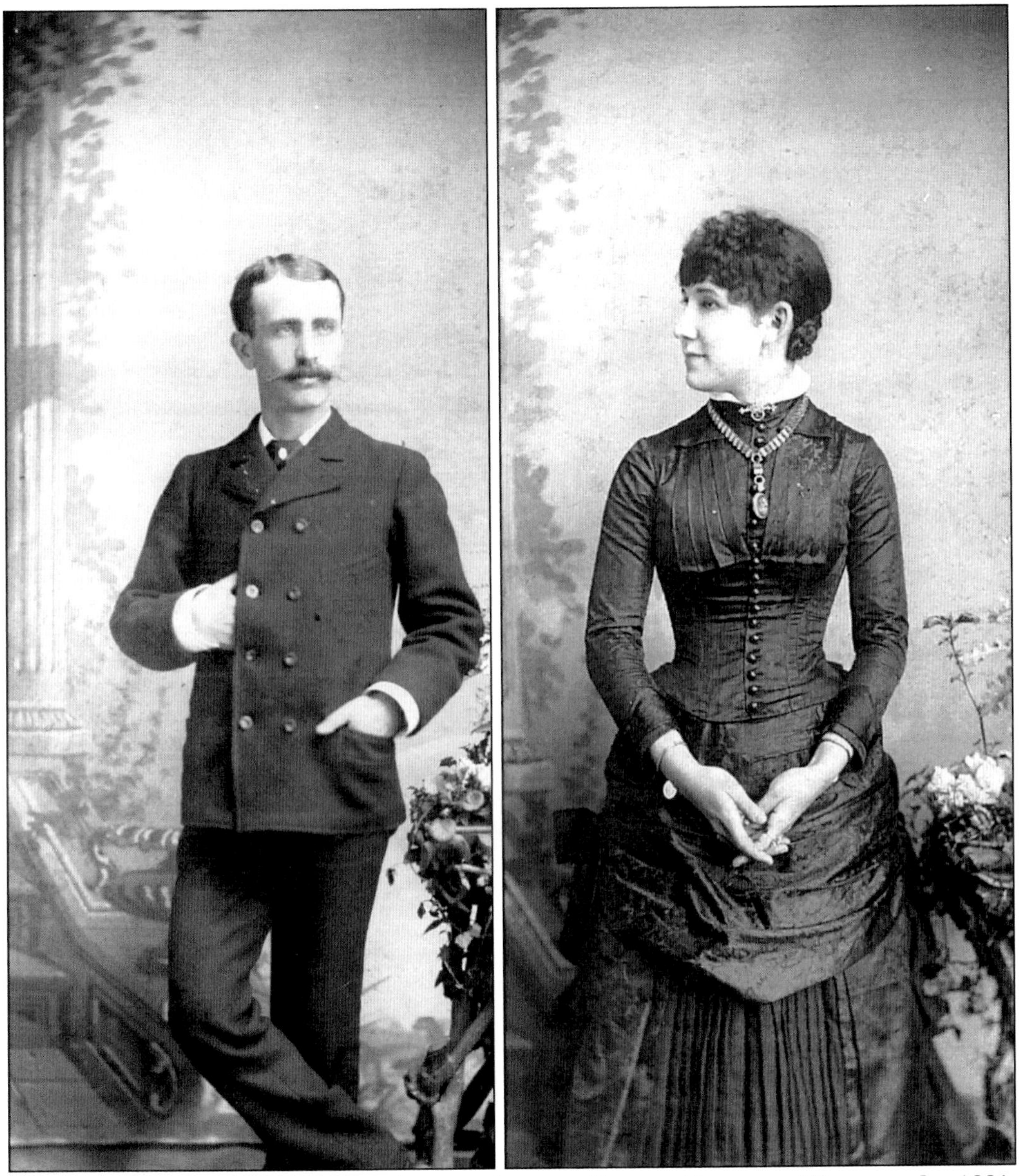

HANDSOME VICTORIAN COUPLE, ADOLPH J. AND FANNIE BARNETT WINTERS. In 1881, the dapper young man seen here opened a jewelry store on the Courthouse Square in Paris named A.J. Winters & Co. that advertised "Everything First Class." He received his training as a jeweler from A. Shire. The store, which was known across Central Kentucky, provided exceptional quality merchandise and service. These photographic portraits are very typical of the Victorian period and show the clothing styles prevalent at that time. The Winters' son, Barnett, took over the store in 1915 when his father died and finally sold the business in the 1970s.

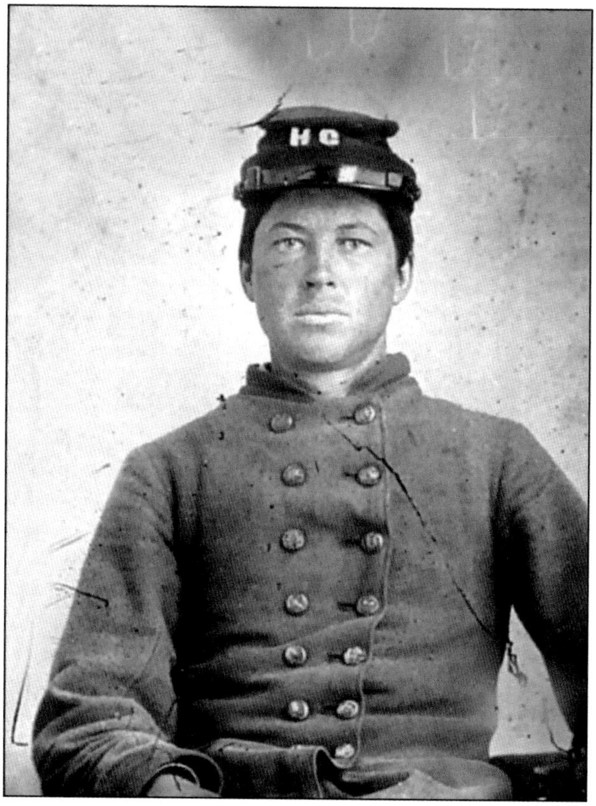

Members of the Hamilton Guard. In 1860 when the drums of war were beginning to beat across the United States, a number of state militia units were formed across Kentucky, many of them Confederate sympathizers. In Bourbon County such a unit was organized by Archibald W. Hamilton and named the Hamilton Guards (note the "H G" on the caps.) They became Company G of the Kentucky Second Infantry Regiment, CSA.

Benjamin F. Batterton. Fourth Sergeant Batterton was 21 when he enlisted. He was captured at Fort Donelson in February of 1862 and was exchanged along with other members of the company seven months later. He was selected to the Roll of Honor for his conduct at Chickamauga and surrendered with the company at the end of the war in 1865. He is buried in Ruddles Mills.

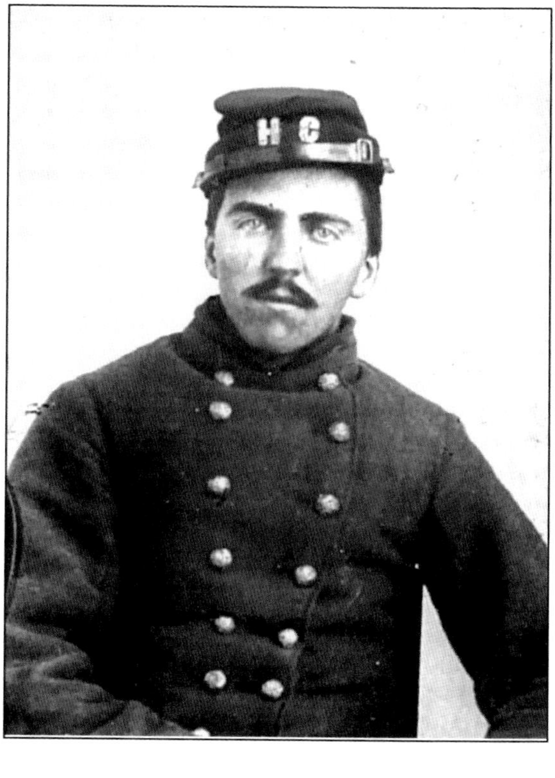

Daniel E. Turney. First Lieutenant Turney was a native of Paris and enlisted at the age of 24. He was named to the Confederate Roll of Honor for conduct at the Battle of Stones River in December of 1862. He was made Captain of Company I in 1863, which he commanded until being wounded and captured in Jonesboro, Georgia in 1864.

COMPANY G PART OF THE "ORPHAN BRIGADE." We know these pictures were taken before the unit marched off to war because they were members of Kentucky's famous "Orphan Brigade," a group that did not have the luxury of coming home on leave during the war. They fought in most of the major battles of the Western Campaign. There is an exhibit about Company G at the Hopewell Museum in Paris.

GEORGE W. MCINTIRE. Private McIntire was a Bourbon County resident and a 42-year-old, Mexican War-veteran when he answered the Confederate call. He was discharged in November of 1864, "due to age and disability."

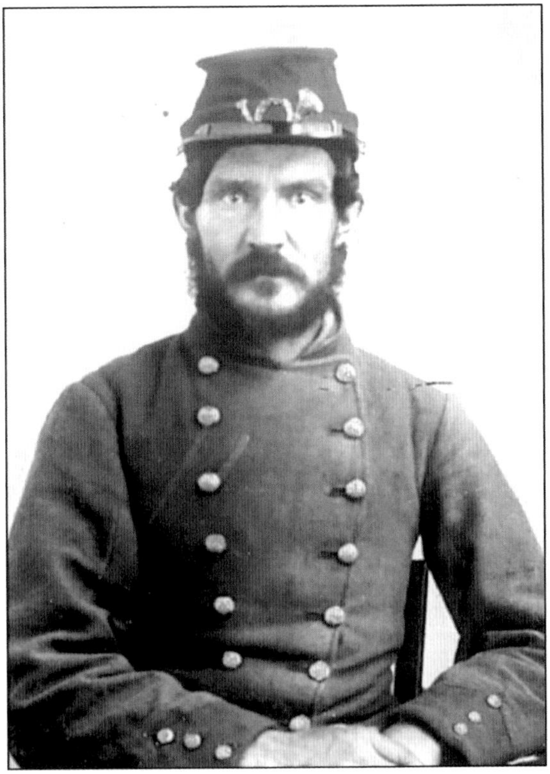

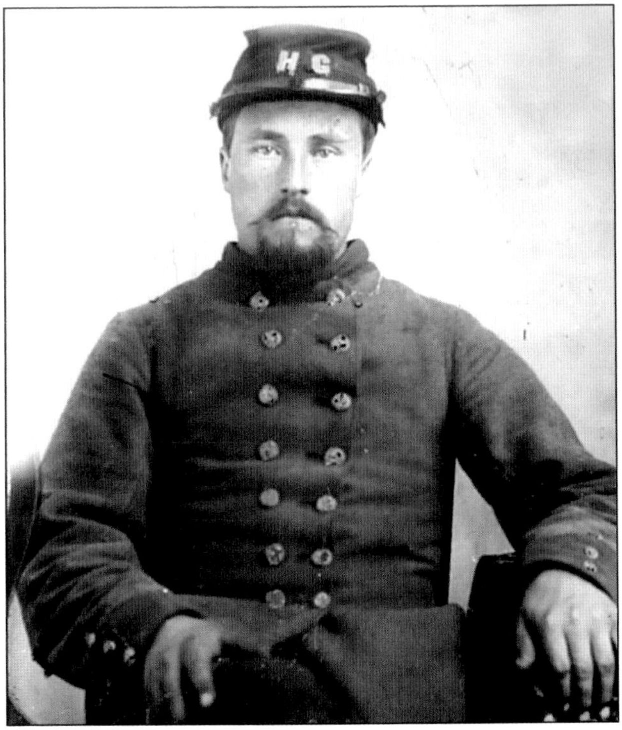

PETER MURPHY. Second Corporal Murphy came from Bourbon County and was 21 in 1861. He was wounded at the Battle of Chickamauga and died of his wounds a few days later. He was one of nine men in Company G who died due to that battle. The 2nd Kentucky Regiment lost 146 of 282 men engaged at Chickamauga.

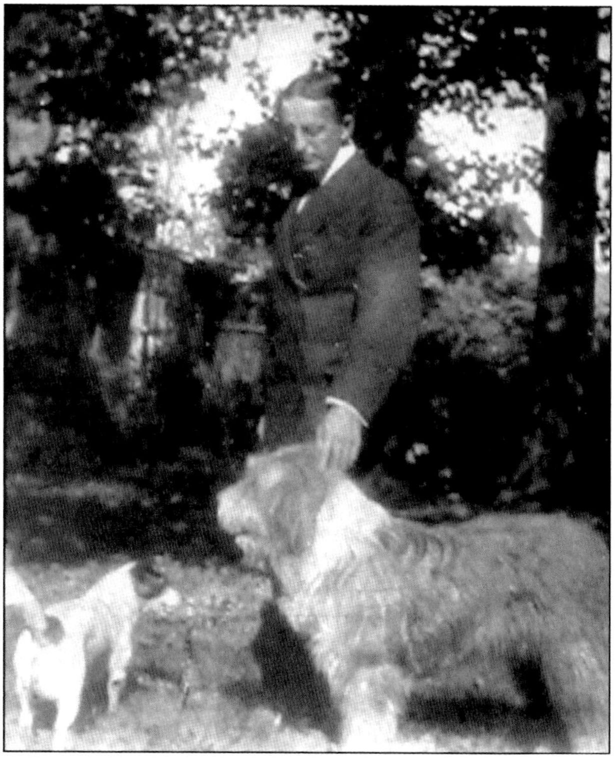

Famous Author With His Dogs. John Fox Jr. was born in 1862 at Stony Point in eastern Bourbon County where his father was schoolmaster at Stony Point Academy. After attending Transylvania University and graduating cum laude from Harvard, he went on to write a number of popular books about Appalachian Mountain life, including his 1903 novel *The Little Shepherd of Kingdom Come*. That book became America's first "million-seller." (U.K. Collection.)

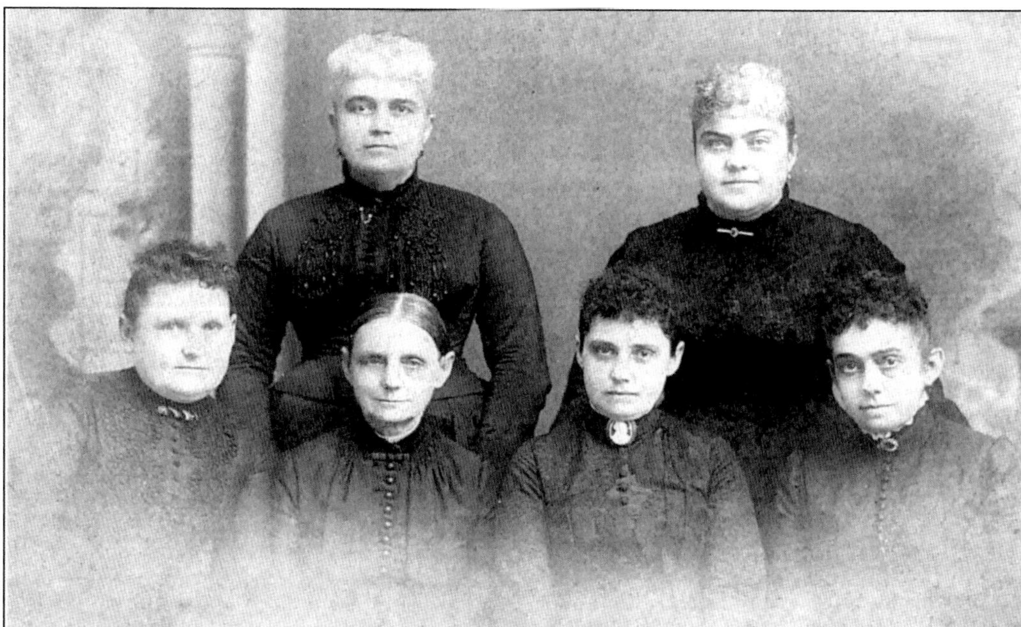

The Six Hutchcraft Sisters. This photograph was taken about 1890 at Lafayette Grinnan's studio on Main Street in Paris. The six daughters of James and Eliza Hutchcraft, pictured from left to right, are (front) Kate (m. Russell Mann); Fanny (m. Henry Hedges); Martha (m. Dr. William Miller); and Margaret "Mug" (m. Dr. J. Edward Ray); (back row) Anna (m. Dr. Charles Hart); and Harriet "Hattie" (m. William A. Hill), who was an internationally known artist.

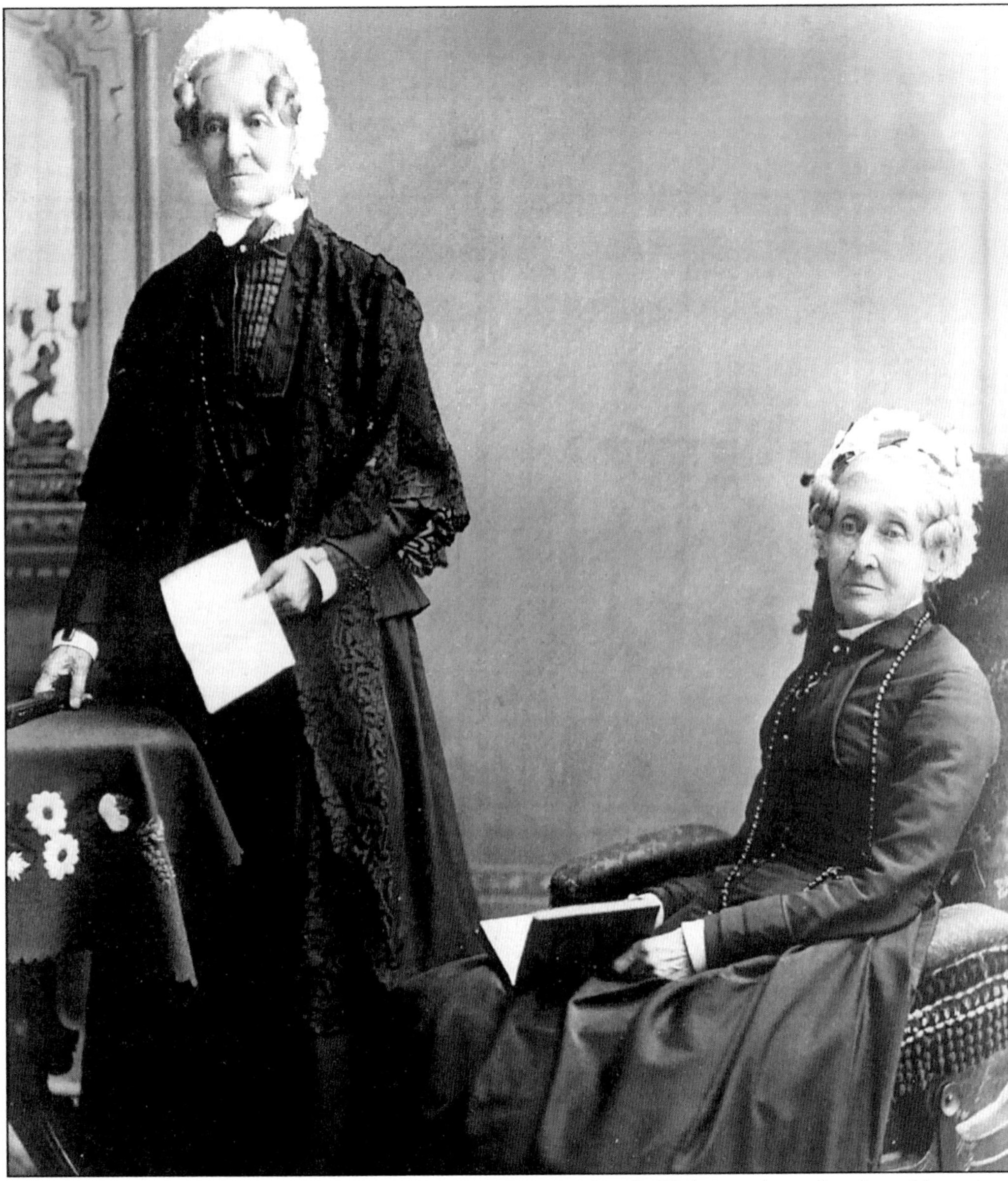

EMILY TUBMAN, ABOLITIONIST AND PHILANTHROPIST. Emily Tubman (standing) and her sister Louisa Keiningham spent summers in their home on Vine Street in Paris late in their lives when this photo was taken. Emily was only ten in 1804 when her father, Edmund Thomas, registrar of the Kentucky Land Office, died. He had been a close friend of statesman Henry Clay, who became the sisters' legal guardian and Clay's abolitionist feelings possibly had an influence on them. In 1818, Emily moved to Georgia and married Richard Tubman. When he died in 1836, she inherited several plantations. In 1842 she gave her slaves the choice of remaining in her household as paid servants or being freed to join a colony that American emancipationists had established in Liberia on the west coast of Africa. Of her 144 slaves, 75 chose to stay and the remainder went to Liberia. Mrs. Tubman also started a free school in Paris behind the Christian Church and donated generous sums to orphanages, colleges, and both the Frankfort and Paris Christian Churches. She died in 1885.

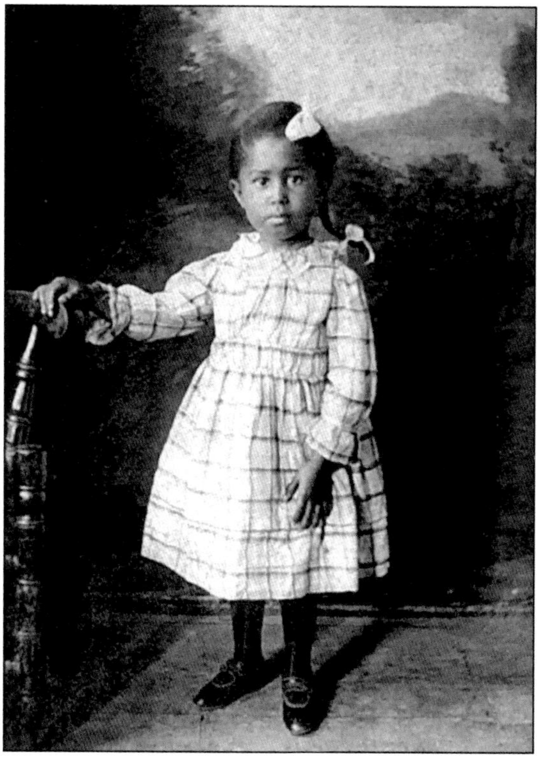

DRUSILLA ALLEN'S PHOTO, TAKEN MORE THAN A CENTURY AGO. This photo of little Drusilla Allen of Paris was probably taken before 1900. Even though the art of photography was fairly new in the 1890s, a town like Paris could support several professional photographers and the images they captured bring us invaluable information about people and places of the past.

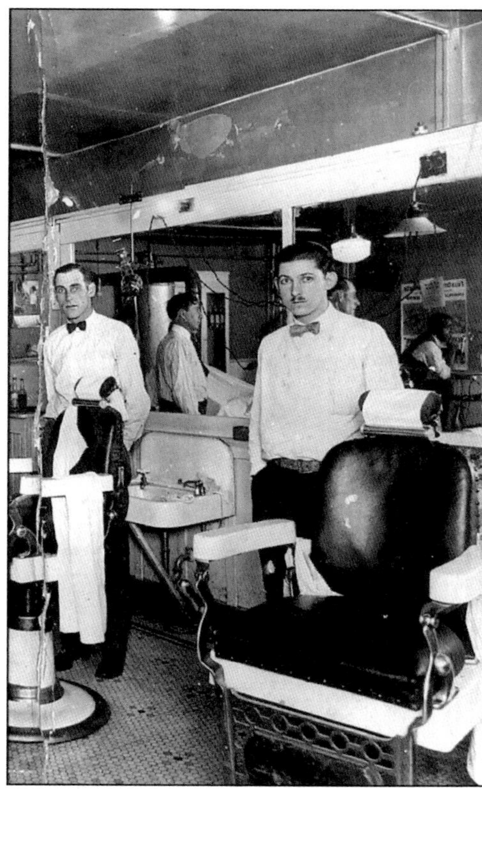

SHAVE AND A HAIRCUT? In 1923, Bill Morris (left) and Bob Harney (right) came to the popular Fordham Hotel in Paris to cut hair in the barbershop in its lobby. Harney did so until 1932 when fire destroyed the hotel. He continued to operate barbershops on Main Street until he passed away at the age of 76 in 1981 after cutting hair for 59 years.

UNITED STATES SENATOR FROM PARIS, VIRGIL CHAPMAN. Born in Southern Kentucky's Simpson County, Chapman moved to Paris and became a prominent Democratic Party leader after he assisted in organizing the tobacco growers of Kentucky and nearby states into cooperative marketing associations. He was elected to ten terms as United States congressman between 1925 and 1948. Chapman was elected to the Senate in 1948 and served until his death following an automobile accident in 1951. (U.K. Collection.)

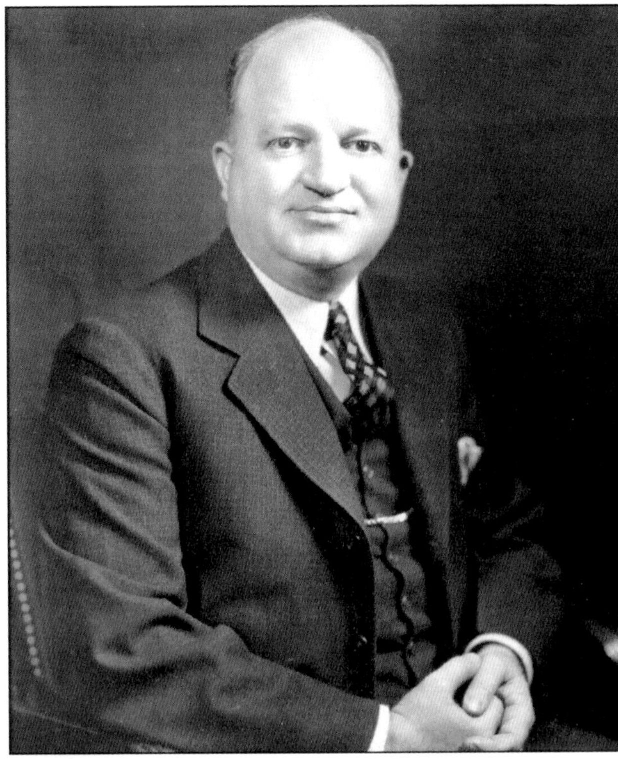

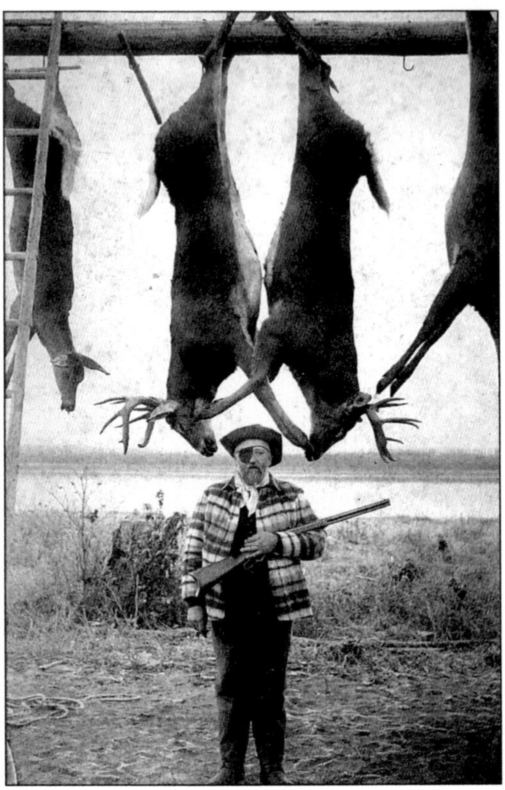

A BAD DAY FOR DEER. Losing an eye during the Civil War in a battle near Paintsville did not keep Col. Ezekial F. Clay from being a good shot. Clay was commander of the Confederate First Kentucky Rifles. Besides being a successful horse breeder, he was also a supporter of some of the local early sportsmen's and shooting clubs. This picture was not taken in Bourbon County, but in Florida where he often went to hunt.

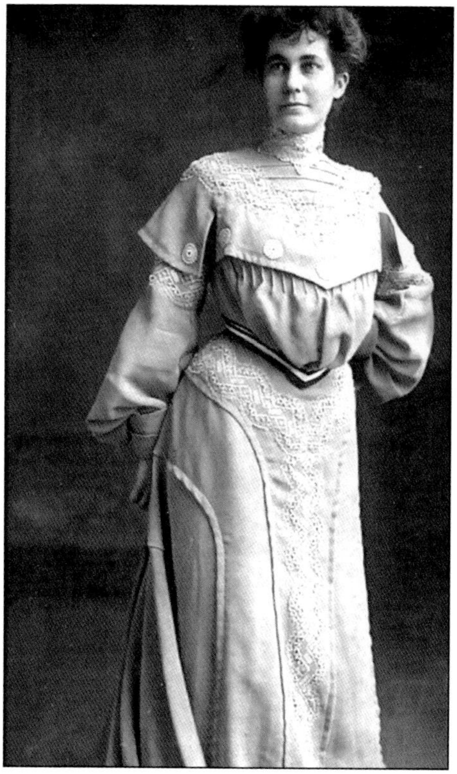

When Irish Eyes are Smiling. This photo was taken of Miss Julia O'Brien in 1896. She taught sixth grade and music at the Paris City School and was remembered fondly by former students. "She always looked beautiful to us children, with her typical Irish beauty enhanced by as typical Irish wit and good humor—what child could not be happy in school under such an influence?" wrote one student, years later.

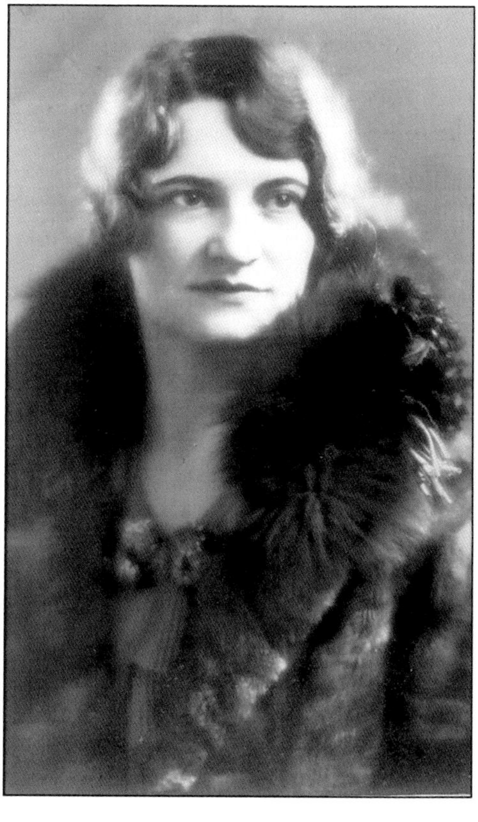

PHS Grad Became Successful Businesswoman. Josephine Ewalt, Bourbon County native and Paris High School graduate, went on to become a public relations executive and board member of the U.S. Savings and Loan Association. She worked out of the association's offices in Chicago and Washington, D.C. and later traveled around the world when she was elected as the secretary-general of the International Union of Loan Associations, a position she held from 1965 to 1971.

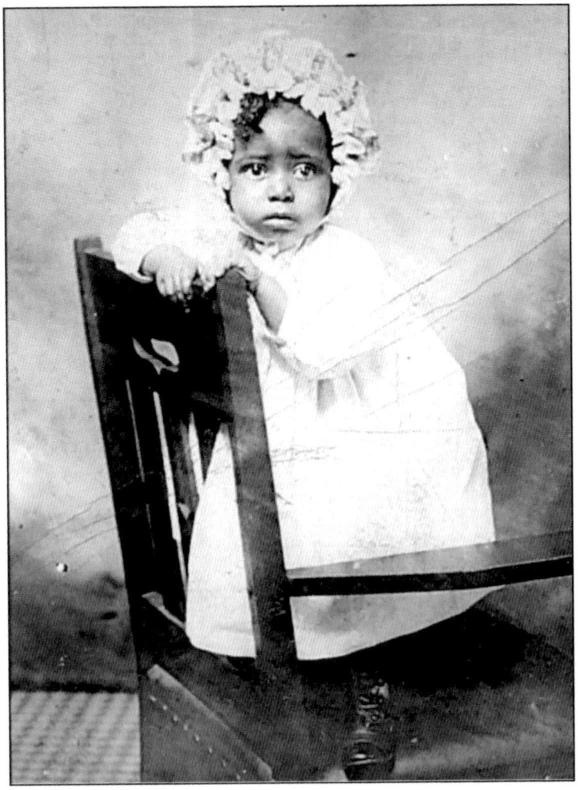

1912 Baby Photo of Edna Patterson Wright. This cute mop-capped baby grew up to graduate from Western High School in Paris and then from Kentucky State University. She taught school for more than 45 years—first in Eastern Kentucky and then in Michigan after earning a graduate degree at the University of Michigan. In the early 1990s, she retired and came home to Bourbon County to live.

Dick Family Amid Spring Flowers. It looks like it was a sunny spring day when this photo was taken in 1930 of Lucile Barnes Crouch Dick of North Middletown and her three children: Florence, David, and Jane. David Dick graduated from North Middletown High School and the University of Kentucky and became an award-winning newsman at CBS News. He is the author of numerous books—several focusing on his Bourbon County home.

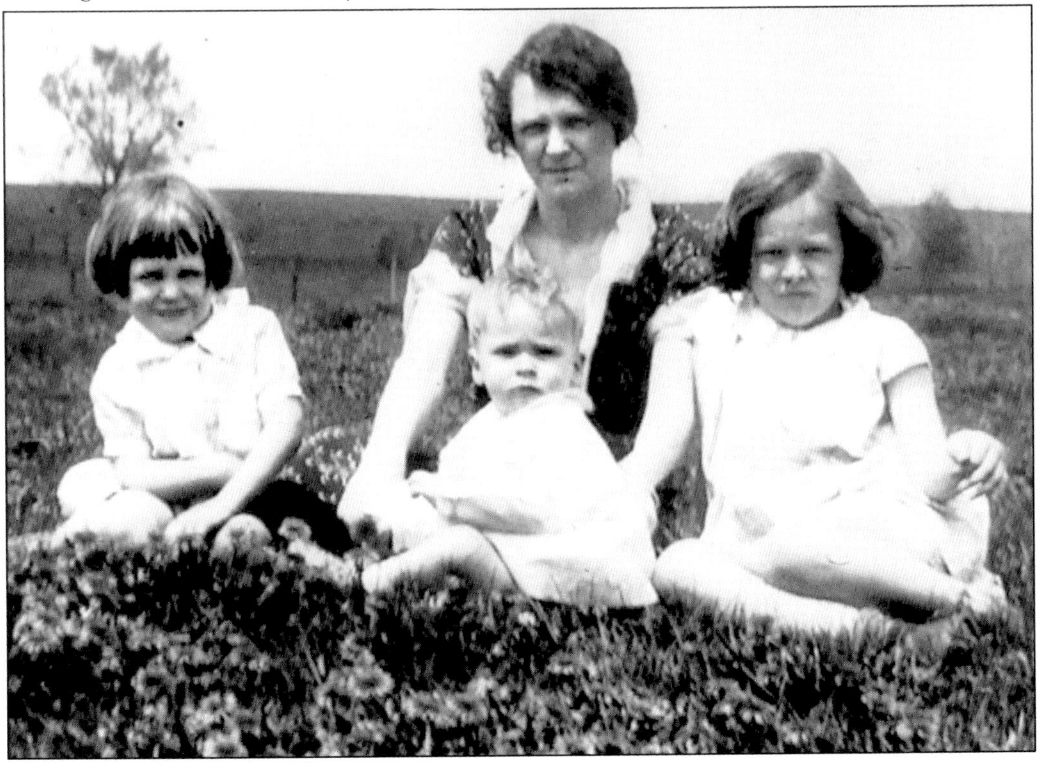

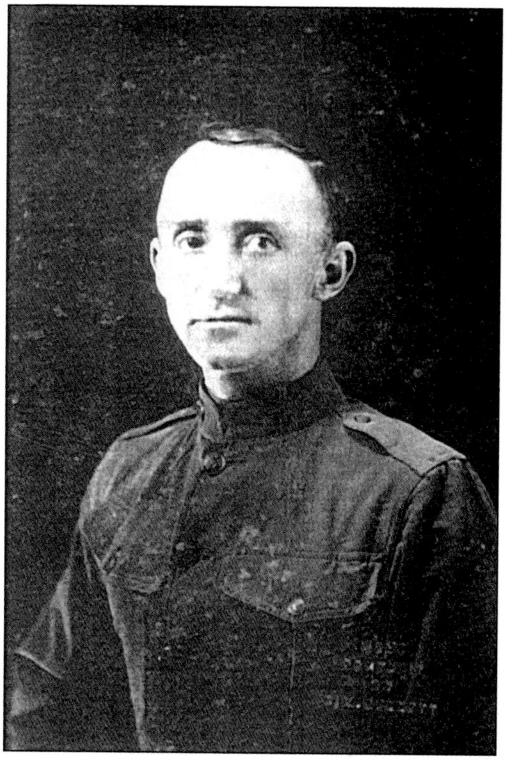

MMI Alumnus in World War I. John Allen Mason of Bourbon County attended Millersburg Military Institute and was drafted into the army in 1918 along with his friend Isaac Eurove (Mason is seen here in his U.S. Army uniform.) Both were sent to Europe and on the bloody battlefield of Argonne they met up with another Millersburg friend, Jim Miller. All three returned safely to Bourbon County.

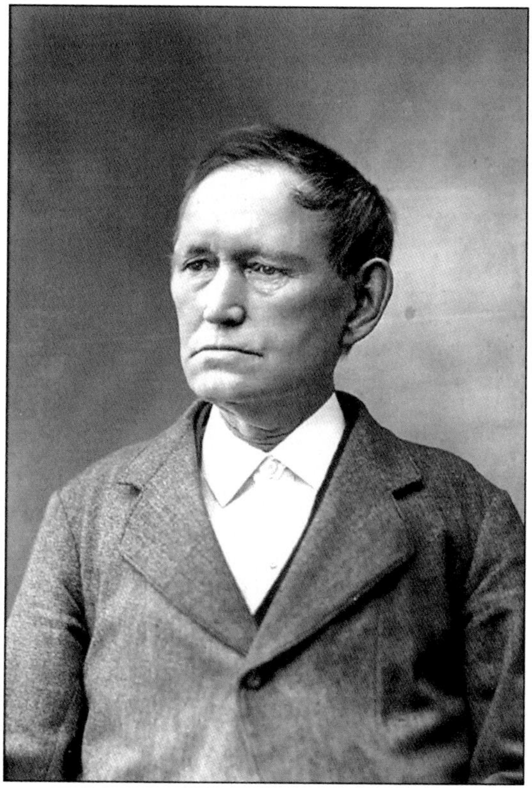

Unidentified Man With Expressive Face. This man's name has been lost over time, but his face still tells a story of possible hardships and difficulties overcome. The photo is sharp and clear and was the work of one of the many photographers who worked in Bourbon County—unsung heroes for those who treasure historical photographs. The photographer who took this photo is listed as Mrs. J. Walker on an 1879 list.

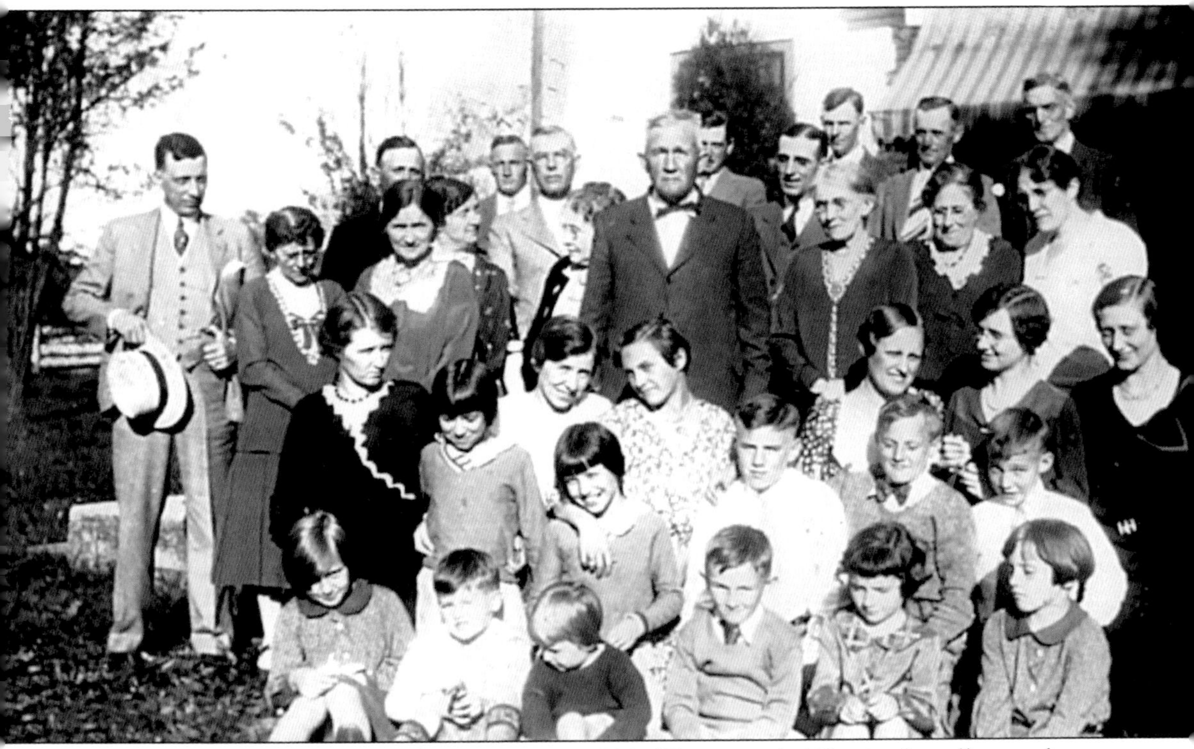

50TH WEDDING ANNIVERSARY GATHERING IN 1931. The extended Burris clan all turned out for the 50th wedding anniversary of Jonathan and Mary (Mollie J.) Burris who were married on October 18, 1881, and are centered in the photo above. This photo, which shows the strong family resemblance among the Burris family, was taken in the front yard of their home. Pictured from left to right are (first row) Bessie Burris, Carlton Lambert, Gay Lambert, John Curtis Burris, Edwina Burris, and Charleen Burris; (second row) Betty Tripp, Mollie Tripp, Francis C. Bryan, James B. Clark, and Bill Burris Bryan; (third row) Mollie Lambert, Sidney Burris Tripp, Helen Clark, Mary Margaret Clark, Alleen Burris, and Minerva Lambert; (fourth row) Arthur J. Willey, Willie B. Willey, Aimee Burris Bryan, Elizabeth Burris, Fannie Lambert, Jonathan Burris, Mary (Mollie J.) Burris, Lizzie Myers, and Irene Burris Clark; (fifth row) Finley Burris, Charles Burris, Carlton Lambert, Boardman Lambert, Oliver Lambert, James C. Bryan, Troup Clark, and Herdy Myers.

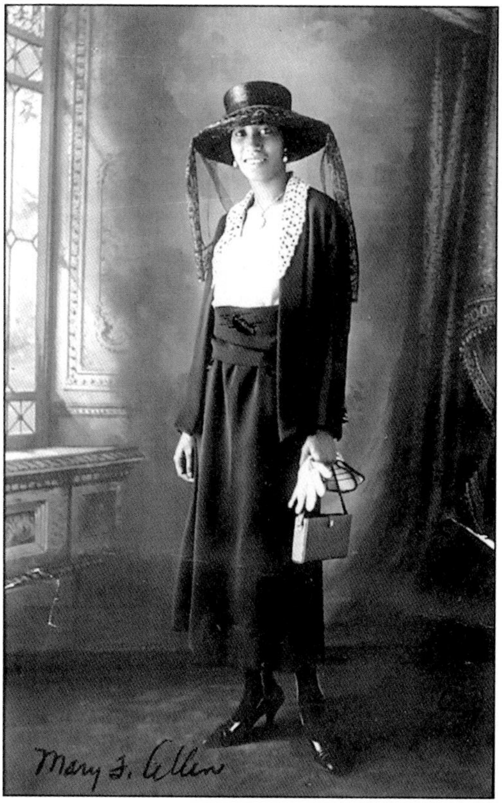

Vintage Picture of a Fashionable Lady. This photo, taken in the 1920s of Mary Florence Allen, illustrates the fashions of the day as she is pictured in an ensemble perfect down to her white gloves and gleaming, patent leather shoes. Mary Florence Allen lived near Little Rock and is representative of the prosperous, African-American middle class in Bourbon County in the period between the two world wars.

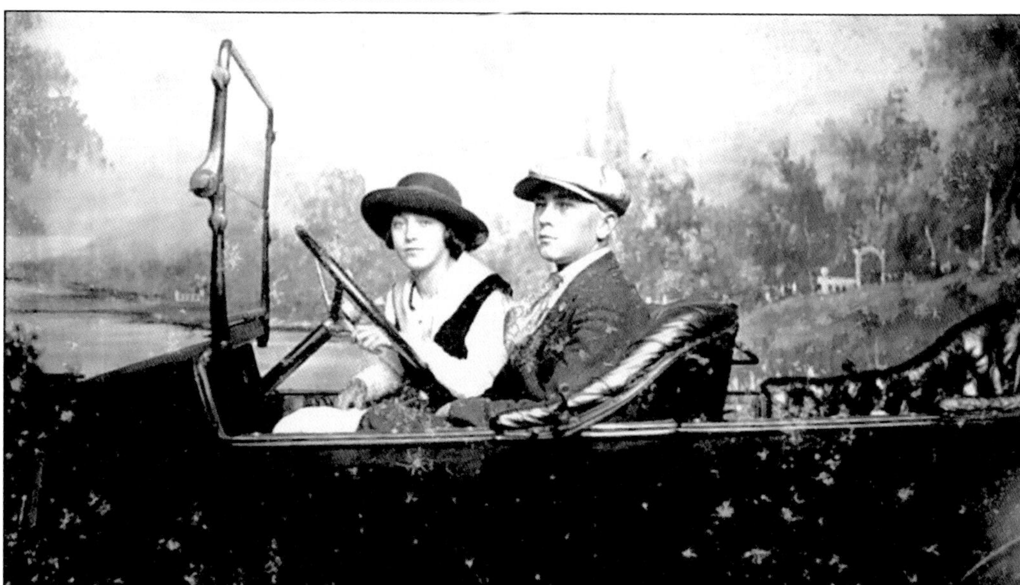

Driving a Make-Believe Car at Joyland. Parisian Lula Lytle Doty and a boy friend had this picture taken in an automobile in front of a painted background at Joyland Amusement Park. Joyland opened in 1923 and was situated on 25 acres just north of Lexington on the Paris Pike. Bourbon Countians could reach the park on the interurban line that stopped at the park's entrance. Joyland closed in the 1960s after two fires.

JULIA SPENCER ARDERY AT FOUR. Young Julia Spencer grew up and married William Ardery. She lived in Bourbon County most of her life and was a renowned genealogist and local historian. She compiled the two-volume *Kentucky Court and Other Records* and was the driving force in the fight by the local chapter of the Daughters of the American Revolution to save historic Duncan Tavern on the courthouse square. (U.K. Collection.)

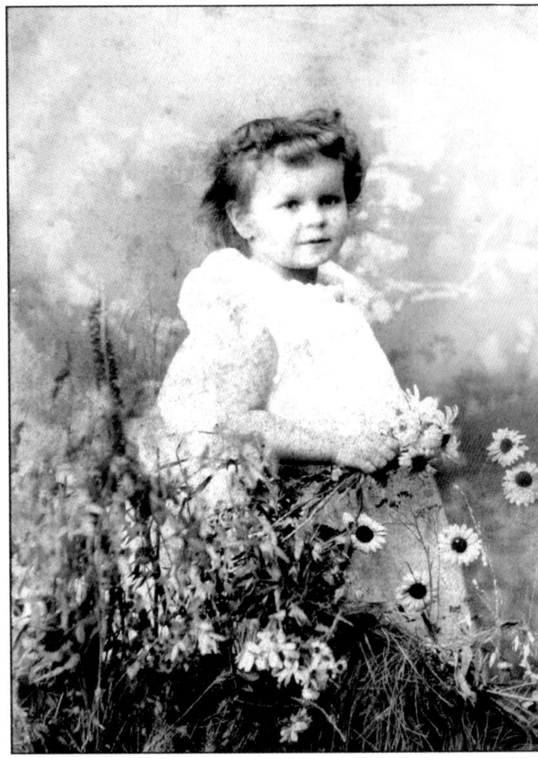

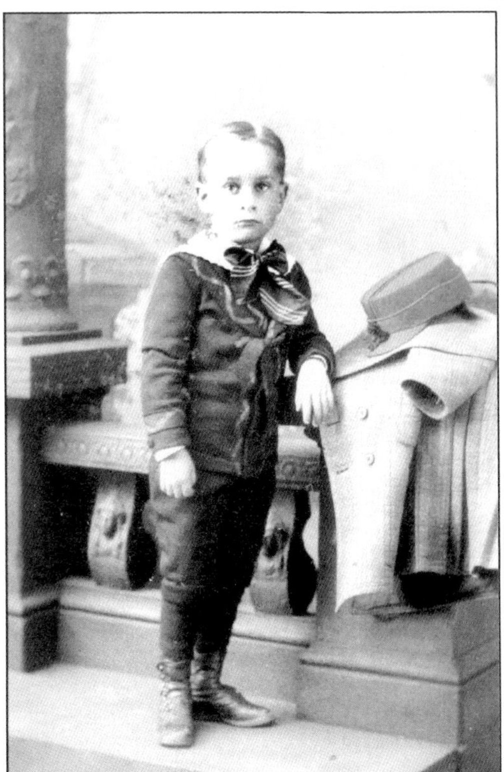

WILLIAM BRECKINRIDGE ARDERY BORN IN 1887. That means this photo was taken around 1890. When he was quite a bit older, Ardery became the owner/editor/publisher of the *Paris Democrat*, a weekly newspaper. As is obvious from the name of his newspaper, he was very active in local and state politics. He served in the state legislature and was elected circuit court judge in 1936. He served as judge for more than 20 years. (U.K. Collection.)

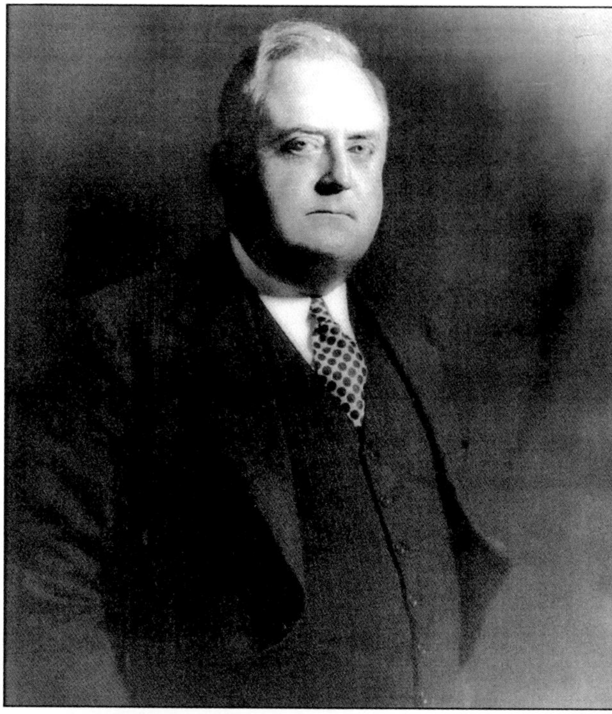

George Batterton, County Judge for 32 Years. Serving a record 32 years as Bourbon County judge, Batterton was first elected in 1918 and served eight, four-year terms before retiring in 1949. A graduate of Centre College Law School, he served as county attorney for eight years before he was judge. A dominating Democratic leader for decades, he is remembered for his tight fiscal policies and his determination to see a local hospital opened.

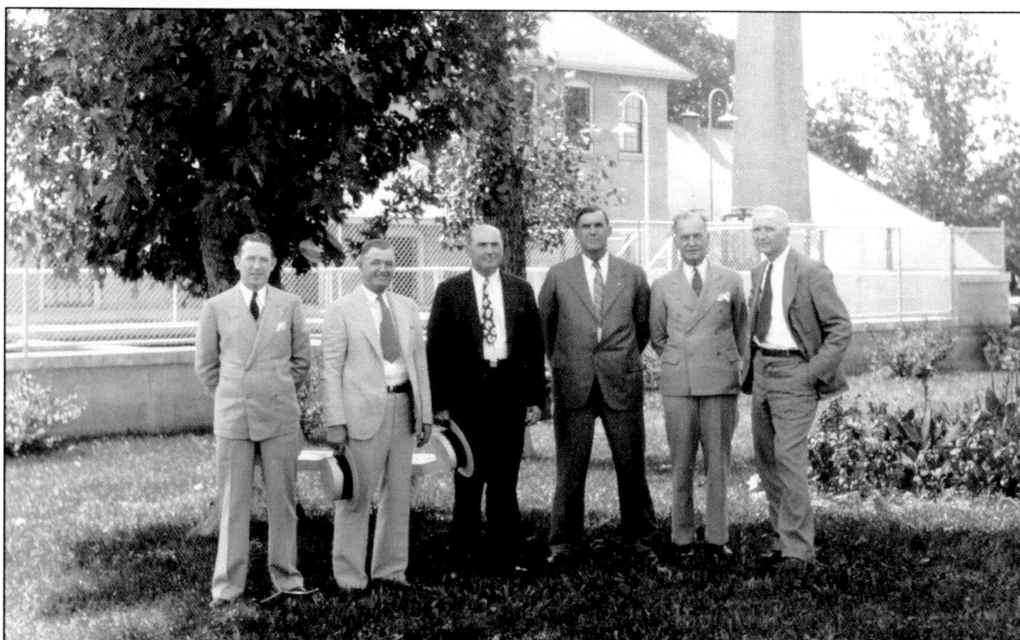

Paris City Commissioners at New Municipal Water Plant. Pictured in 1932, these community leaders guided Paris during much of the Depression era. Pictured from left to right are Commissioner Raymond Connell, City Manager Boone Baldwin (served 24 years), Commissioners McClanahan, Jeff Denton, Withers Davis, and Mayor George Doyle (six-term mayor). The construction of the water plant and the city power facility are considered pivotal accomplishments in the growth of Paris. (U.K. Collection.)

Five

Education in Black and White

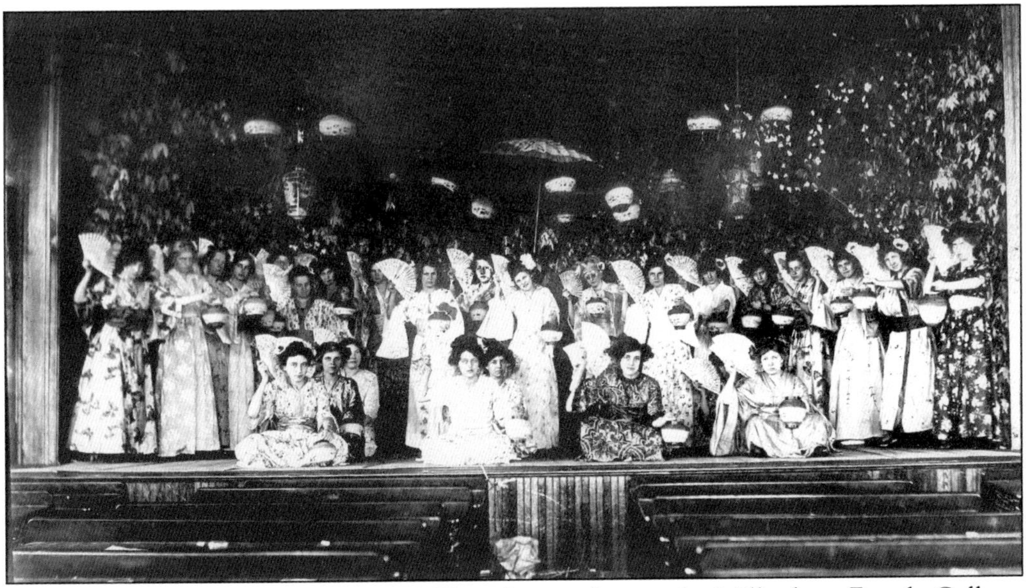

Mini-Mikado in 1914 Millersburg? This photo, taken at the Millersburg Female College, was identified as "A Chinese Operetta-Commencement 1914." It illustrates both the school's popularity during that era and the prevalence of large, costumed set pieces put on by the students for family, friends, and classmates. Millersburg Female College was founded in 1860 and lasted well into the 1920s. The year 1914 brought big changes for the institution. That summer, a large annex was constructed containing a gymnasium, a swimming pool, a "society hall," studios, and dormitory rooms according to the 1915 announcement bulletin. Also in 1914, the word "Female" was dropped from the name of the school as the word was not "in as good repute as in former days, according to the same bulletin."

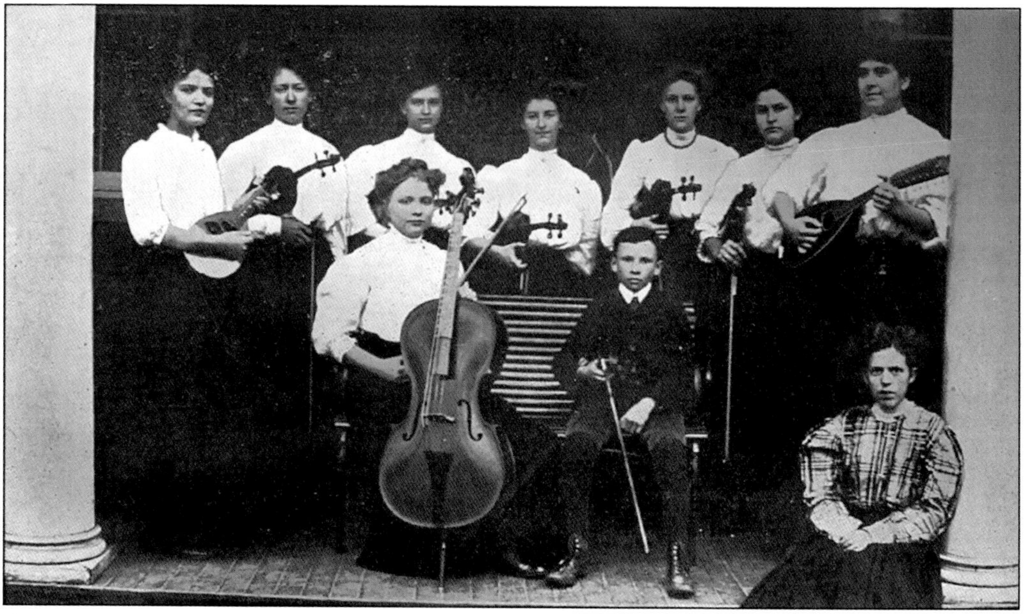

String Music in Millersburg, Kentucky. Not only was "book learning" important to the students at Millersburg Female College, the fine arts were also emphasized including music, art, and drama. The stringed instrument students listed in the 1907 register of the MFC included violin students Raymond Booth, Kittie Burberry, Louise Cray, Dorothy Moremen, Carrie Reib, and Anna Webber; cello student Ethel Fisher, and mandolin student Bessie Hardie.

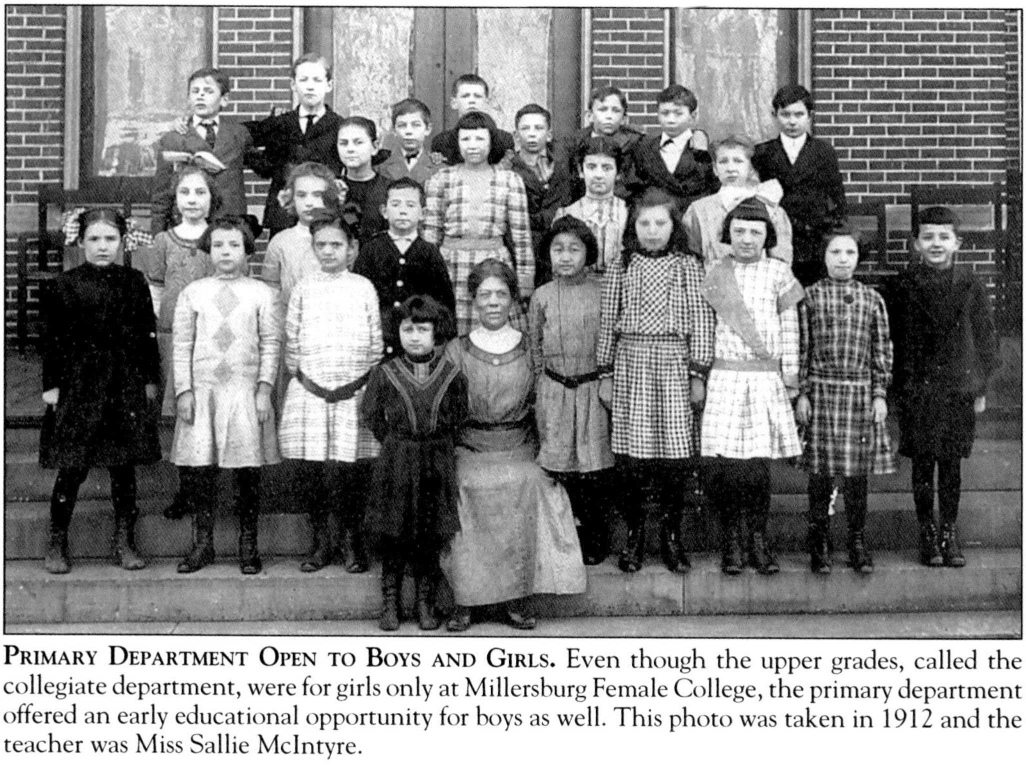

Primary Department Open to Boys and Girls. Even though the upper grades, called the collegiate department, were for girls only at Millersburg Female College, the primary department offered an early educational opportunity for boys as well. This photo was taken in 1912 and the teacher was Miss Sallie McIntyre.

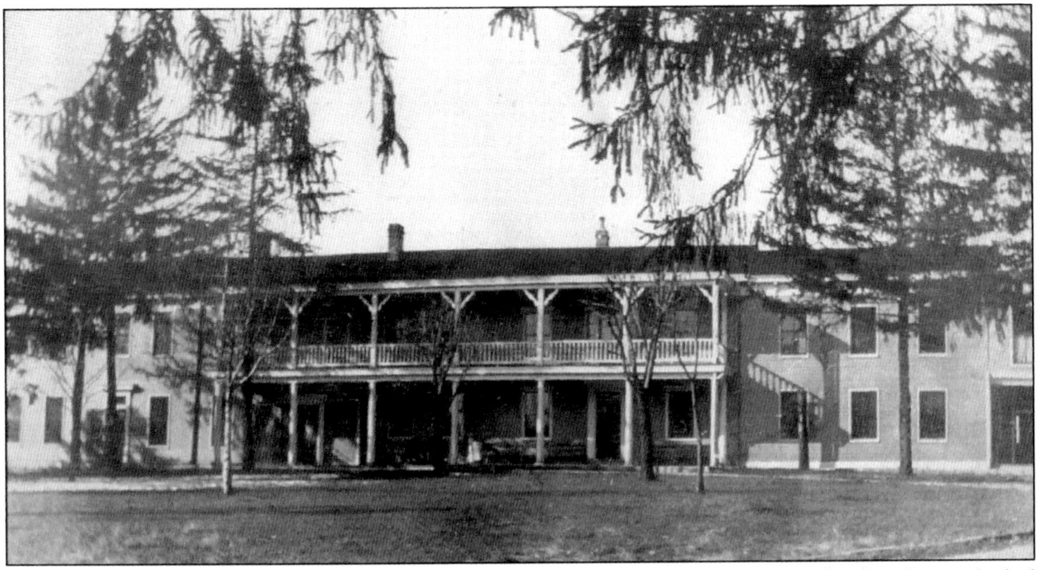

Bourbon Female College Building Still Standing Today. In 1908, the faculty included M.G. Thompson, president and Hattie Hutchcraft Hill, well-known Paris artist, who taught both art and French. The frame building, located off Cypress Street, served as a school until 1914 and is now used as an apartment building. Bourbon Female College boarding students wore academic gowns and mortarboard hats to all public events including church services. (U.K. Collection.)

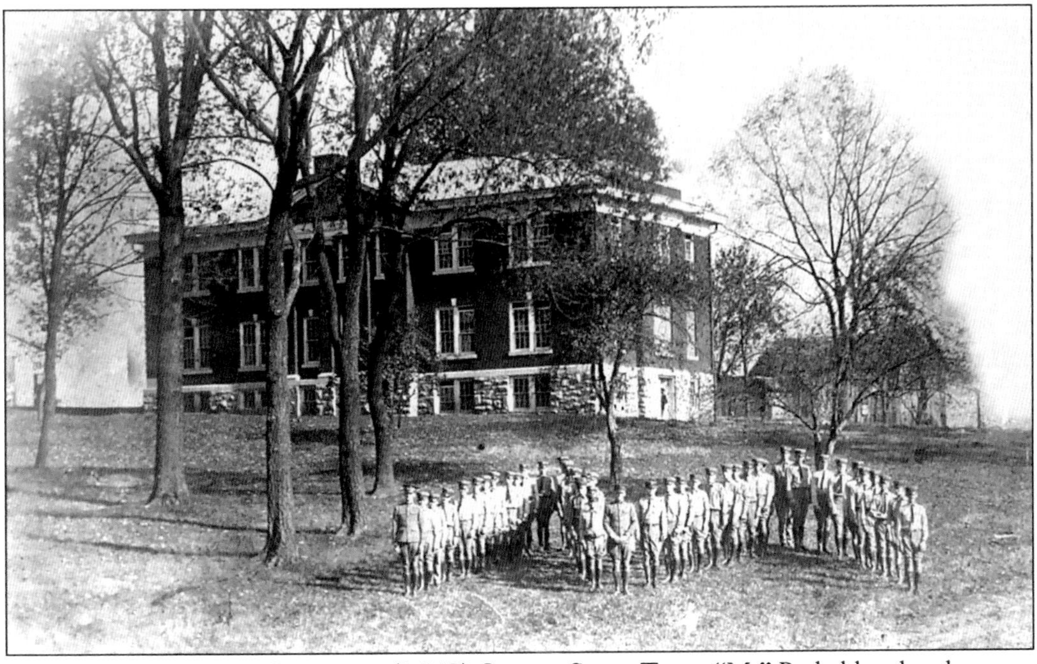

Millersburg Military Institute (MMI) Cadets Show Their "M." Probably taken between 1925 and 1930 in front of Moffett Hall on the campus of MMI, this photo shows the cadets forming the letter "M" in honor of their school. MMI was established by Col. C.M. Best in 1893 and was known as the Millersburg Training School until 1898, when he purchased the school building and changed the name of the school to Millersburg Military Institute.

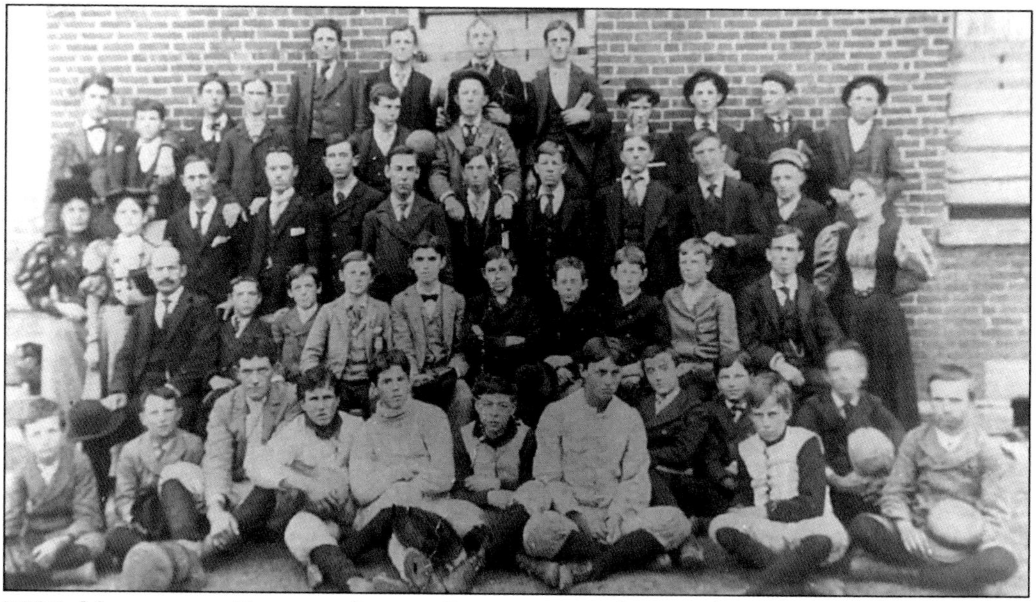

1890s Millersburg Training School Students and Staff. The community of Millersburg was very proud of the schools that brought countless students from across the country to their town. Millersburg residents came out to help Colonel and Mrs. Best make their dream of a military school a reality in 1898 with a barbecue that raised $400 in cash to purchase the necessary swords, rifles, and uniforms to outfit cadets at Millersburg Military Institute.

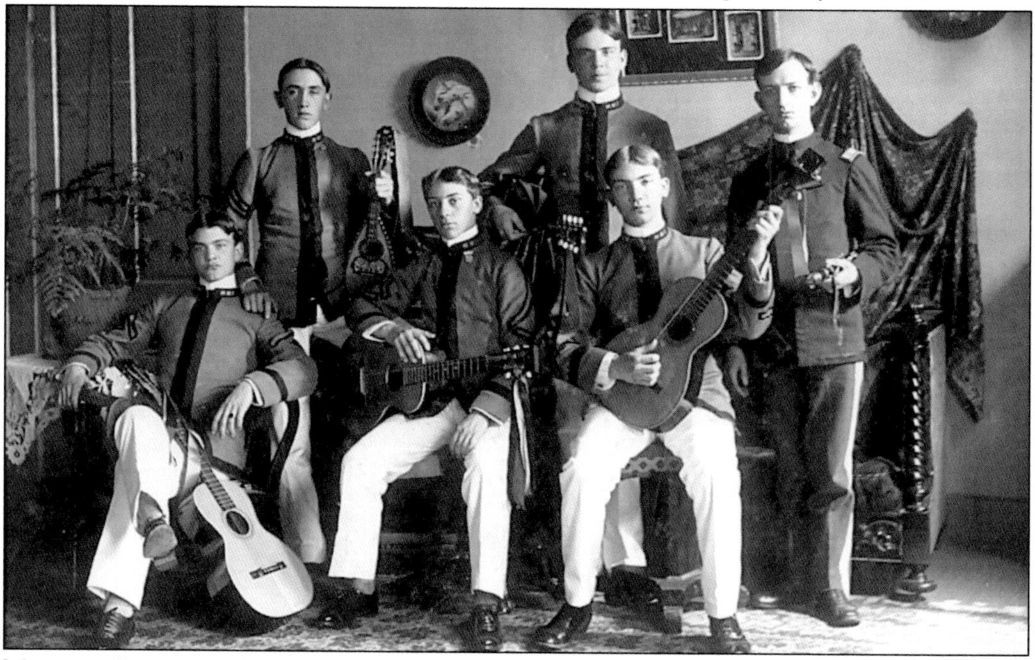

Musical Cadets at Millersburg Military Institute. This group of cadets is shown with their musical instruments—perhaps they were rehearsing. In 1929, MMI purchased the former Millersburg College building and opened a Junior School for younger boys in that facility in 1931. MMI has educated hundreds of boys during the past century and is now a co-educational institution with a new name—Millersburg Military Academy.

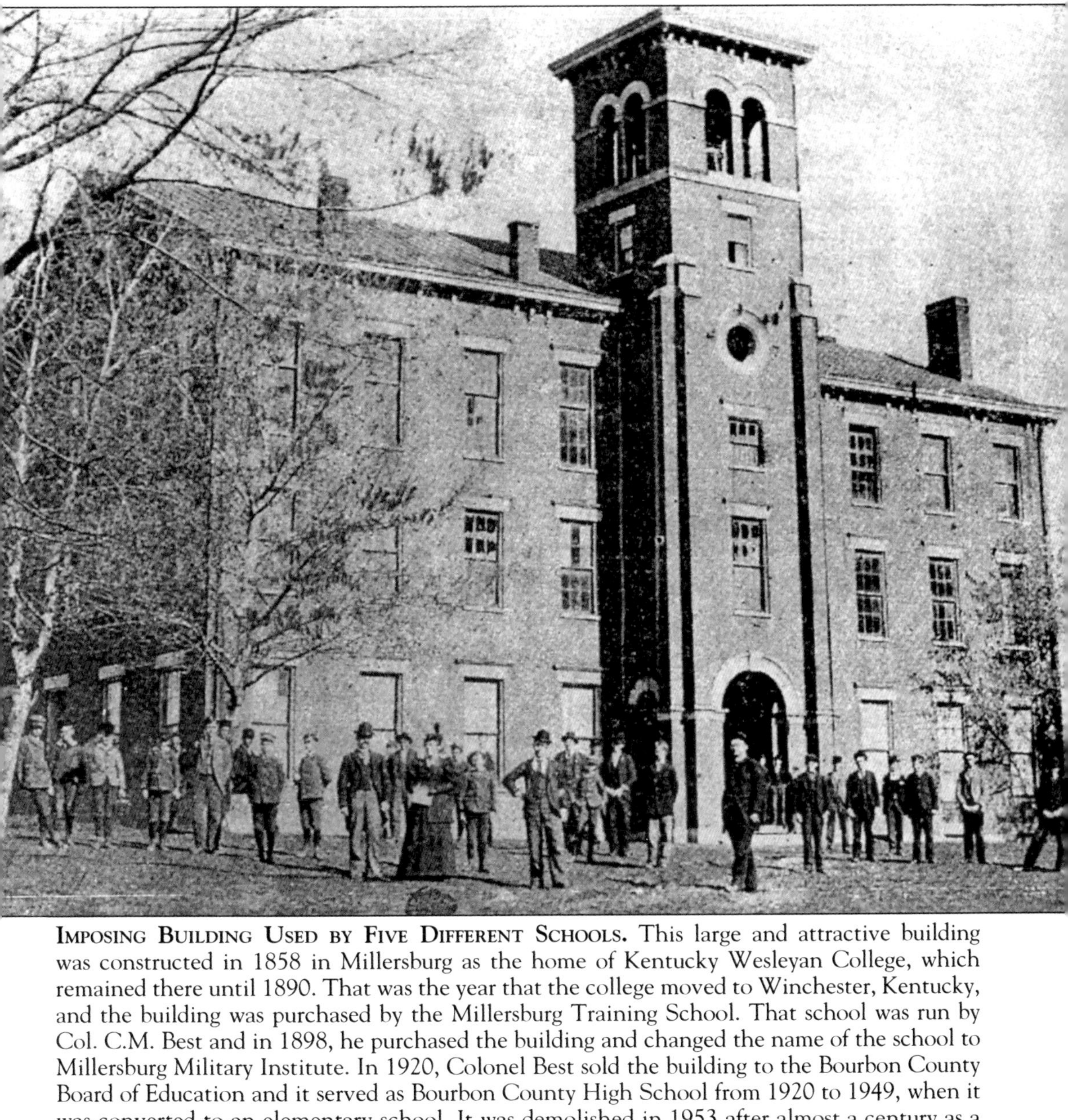

IMPOSING BUILDING USED BY FIVE DIFFERENT SCHOOLS. This large and attractive building was constructed in 1858 in Millersburg as the home of Kentucky Wesleyan College, which remained there until 1890. That was the year that the college moved to Winchester, Kentucky, and the building was purchased by the Millersburg Training School. That school was run by Col. C.M. Best and in 1898, he purchased the building and changed the name of the school to Millersburg Military Institute. In 1920, Colonel Best sold the building to the Bourbon County Board of Education and it served as Bourbon County High School from 1920 to 1949, when it was converted to an elementary school. It was demolished in 1953 after almost a century as a school serving thousands of children.

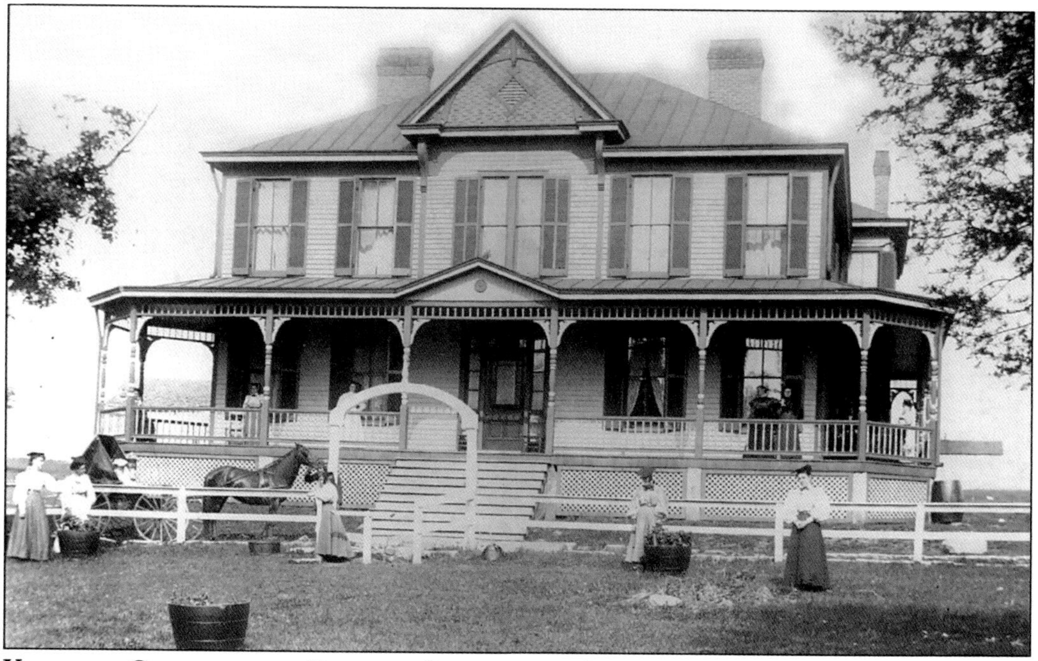

Kentucky Classical and Business College was Located in North Middletown. The school was co-educational but offered boarding facilities only for boys. There were more than 75 students in 1906 including boys and girls from North Middletown, Danville, Lexington, Covington, Clintonville as well as Cincinnati, Ohio, and Springfield, Tennessee. This photo shows the school building that year.

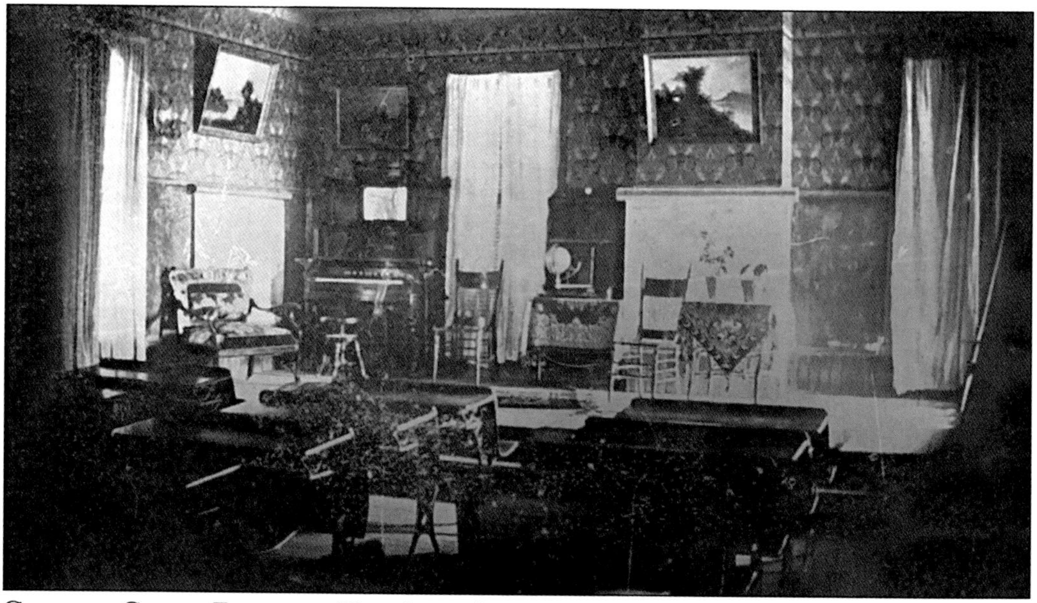

Going to Chapel Everyday. This photo shows a corner of the chapel at Kentucky Classical and Business College in 1906. All the students were required to attend chapel services each morning. Annual tuition fees for the school were modest: $60 for the Collegiate Department; $50 for the Preparatory Department; $40 for the Intermediate Department; and $30 for the Primary Department.

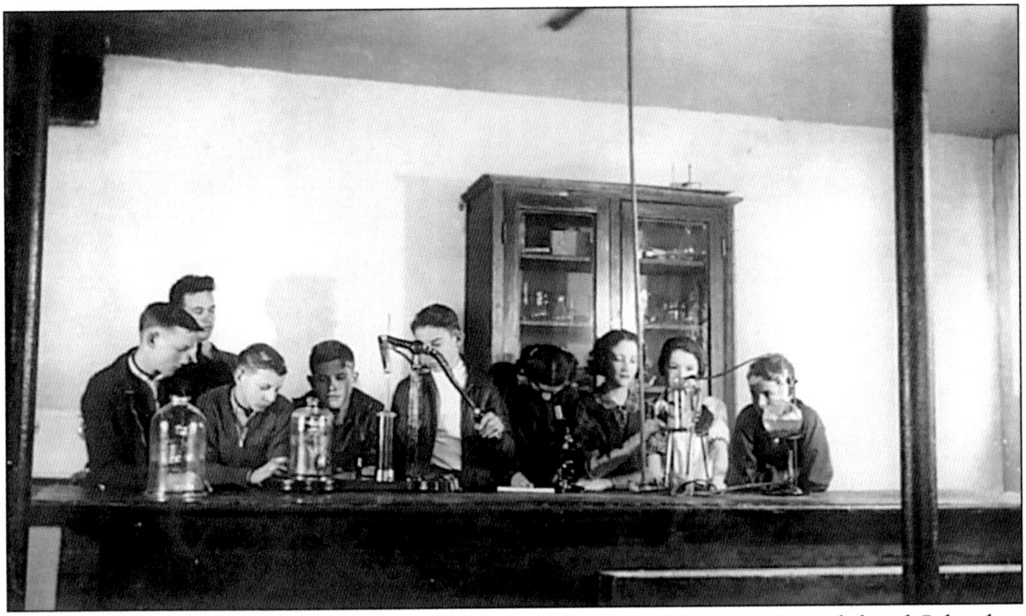

Busy Science Department. This photo, taken at North Middletown Consolidated School in 1937, shows students busy at work in the science department. The school, formed in 1857 by Professor Patterson, had a long history. It became one of the county's graded schools in 1919 and it was made one of the county's six consolidated schools in 1926. A new building was constructed in 1927, during the county school system's building boom.

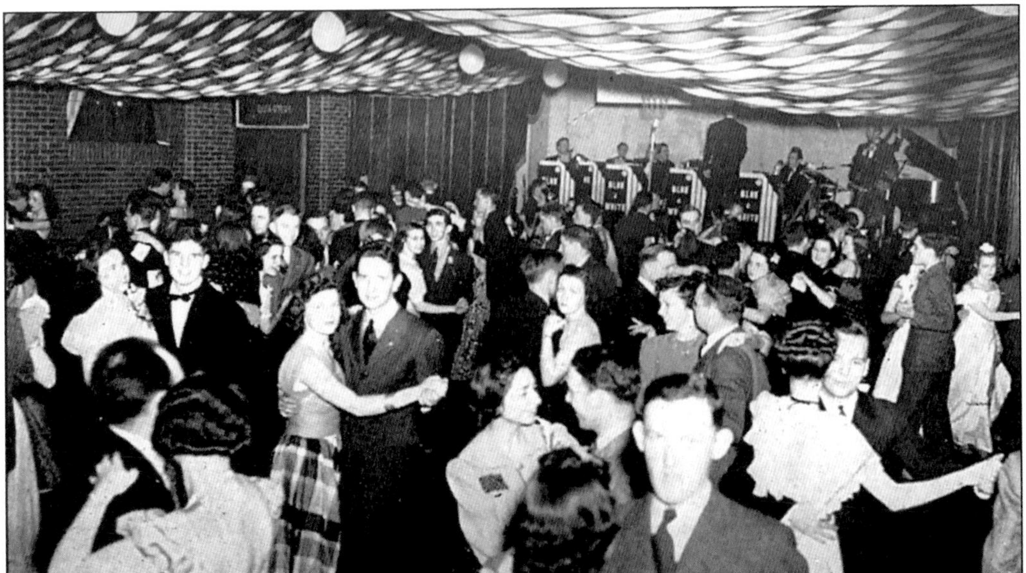

Dancing Cheek to Cheek. In April of 1940, the Athletic Department at North Middletown High School sponsored the fourth annual basketball dance. Seen above is the crowded dance floor. The students partied from 10 p.m. to 2 a.m. to the sounds of the Blue and White Orchestra.

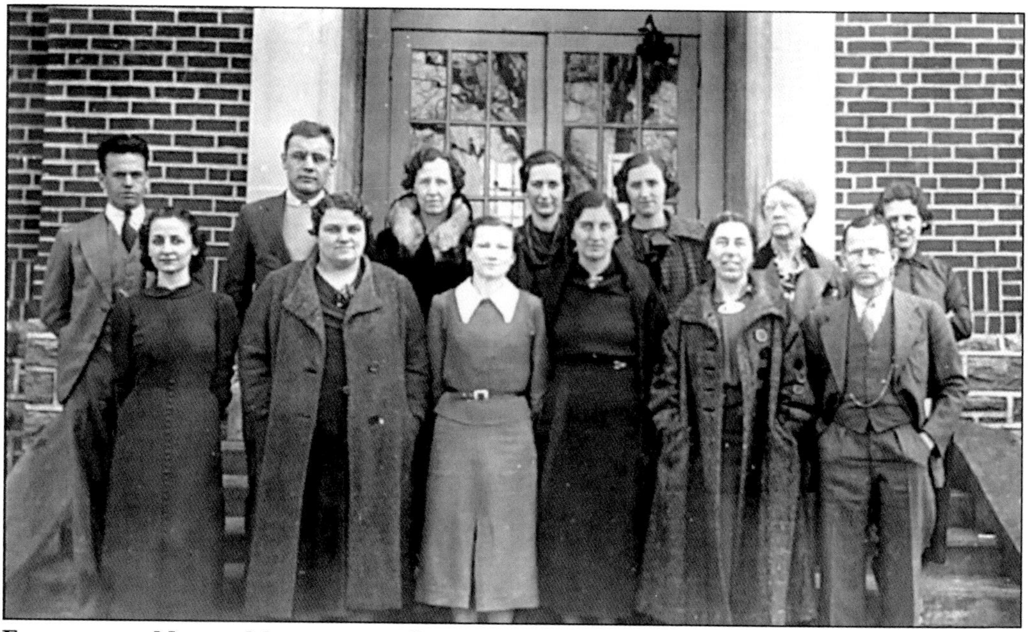

Faculty at North Middletown Consolidated School in 1937. The teachers for all 12 grades and the principal are shown in front of the school building constructed in 1927. Pictured from left to right are (front row) Mildred Laughlin, Mrs. Richard Boardman, Gertrude Talbott, Mamie McDaniel, Delia Tinder, and principal Foster P. Mitchell; (back row) James Gillam, John Gentry, Mary Ellett, Eleanor Payne, Sara M. Thomas, Mrs. John Talbott, and Emily Meng.

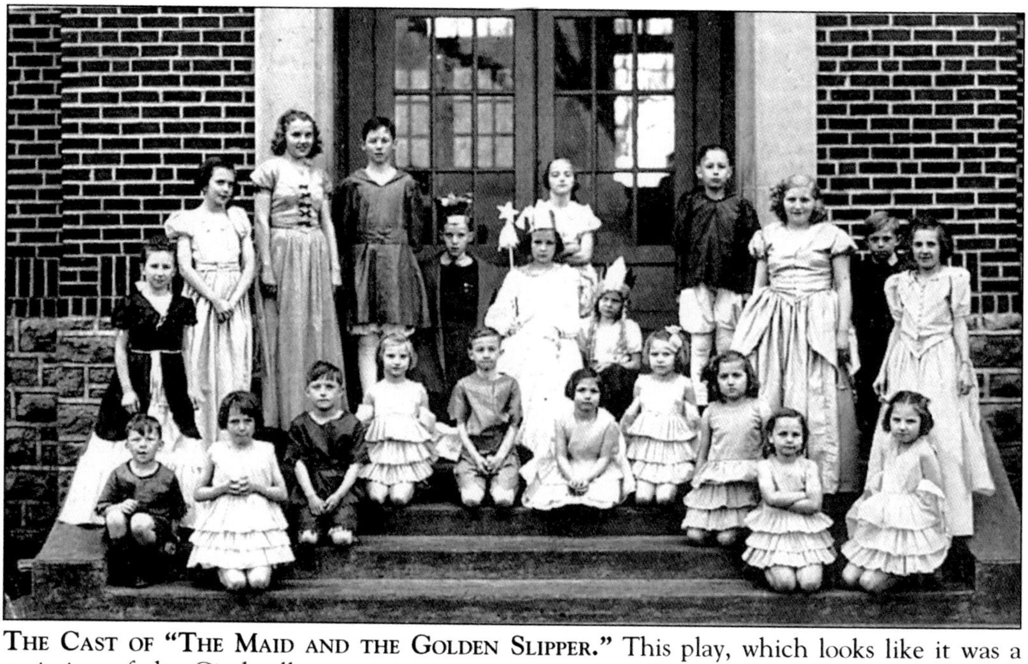

The Cast of "The Maid and the Golden Slipper." This play, which looks like it was a variation of the Cinderella story, was presented by the elementary students at the North Middletown Consolidated School in 1940. Joan Davis played the part of Cinderella and Thomas Sinclair was the prince. David Dick and Stanley Dickson portrayed dukes.

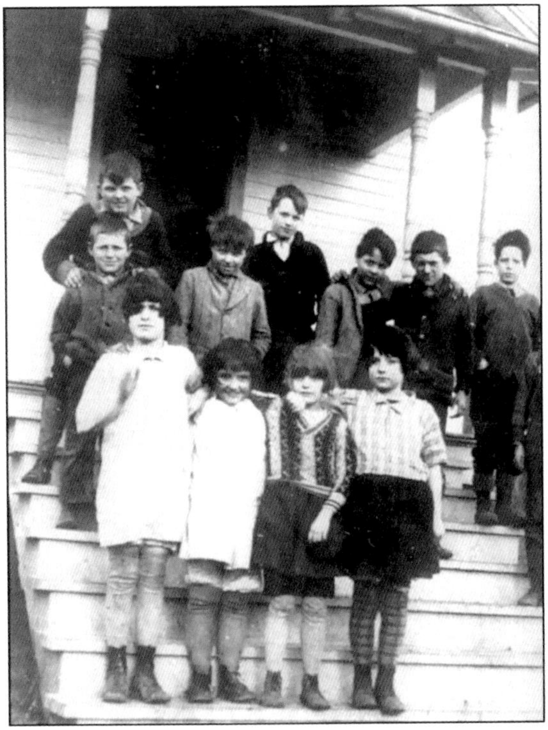

Cane Ridge One-room School Class. The fact that this group of children is all about the same age leads to the premise that this was only one of the grades at the Cane Ridge one-room school in 1929. As can be seen in the accompanying photo of the school, it was a rather large school building for this era and would have served many more students. Nine of the 11 children are identified as follows: (not in order) Bill Wagoner, Ora Wagoner, Vincent Hollar, Stanley Robinson, Pauline Elam, Lillie Hollar, Sarah Wagoner, and the two Clem boys.

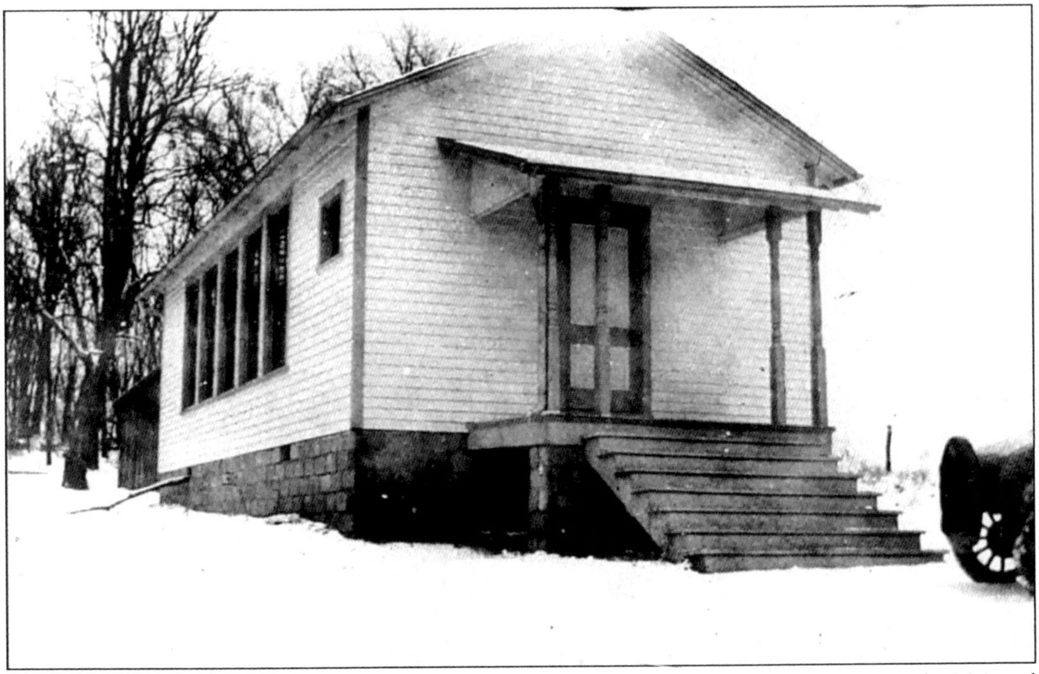

1930 Photo of the Cane Ridge One-room School. This building was in use until 1936 and was located about where the museum building (near the Cane Ridge Meeting House) is today. The one-room schools of this era usually had no electricity or running water and had outdoor privies, which must have cut down on the number of bathroom breaks needed in the winter! This building was torn down in 1940.

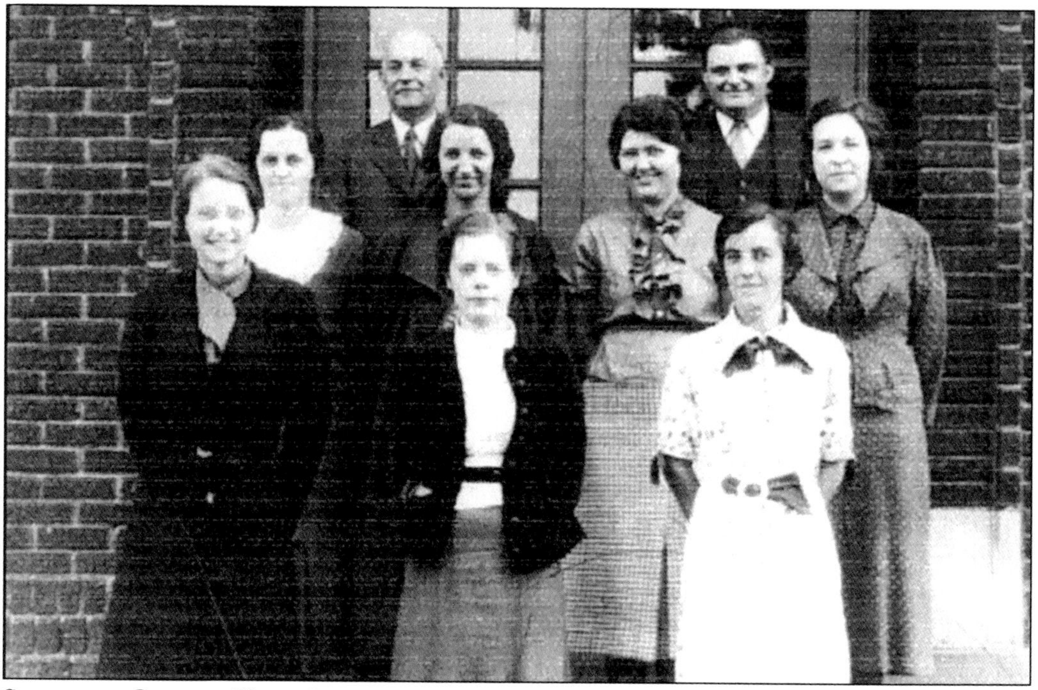

Staff at Center Hill Consolidated School in 1939. Pictured from left to right are (front row) Beatrice Crouch, Ruth Sparks, and Mary Frederickson; (middle row) unidentified, Bernice Shropshire, Sallie Jo Rushmeyer, and unidentified; (back row) Principal A.M. Shelton and Stewart McCray. The school was built in 1924 to accommodate the children who had attended smaller schools in the area including Centerville, Clay's Crossroads, Hill, Hyson, and Jacksonville.

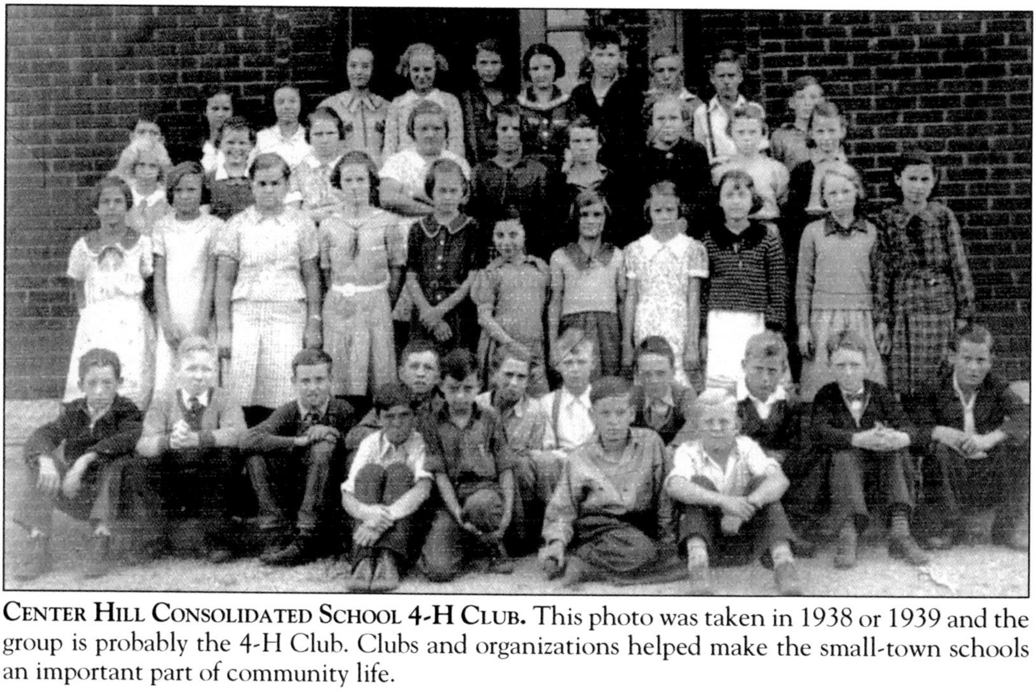

Center Hill Consolidated School 4-H Club. This photo was taken in 1938 or 1939 and the group is probably the 4-H Club. Clubs and organizations helped make the small-town schools an important part of community life.

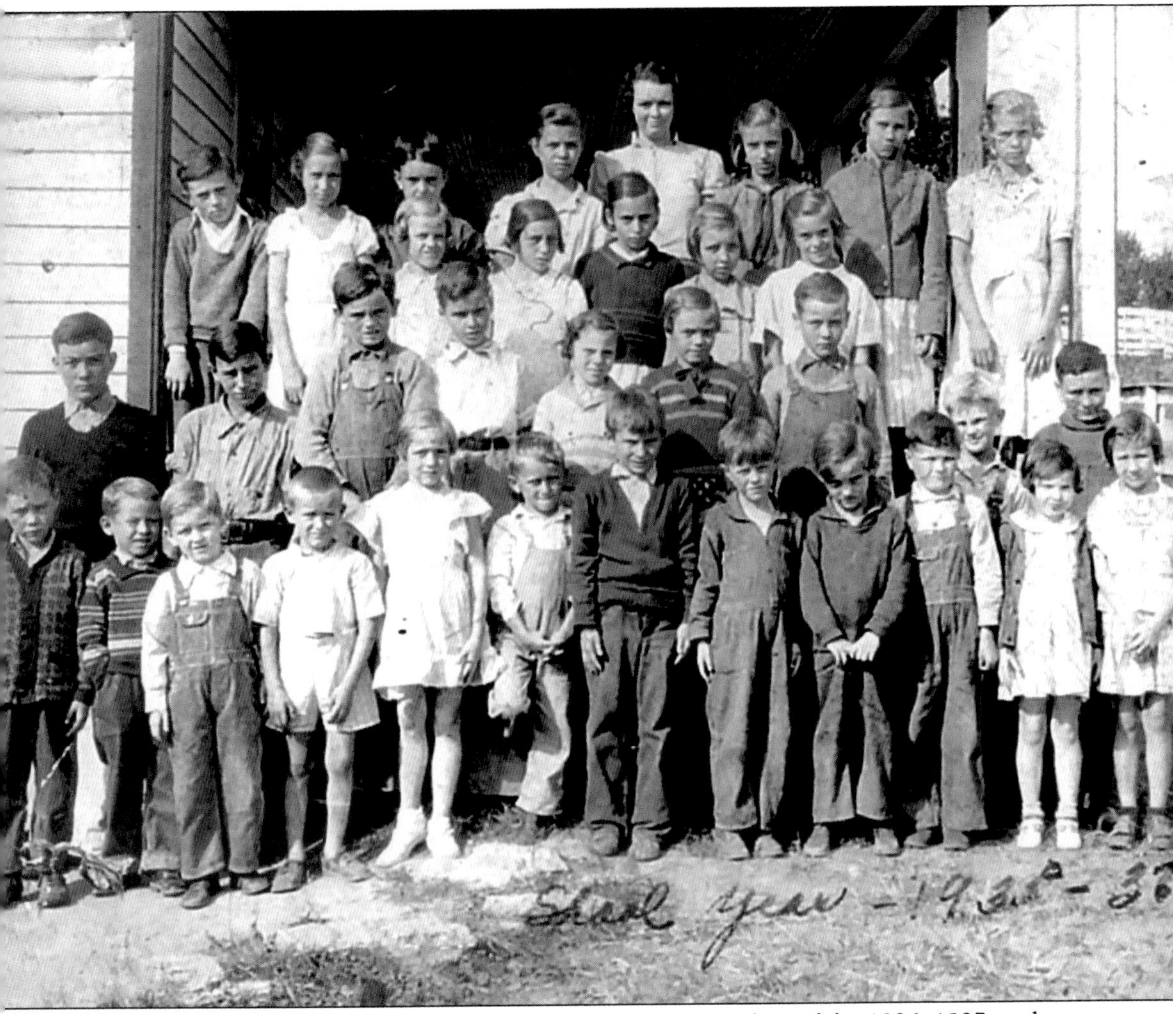

LAST CLASS AT CLAY'S CROSSROADS SCHOOL. This photo was taken of the 1936–1937 students at Clay's Crossroads School. The next year the school closed and the students were sent to the Center Hill School. Shown from left to right are (front row) first three unidentified, Charles Shumate, three unidentified, J.C. Hash, Millard Collins, Harold Clough, James Thomas Hash, Dorothy Juette, and Christine Shumate; (second row) unidentified, J.R. Shumate, Frank Collins, unidentified, Mable Acke, Mary Roberts, and unidentified; (third row) Pauline Harp, Anna Ruth Acke, Geneva Hartman, and Louise Hash; (fourth row) Harold Ralls, Marie Shumate, Billy Lang Wright, Helen Harp, unidentified, Florence Shumate, unidentified, and Ellen Harp. Teacher Susie Clay can be seen looking out the door.

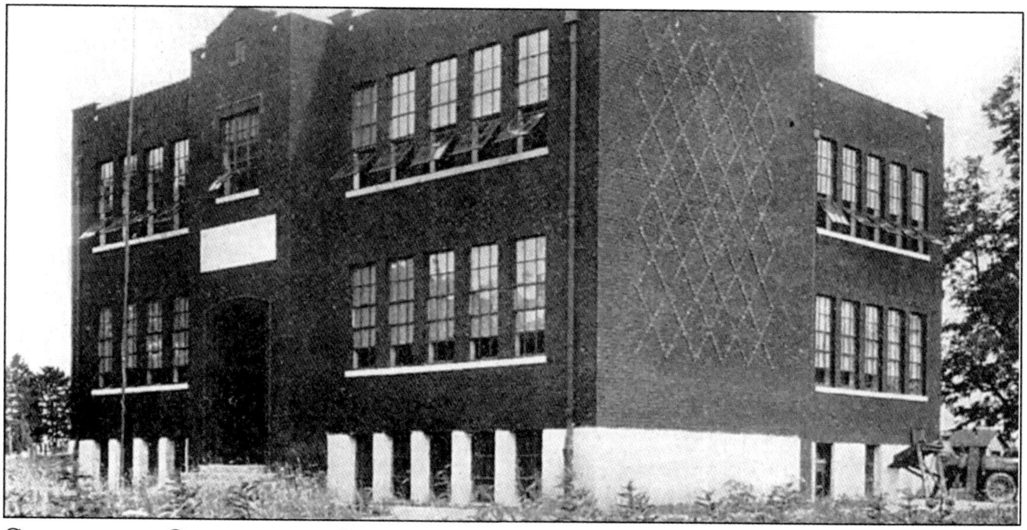

Clintonville Consolidated School, Almost Brand New. This photo was taken in 1927, just two years after the Clintonville Consolidated School was built to serve the children from the Bethlehem, Stony Point, and Hutchison Station schools. The school was constructed on the site of the DeWitt Clinton Masonic Lodge building, which gave the area its name. In 1847, Clintonville was described as containing "two churches, one tavern, two stores, one doctor, and several mechanics."

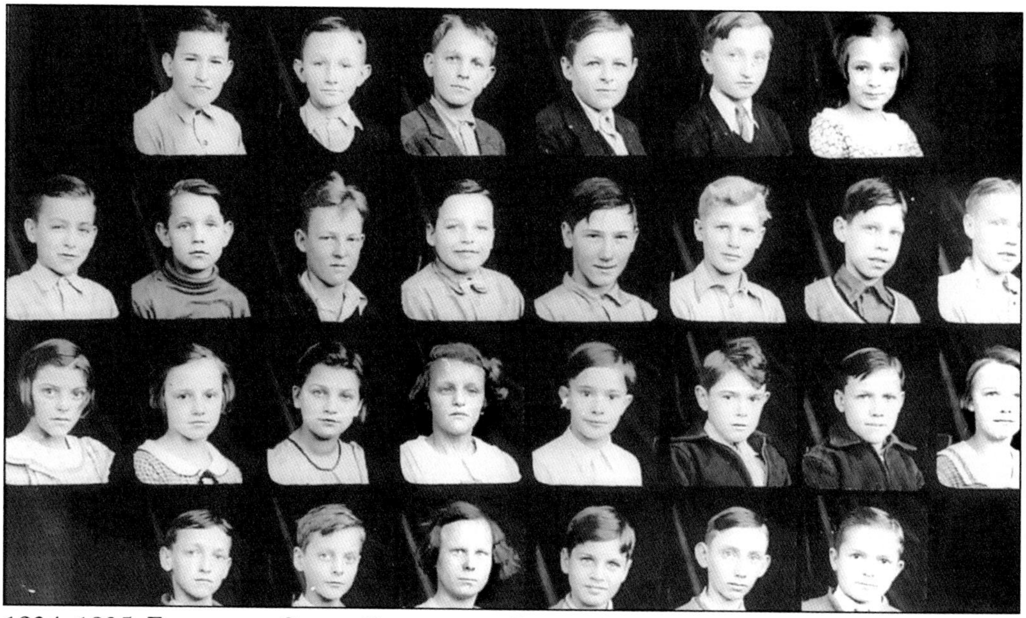

1934–1935 Fifth and Sixth Graders at Little Rock Consolidated School. These two grades shared a homeroom at the Little Rock School. Shown from left to right are the following: (top row) Bill McKenzie, John Curtis Burris, Lou Wassen, Eugene McCord, Lowell Vice, and Lillian Terrell; (second row) Jack McKenzie, N.H. Fletcher, Bob Marshall, J.W. Soper, Lee Gray, Owens Atchison, Woodrow Ishmael, and Carrol Bryant; (third row) Helen Reid, Charleen Burris, Katherine Hawkins, Opal Gaunce, Frank Crouch, Charles Ray Hinkle, Bill Preston, and Ruby Florence; (fourth row) Alley Vice, Templine Wasson, Geneva Wasson, Roger Lowry, Charles Hamilton, and Marion Clark Prather.

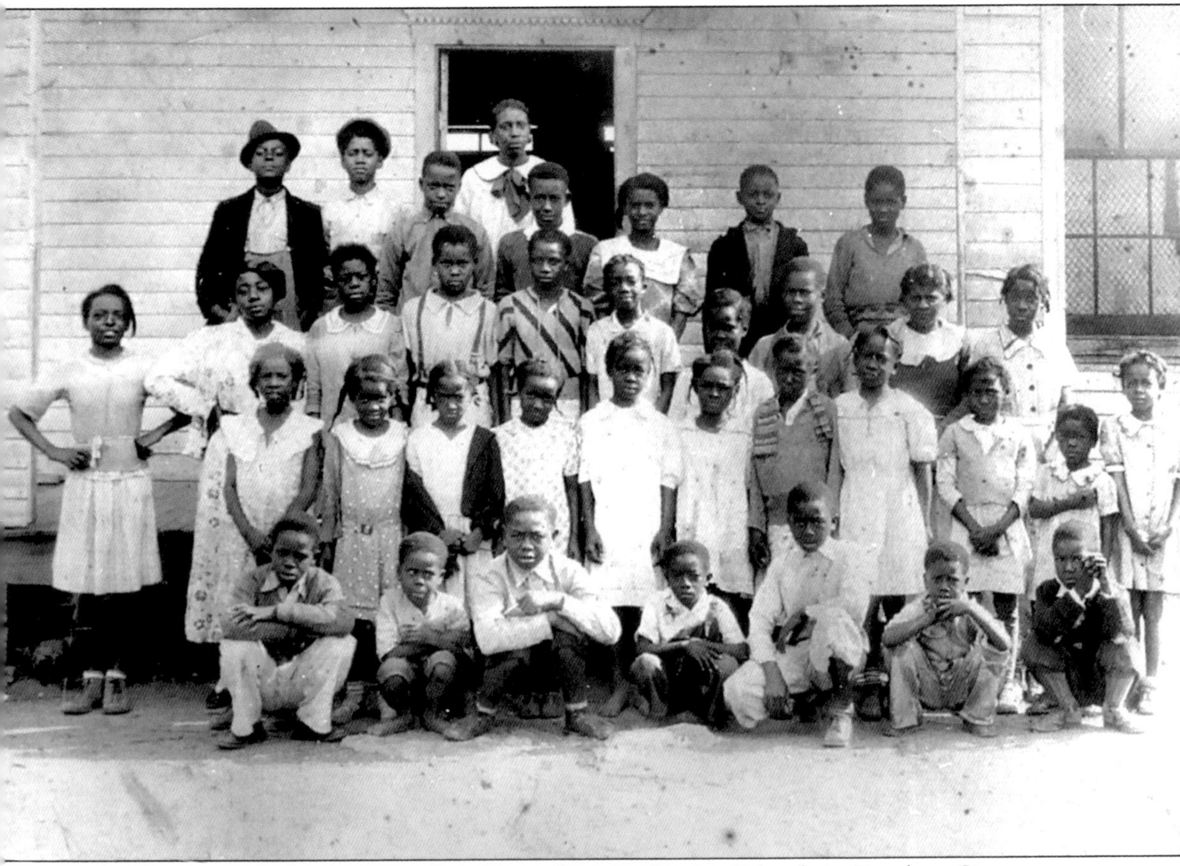

1923 Centerville Segregated One-room School Class. Schools in Bourbon County were segregated until the 1960s as they were in the rest of the state. The county schools for black and white children were all administered by the Bourbon County Board of Education. Other schools for African-American students in the 1920s were located in Ementsville, Brentsville, Mt. Olivett, Clintonville, Currentsville, Ruddles Mills, North Middletown, Millersburg, and Little Rock. Shown from left to right are the following: (front row) Dewey Reed, Oscar Burrell, J.T. Williams, Estell Franklin, William Nutter, Diller J. Hawkins, and John Nutter; (second row) Florence Collins, Frances Brown, Betty Jean ?, Rosa Berry, Ella Burrell, Verline Hersey, Martha Booker, Fannie ?, Mary Reed, Sara Franklin, and Edna Collins; (third row) Ida Hersey, Molly Franklin, Eliza Franklin, Willie Burrell, Nancy Franklin, Virginia Franklin, Mary Burrell, John Burrell, Dorothy Fields, and Helen Reed; (fourth row) Edward Allen, Feliz Reed, William Sparks, John B. Smarr, Dorothy Sparks, John Givens, Phillip Reed, and teacher Nannie Butler.

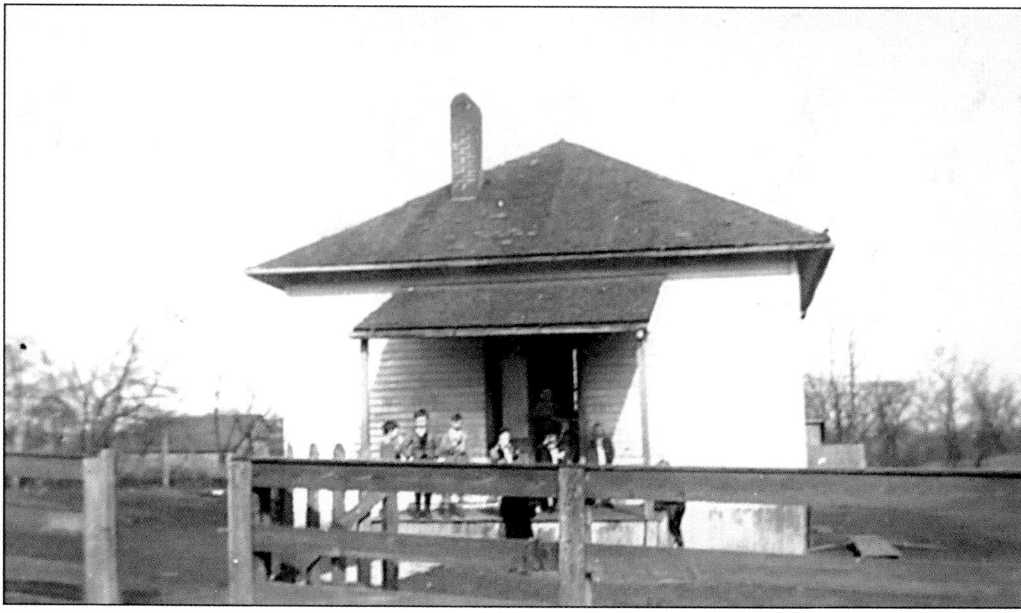

FORD'S MILL ONE-ROOM SCHOOL. This one-room school was just one of many county schools in 1935. The school was located approximately where the intersection of the Paris Bypass, Cypress Street, and the Ford's Mill Road is today. Other one-room schools for white students during this era included Center Hill, Clay's Cross Roads, Hutchison, Bethlehem, Dudley, Monterey, Houston, Escondida, Clintonville, Stony Point, Shawhan, Palmer, Spear's Mill, Deavers, Ruddles Mills, Colville, Purdy, Tarr, Cane Ridge, Letton, Millersburg, Plum, and Burris.

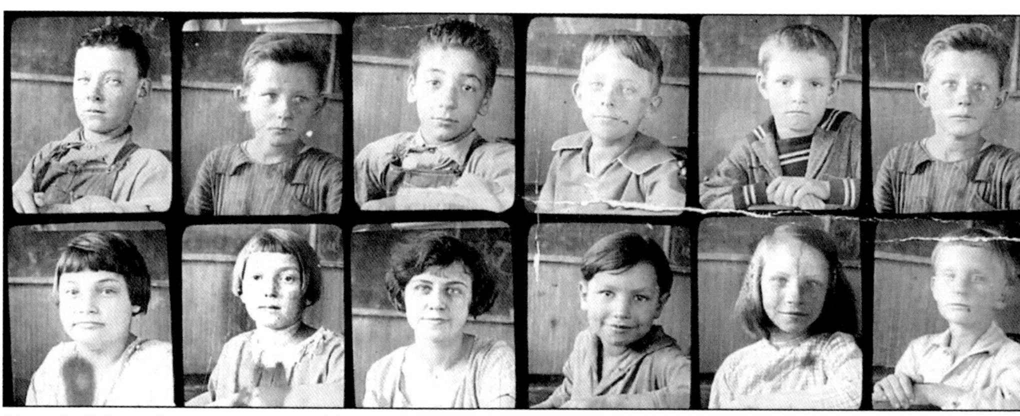

FORD'S MILL STUDENTS AND TEACHER. This photo shows some of the students at the Ford's Mill school in 1925 and their teacher. Shown from left to right are the following (top row) unidentified, Charles Buckler, Billy Longo, Brown Lee Yates, Zonie Soard, and Charles Buckler (again!); (bottom row) Bertha Buckler, Catherine Bowman (Lytle), Laura Belle Smith Bogie (teacher), Clarence Guy, ? Blythe, and C.W. Earlywine. Catherine Lytle taught at the Ford's Mill school from 1932 to 1937. Her first year, she had more than fifty-three students in grades one through eight.

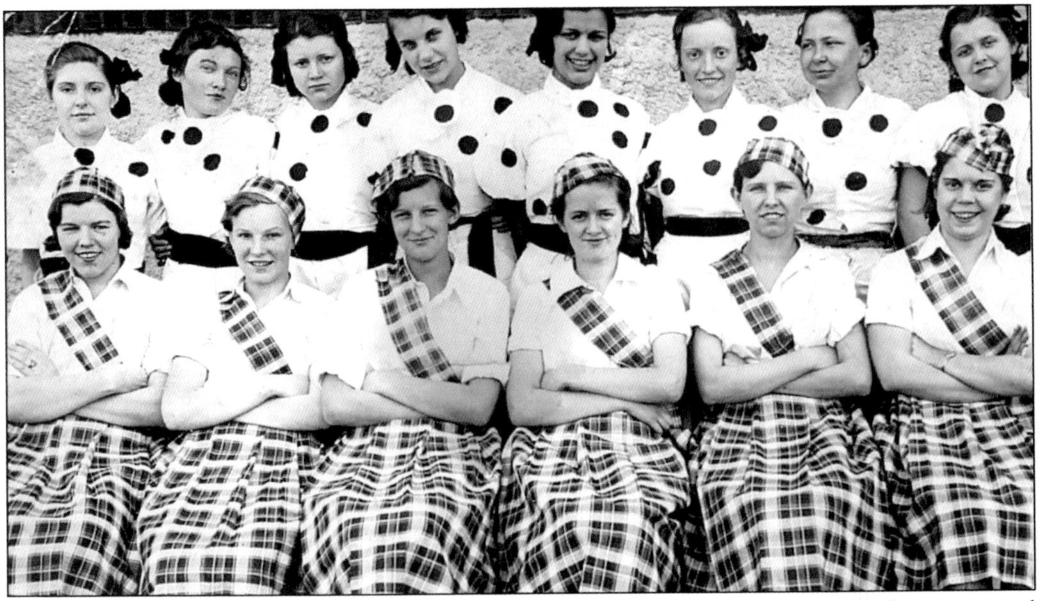

Scottish Lassies and Chorus Girls. These girls are shown in costume for a musical performance at Ruddles Mills Consolidated School in 1933. Pictured from left to right are the following: (lassies in front row) Cecilia Fritz, Elizabeth Moore, Ruby Lemons, Billy Price, Frances Buchannan, and Elizabeth Berryfield; (chorus girls in back row) Betsy Anderson, Mary Ida Owsley, Lucille Watkins, Pauline David, Mary Sue Morrison, Davis Burden, Nina Harney, and Minerva Speaks.

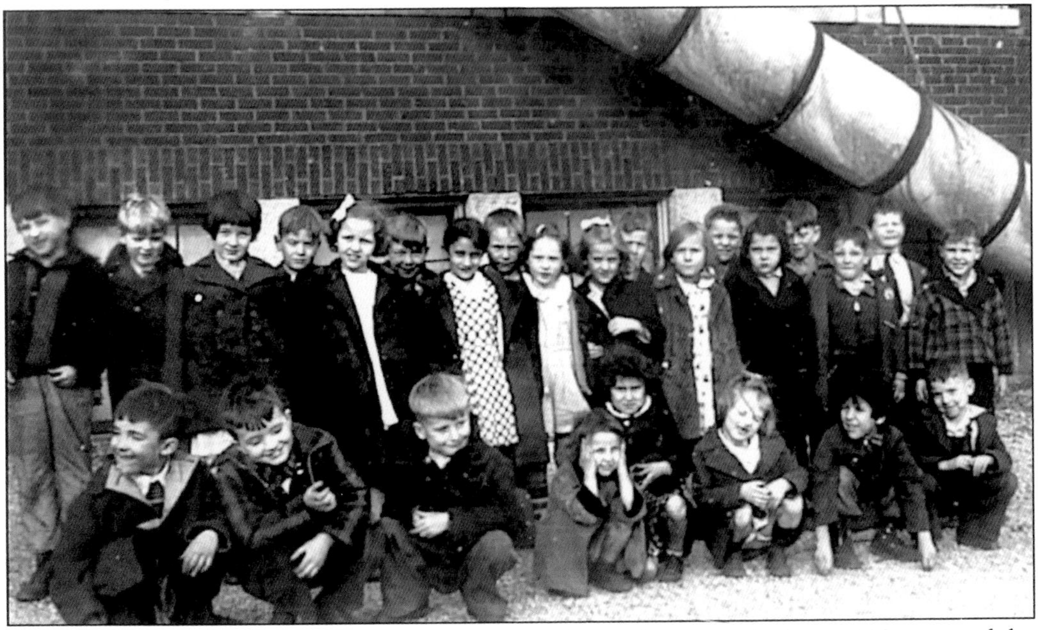

First Grade Class at Ruddles Mills School. This school was built in 1923—part of the building boom aimed at replacing the many small schools in the county with a handful of consolidated schools located in population centers. This 1939 photo shows one of the school's fire escapes. Every week the students had a fire drill and got to slide down the long slide from the second floor.

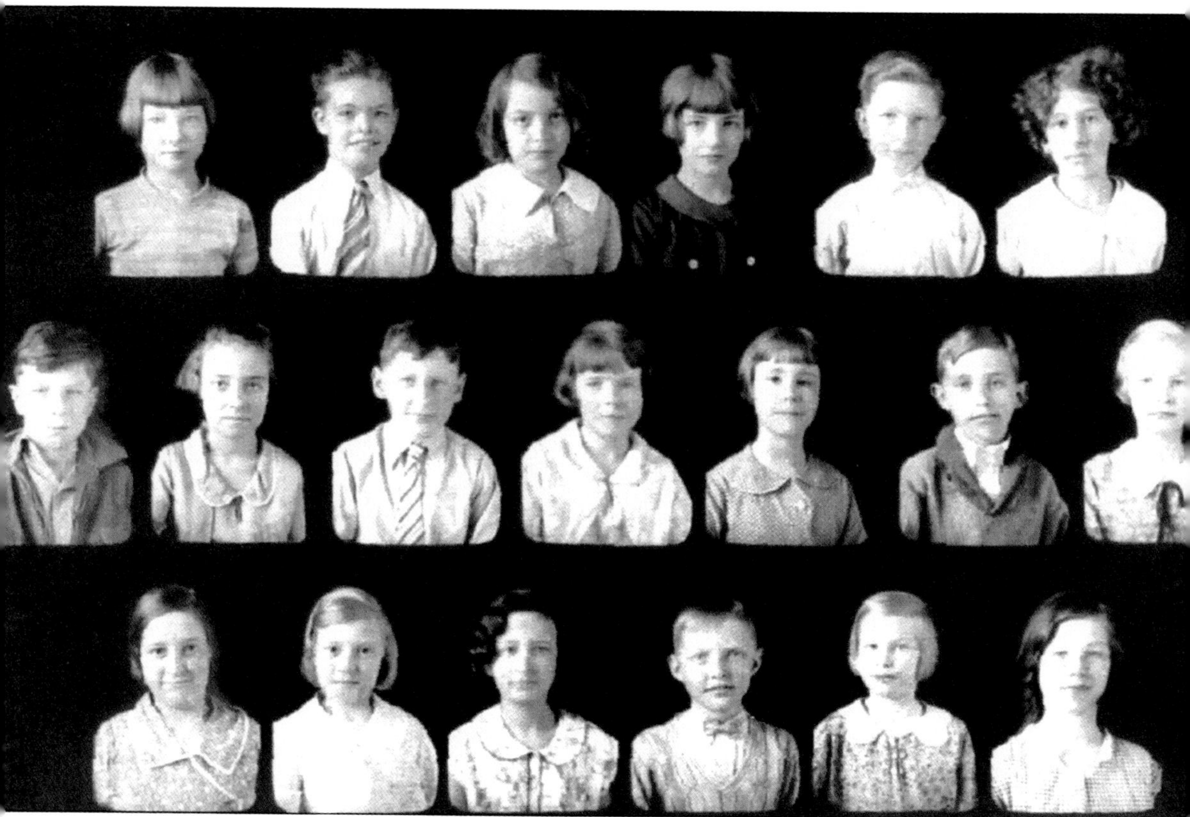

First Southside School was Next to Cemetery. This southside elementary school was located at the corner of 16th and Main, the current site of the Paris Monument Works. During the 1932–1933 school year, the teachers included Sallie Whaley, Julia Clark, Mrs. Harris, and Daisy Detwiller. Ed and Rose Fields operated the lunchroom. The third grade class is pictured above, from left to right, as follows: (front row) Ruby Swim, Hazel Lyons Violett, Karola Castle, George Sidney Tate, Adele Hazelrigg, and Viola Mitchell; (middle row) Eugene Smith, Mary Lou Jones, Rex Lyons, Margaret Pope, Bernadine Poplin, Charles Crawford, and Ann Jeanette Doty; (back row) Lorraine Feeback, Alfred Determan, Ann Hopkins, June King, J.C. Watson, and Nellie Crump.

Brentsville One-room School Students. This school was one of several small schools located throughout the county for black students during the first half of the 20th century. The students in this photo taken around 1939 from left to right are as follows: (front row) Silas Jones, Isaiah Fields, and Marvin Johnson; (back row) John Tom Dickerson, Paul Jones, Ann Tom Bradley, Josephine Nichols, and Ann Eliza Speaks.

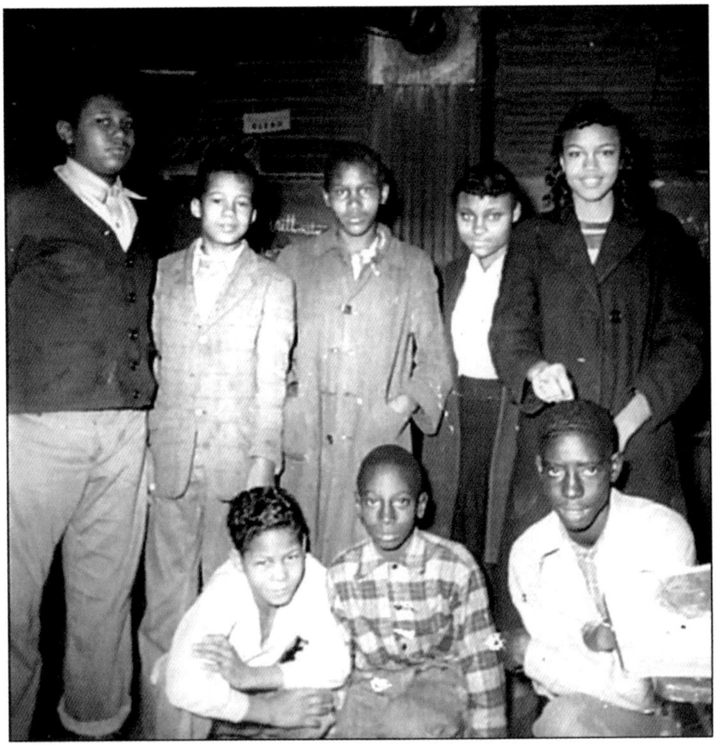

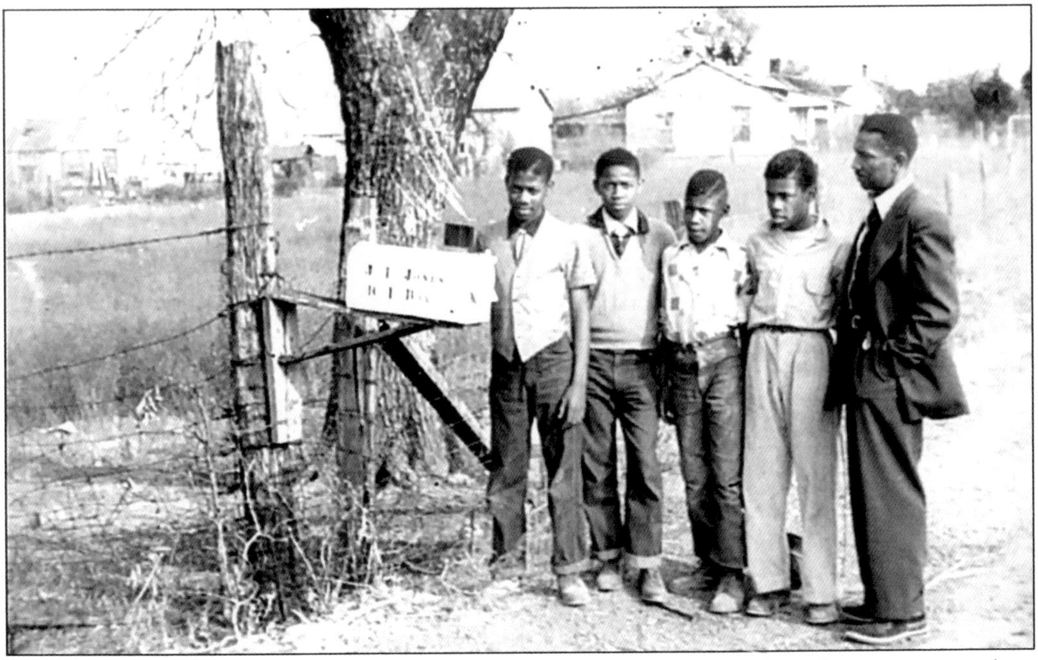

Brentsville School's 4-H Community Improvement Project. These boys were members of the 4-H club at Brentsville School led by teacher Thomas Jacobs. One of their community projects during the 1939–1940 school year was painting and lettering mailboxes. Shown from left to right are William Jackson, Lockhart Bredley, unidentified, Wesley Johnson, and teacher Thomas Jacobs.

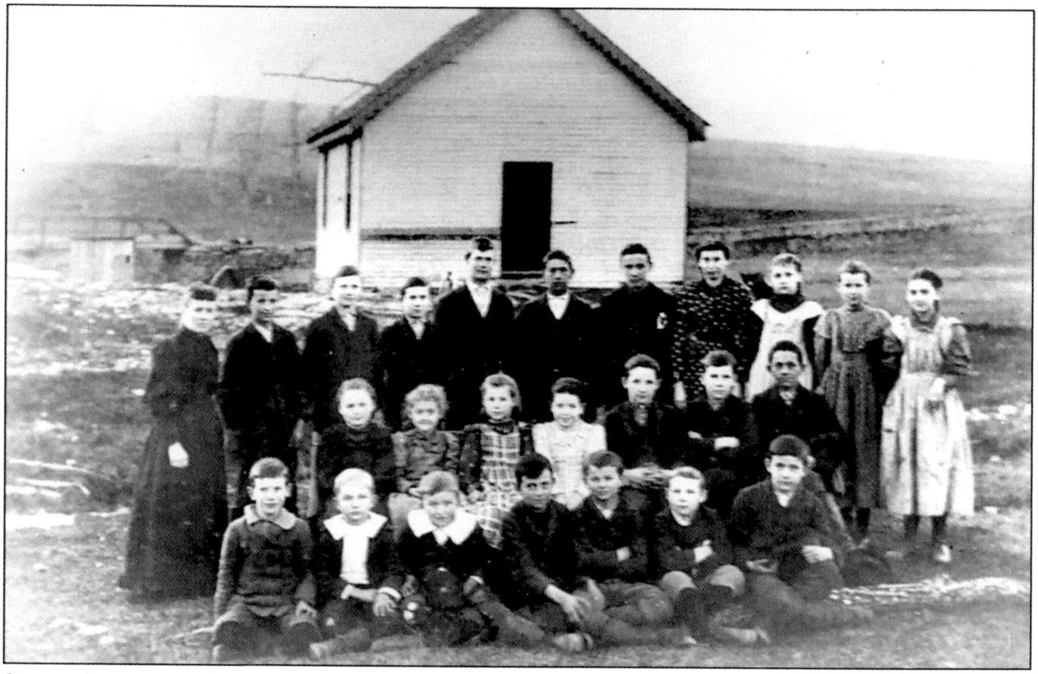

Soper One-room School. This photo was taken around the turn of the century at the Soper School. The school was located on Jackstown Road near Soper Road and Miss Sue Tuttle (far left, back row) was the teacher. The school is representative of the one-room schools that were common throughout the county. In 1902, there were 57 free county schools (35 for white children and 22 for African-American children) with a total annual enrollment of more than 3,800 children.

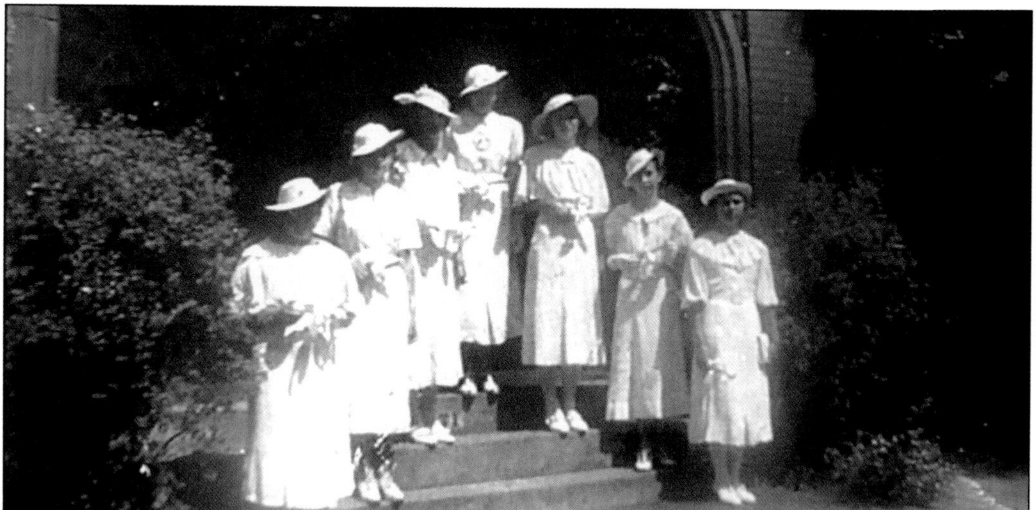

1936 St. Mary's Eighth Grade Graduation. St. Mary's parochial school was established in 1888 by the Sisters of Charity and has educated thousands of local children. In 1936, the school included grades one through eight; after completing the eighth grade, students "graduated" and went on to public high school. Pictured from left to right are Mabel Fudold, Joanna Maher, Nell Coughlin, Lona Howerton, Rose Marie Sidener, Helen Webber, and Carrie Leach.

TEACHERS AT PARIS WESTERN SCHOOL IN 1926. Western School opened in the late 1800s as a school for African-American children living in Paris. In 1922, students from two smaller primary schools in Paris—Claysville and Ruckerville, were absorbed by Western. Paris Western received a "B" ranking in 1928 from the Southern Association at a time when few white schools were ranked at all. Shown from left to right are Martha Bishop, Della M. Garner, and Pauline Fisher. Professor E.B. Toles, Western principal, is in front.

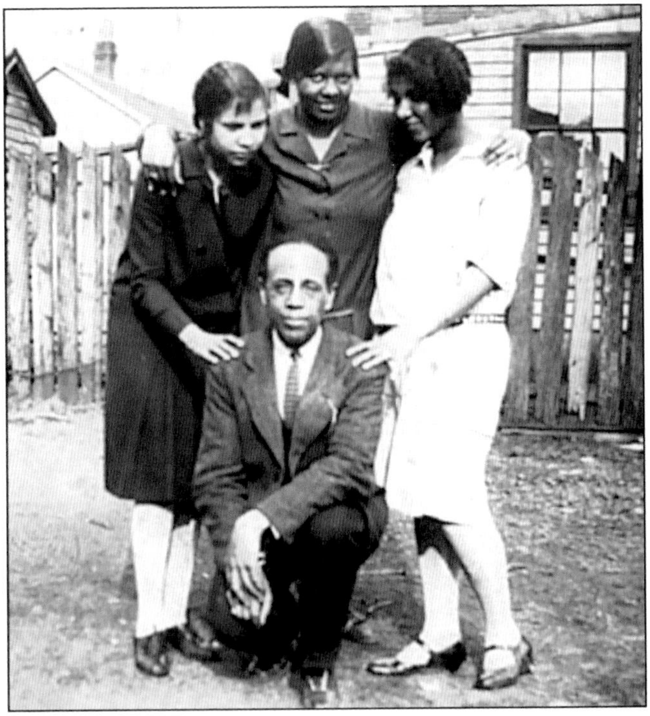

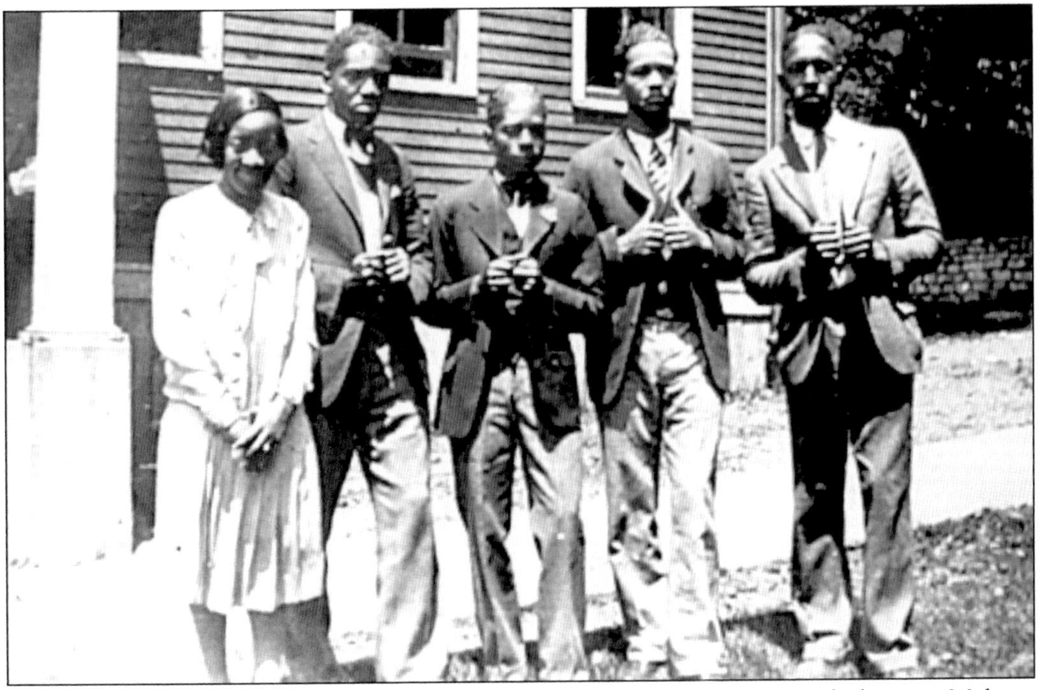

WESTERN MUSIC TEACHER AND STUDENTS. This photo was taken in 1928 of Christine Mebane Hamblen, music teacher at Paris Western. Pictured along with several of her students, from left to right, are Miss Hamblen, Charles Buckner, Lewis Livas, Vernon Mack, and James Ross Wilson. Music was an important part of Western's curriculum beginning in 1912, when the music department was started under the direction of Willa B. Stevenson.

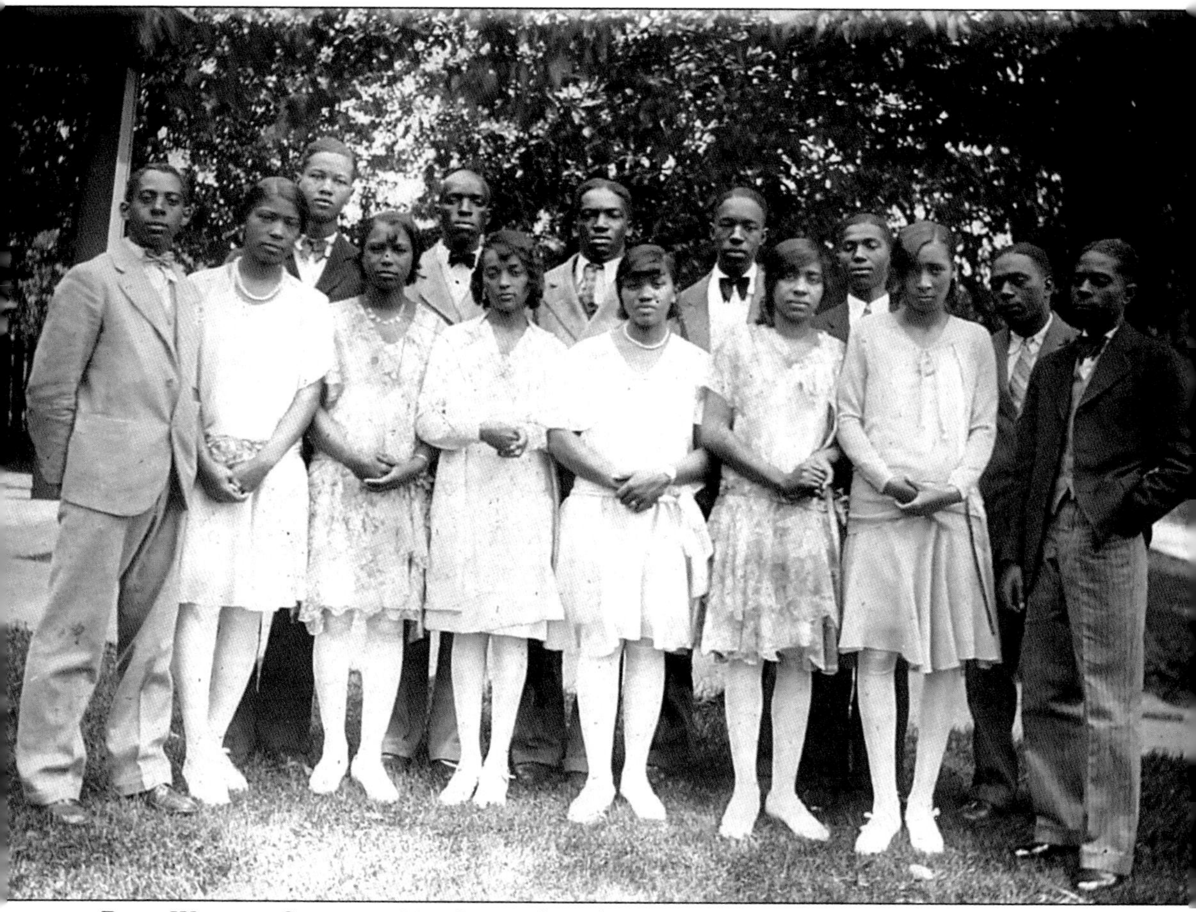

PARIS WESTERN CLASS OF 1929. Pictured are the 1929 Western High School graduates. Shown from left to right are the following: (front row) Houston Hutchison, Ella Brooks Scott, Kitty Sparks, Gertrude Ranson Hutsell, Ora Del Jacobs, Mary Scroggins Hunter, Edna Patterson Wright, and Lewis Livas; (second row) Vernon Mack, Charles Patterson, Charles Buckner, James Ross Wilson, and John Frank Wilson. Paris Western was located on Seventh Street in Paris and was part of the city school system. Several distinguished men had served as principal of Paris Western by 1929 including Professor F.M. Wood, who was principal from 1911 to 1923 before being named president of Kentucky State University. Prof. E.B. Toles, who was principal after Wood, was the grandson of Samuel Buckner, founder of the Little Rock Christian Church.

STATE CHAMPIONSHIP DEBATE TEAM. This Paris High School debate team, are, from left to right, Louise Dailey, Earl Boen, and Sarah Bradley. They won the state championship in debating in 1925. The handsome trophy must have made a nice addition to the school's trophy case. Debating was added to the course of study at Paris in 1921.

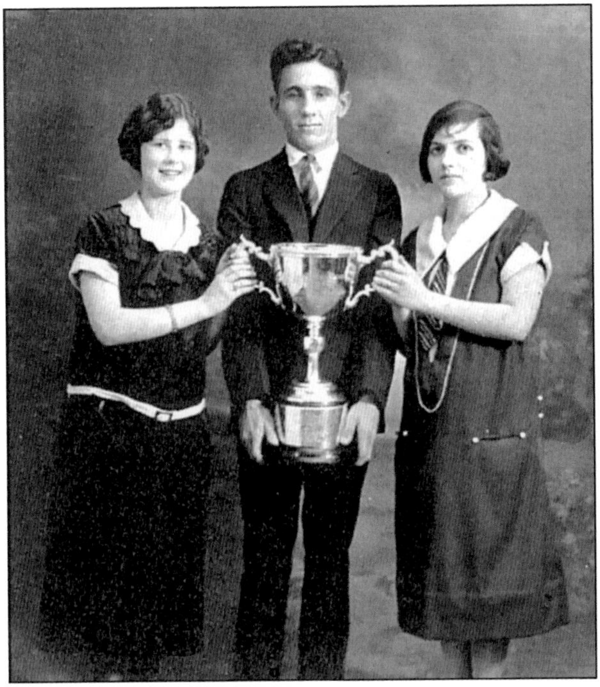

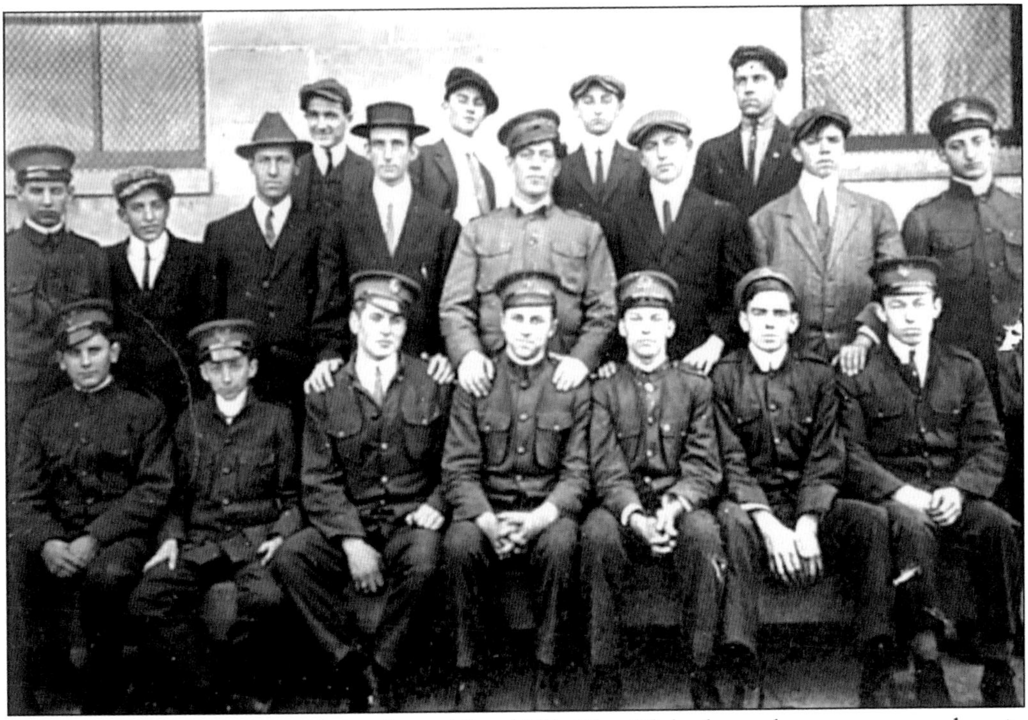

1911 PARIS HIGH SCHOOL GLEE CLUB. This 1911 Glee Club photo shows some members in "civilian" clothes and other boys in the uniform of the PHS Military Science Department. According to the 1912 Report of Paris Public Schools, the governor "has authorized the issue of rifles and equipment for the High School boys, and given his permission for them to bear arms." Two boys out of that group of approximately fifty boys went on to reach the rank of general.

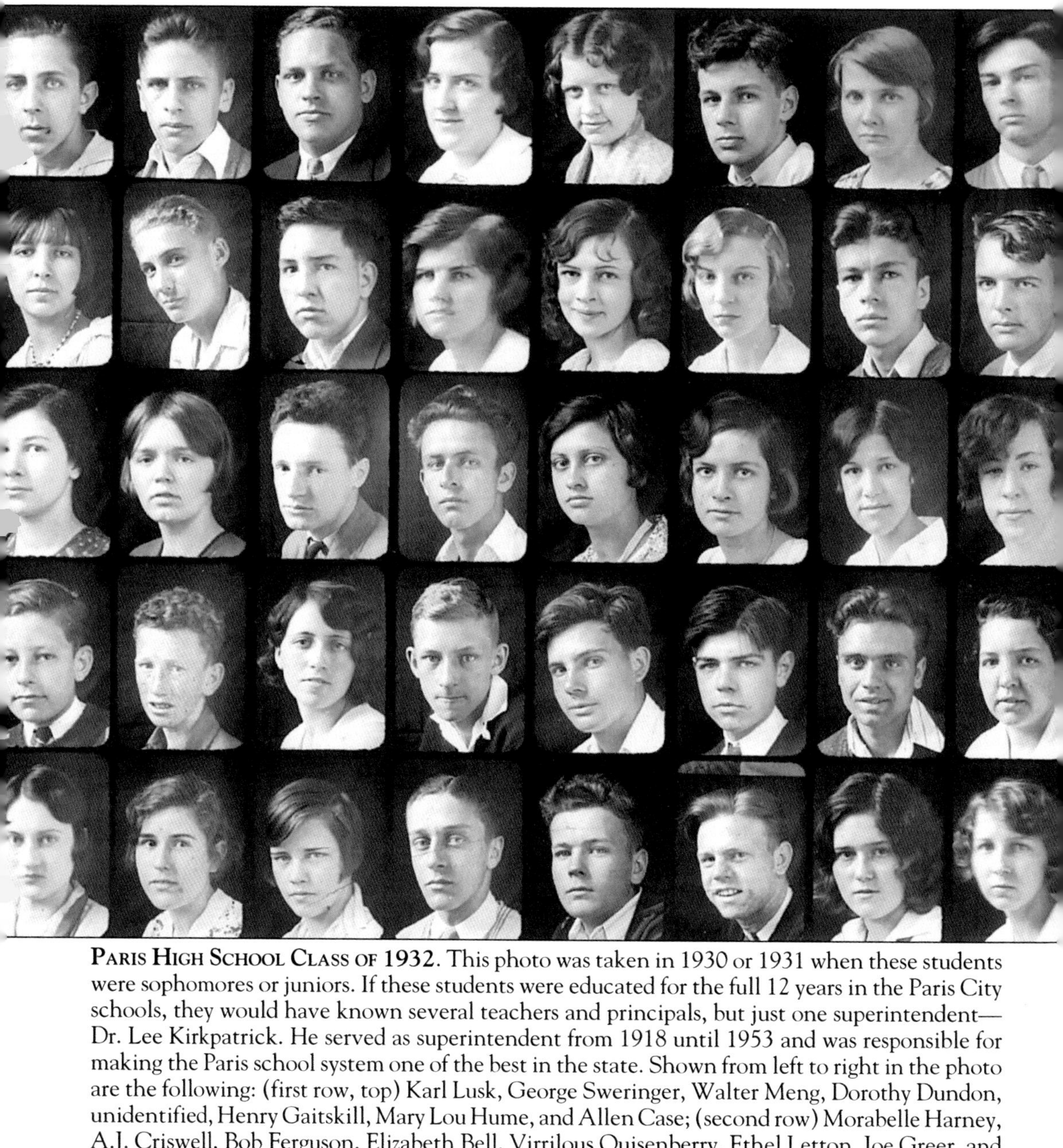

Paris High School Class of 1932. This photo was taken in 1930 or 1931 when these students were sophomores or juniors. If these students were educated for the full 12 years in the Paris City schools, they would have known several teachers and principals, but just one superintendent—Dr. Lee Kirkpatrick. He served as superintendent from 1918 until 1953 and was responsible for making the Paris school system one of the best in the state. Shown from left to right in the photo are the following: (first row, top) Karl Lusk, George Sweringer, Walter Meng, Dorothy Dundon, unidentified, Henry Gaitskill, Mary Lou Hume, and Allen Case; (second row) Morabelle Harney, A.J. Criswell, Bob Ferguson, Elizabeth Bell, Virrilous Quisenberry, Ethel Letton, Joe Greer, and Hume Ferguson; (third row) Ann Clay Hinkle, Naoma Isgrig, Buck Hinkle, unidentified, Mary Elizabeth Rose, Mildred Allison, Irma Parker, and Edwina Gorey; (fourth row) Eugene Santen, Marion Powell, Ova Dumas, James Anderson, unidentified, Richard Wills, Raymond Ogle, and Laura Ferguson; (fifth row) Gladys Rion, Margaret Bohn, Esta Briggs, James White, Guthrie Bell, Norman Violett, unidentified, and Martha Marsh.

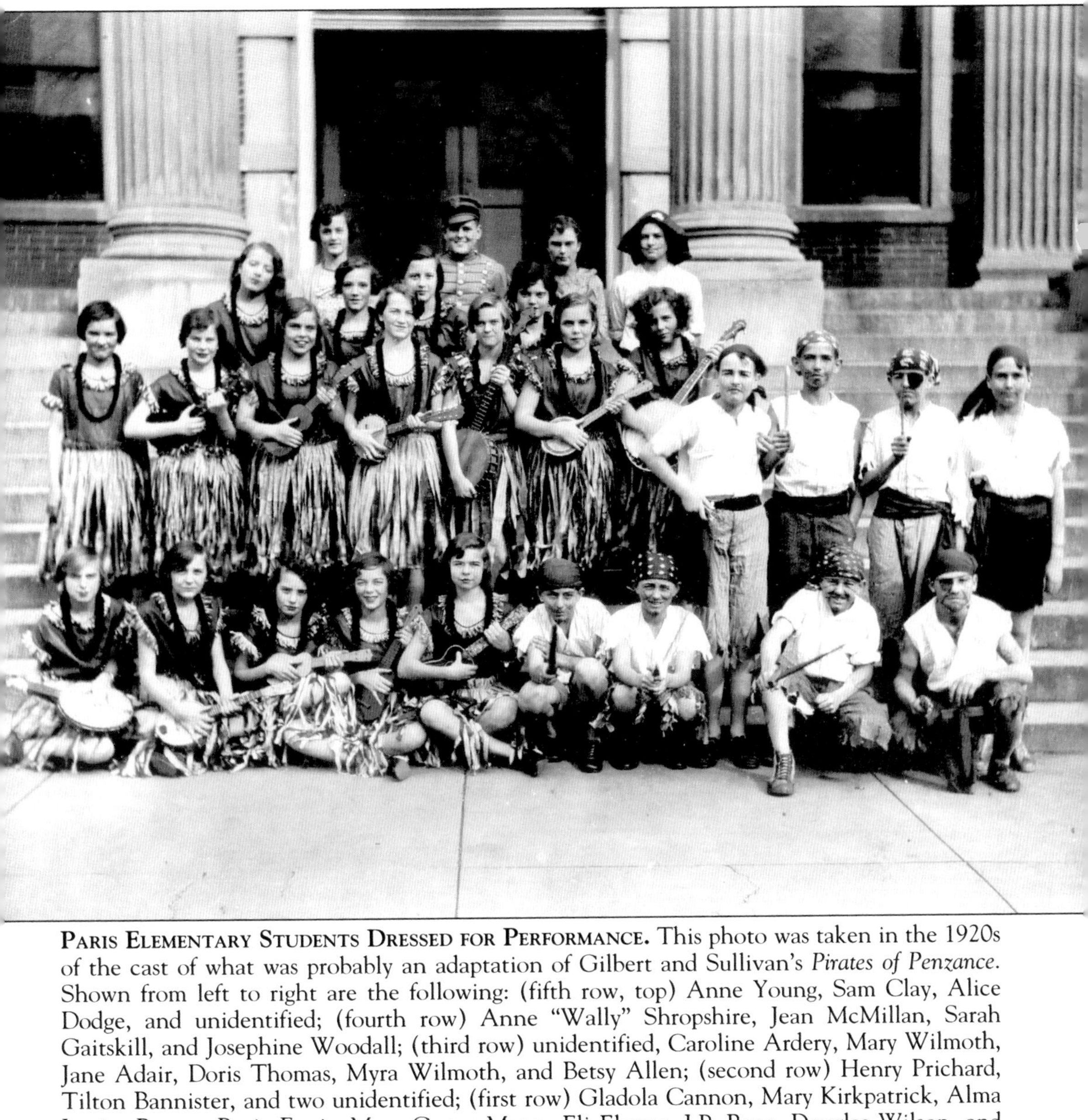

Paris Elementary Students Dressed for Performance. This photo was taken in the 1920s of the cast of what was probably an adaptation of Gilbert and Sullivan's *Pirates of Penzance.* Shown from left to right are the following: (fifth row, top) Anne Young, Sam Clay, Alice Dodge, and unidentified; (fourth row) Anne "Wally" Shropshire, Jean McMillan, Sarah Gaitskill, and Josephine Woodall; (third row) unidentified, Caroline Ardery, Mary Wilmoth, Jane Adair, Doris Thomas, Myra Wilmoth, and Betsy Allen; (second row) Henry Prichard, Tilton Bannister, and two unidentified; (first row) Gladola Cannon, Mary Kirkpatrick, Alma Louise Parent, Pagie Farris, Mary Carter Mann, Eli Elvove, J.P. Rose, Douglas Wilson, and unidentified. (U.K. Collection.)

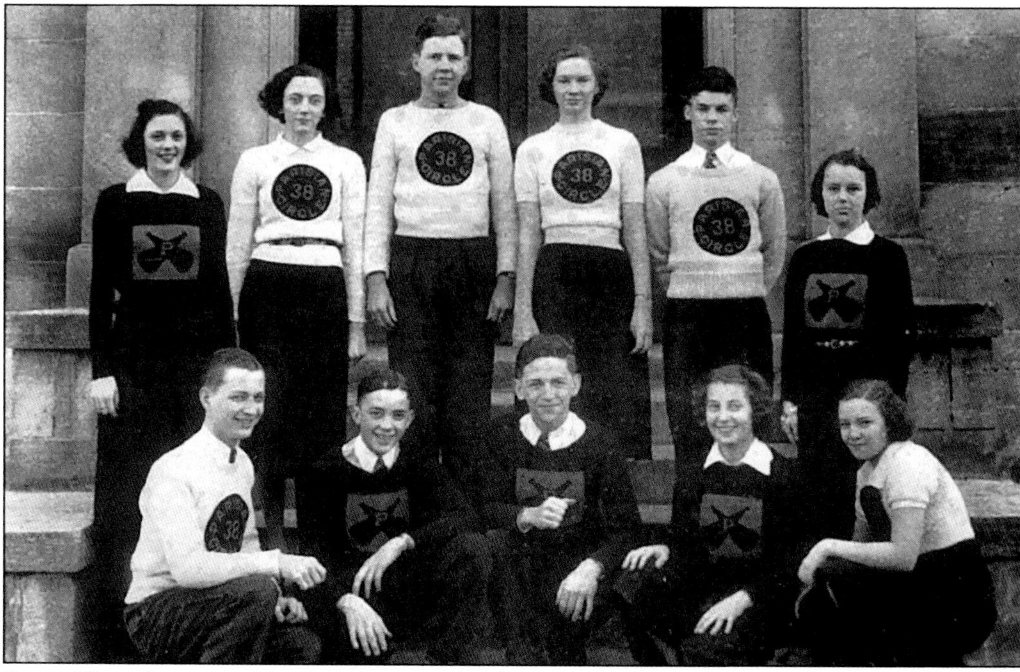

PARIS HIGH SCHOOL 1938 PEP CLUB. School spirit was important and this club, made up of senior Parisian Circle members and cheerleaders, was said to be "one of the most active" in 1938, according to the yearbook. Members shown are (not in order) Catherine Kennedy, Larry Brannon, John Minogue, Jane Clay Sutherland, Jack Baldwin, Betty Lindsay Roseberry, Norma Mae Mastin, A.B. Collins, Charlene Young, Jane White Humble, and Billy Young.

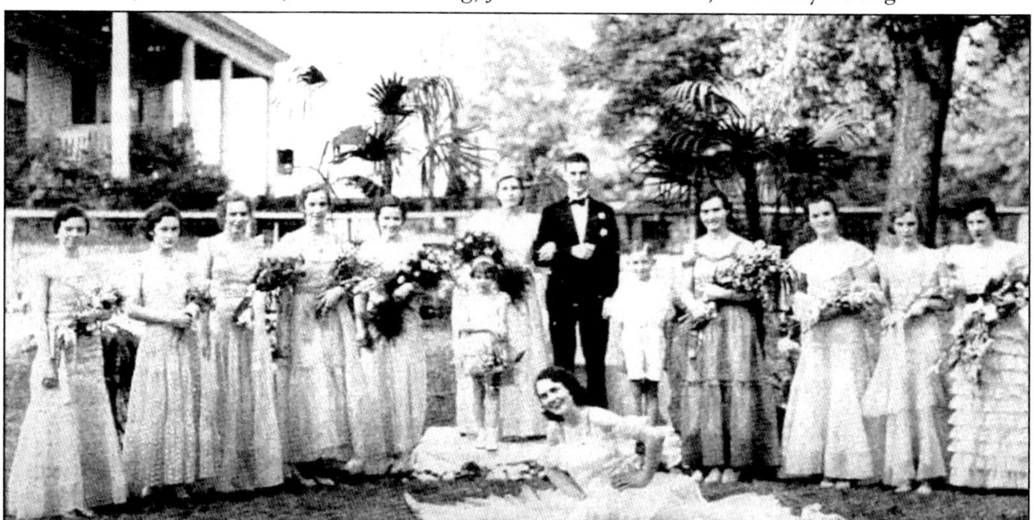

MAY QUEEN AND HER PRINCE CHARMING. Paris High School's May Queen for 1932 was Margaret Bohn, seen in the photo above on the arm of her "Prince Charming" George Swearingen. Other attendants included Esther Briggs, Ann Clay Hinkle, Gladys Rion, Ethel Letton, Virginia Henry, Jean Allen, Nathalie Linville, Martha Williams, Constance Kennedy, Edwina Gorey, Susan Hinkle, Helen Farmer, and Virrillous Quisenberry. Serving as ringbearer was Charles Roberts and crownbearer was Doris Doty.

Six

Agriculture and Industry

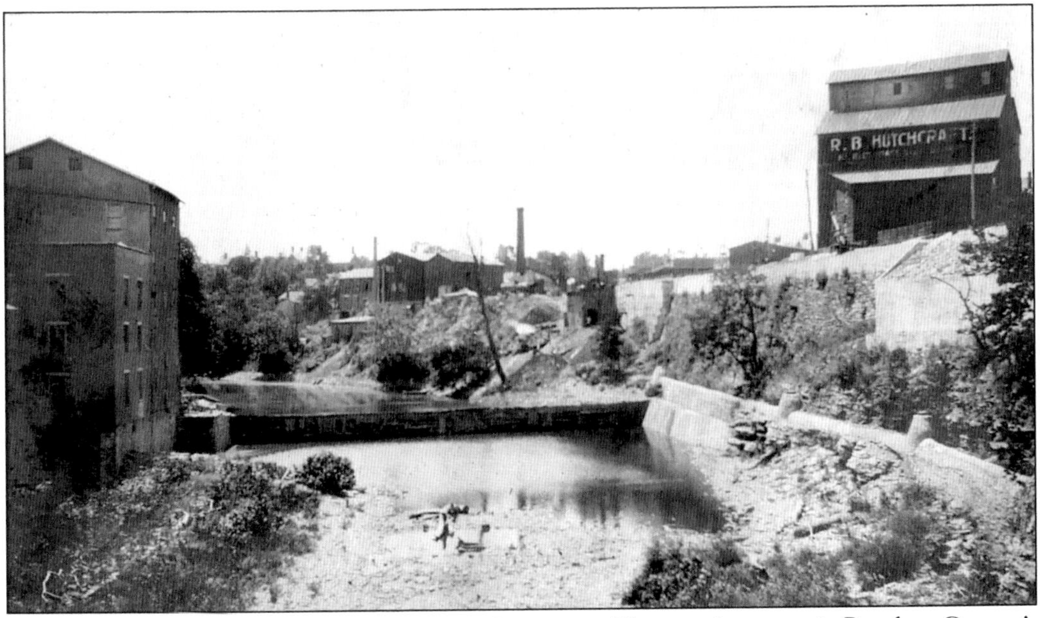

Stream-powered Mills Provided Earliest Industry. The running water in Bourbon County's many streams powered mills like the Paris Cotton Mill seen here on Stoner Creek. Mill works ground wheat and corn and drove looms in both cotton and wool mills. The tall warehouse/factory seen to the right was built by Reuben Brent Hutchcraft at the end of Pleasant Street in about 1880. He sold locally produced wool, blue grass, and other field seeds.

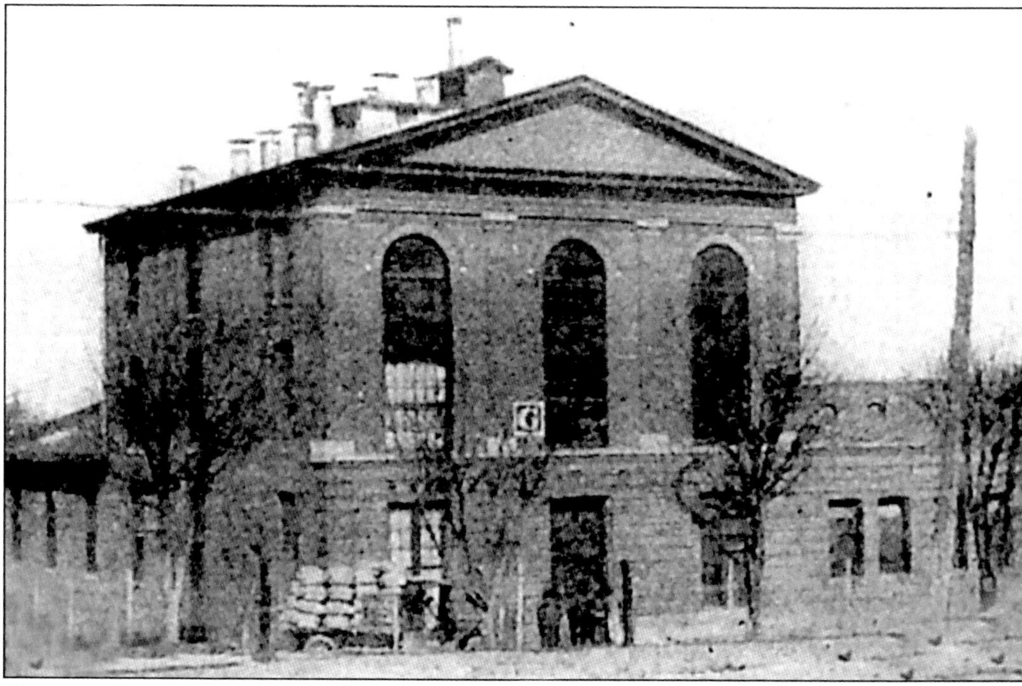

Chicken Cock Distillery in Paris. America's distinctive whiskey, bourbon, was probably first distilled in the county as early as 1785 when whiskey makers like Jacob Spears began using charred oak barrels to age their whiskey. By 1820, the county was full of distilleries. The Chicken Cock Distillery, pictured here, had warehouse space for 30,000 barrels and began operation in 1856. This building was later used as a seed cleaning facility and burned in 1961.

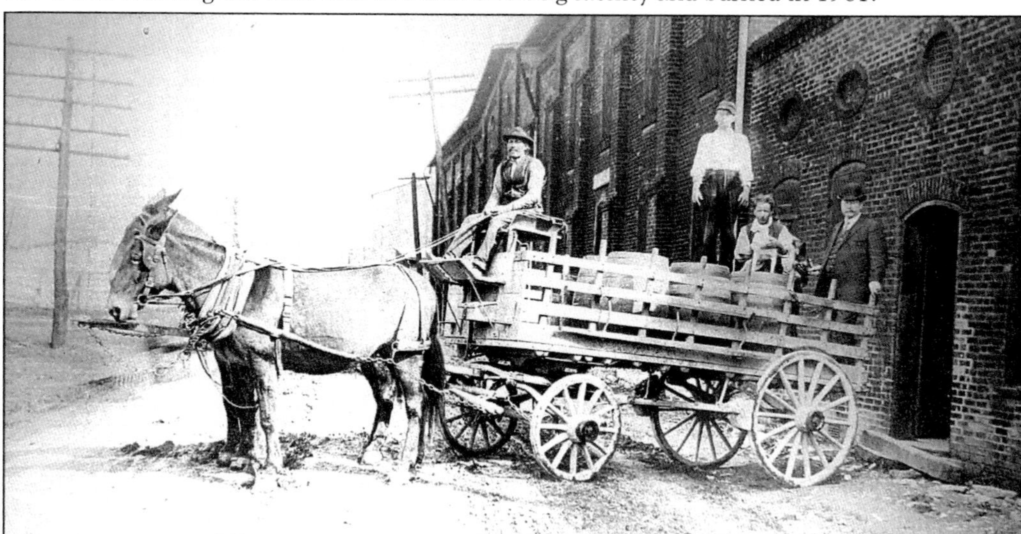

Roll Out the Whiskey Barrel Wagon. Pictured are barrels of whiskey either being delivered or picked up at one of several bourbon warehouses found in Paris in the 1880s. After distilling, the whiskey was placed in charred, white oak barrels and allowed to age for 10 to 15 years. The barrels were then sent to the bottling house where the potent contents were diluted with spring water and poured into bottles and jugs.

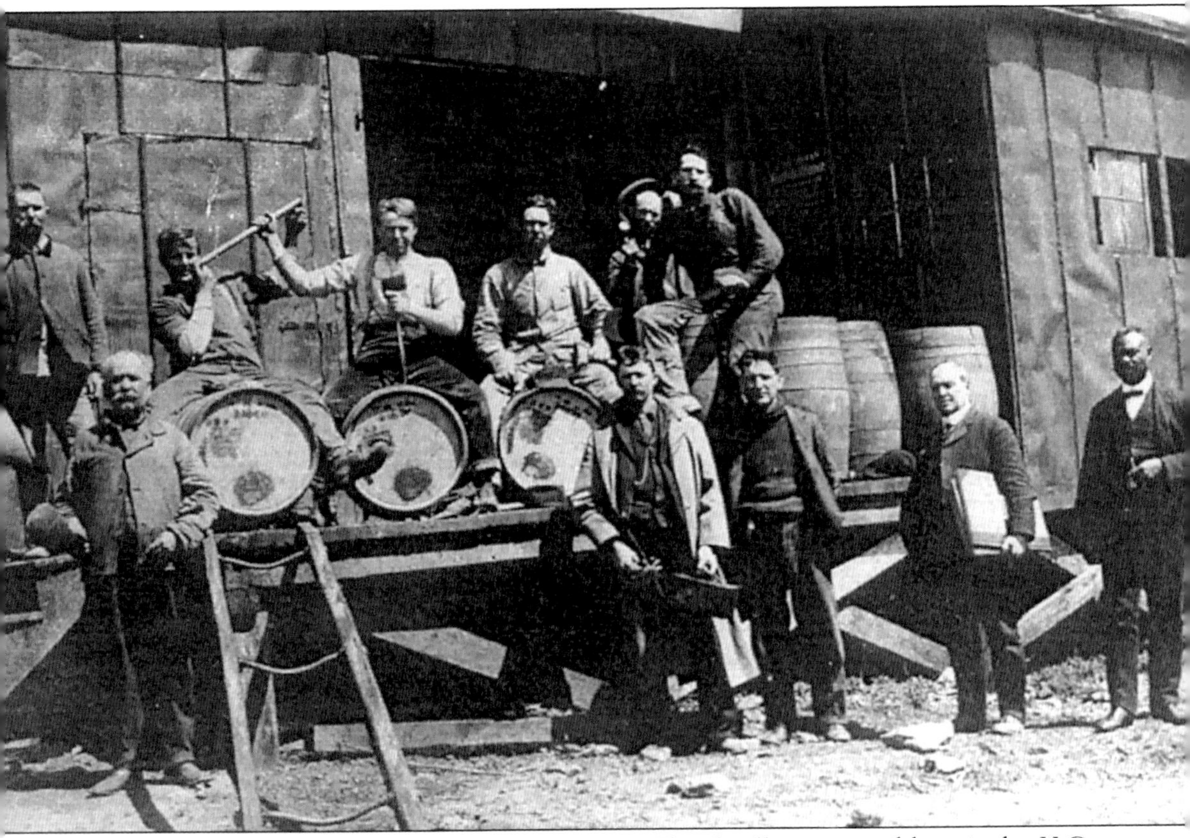

Crew of the Peacock Distillery Barrel House. The distillery pictured here is the H.C. Clay or Peacock Distillery that was located nearly five miles north of Paris on Peacock Road. Originally built in 1857 as the Ford & Bowen's Distillery, it was adjacent to the Kentucky Central Railroad. The large Julius Kessler Company of Cincinnati later bought this and other distilleries in the area and eventually phased them out in favor of larger plants. The long stick-like tool the man astride the barrel is holding (third from left) is a "barrel or bung thief." It was used to sample the whiskey as it aged in the barrels. During this time, the distillery produced 50 to 60 barrels of bourbon a day. Noah Andre Moll (second from right) was Paris Postmaster from 1910 to 1914.

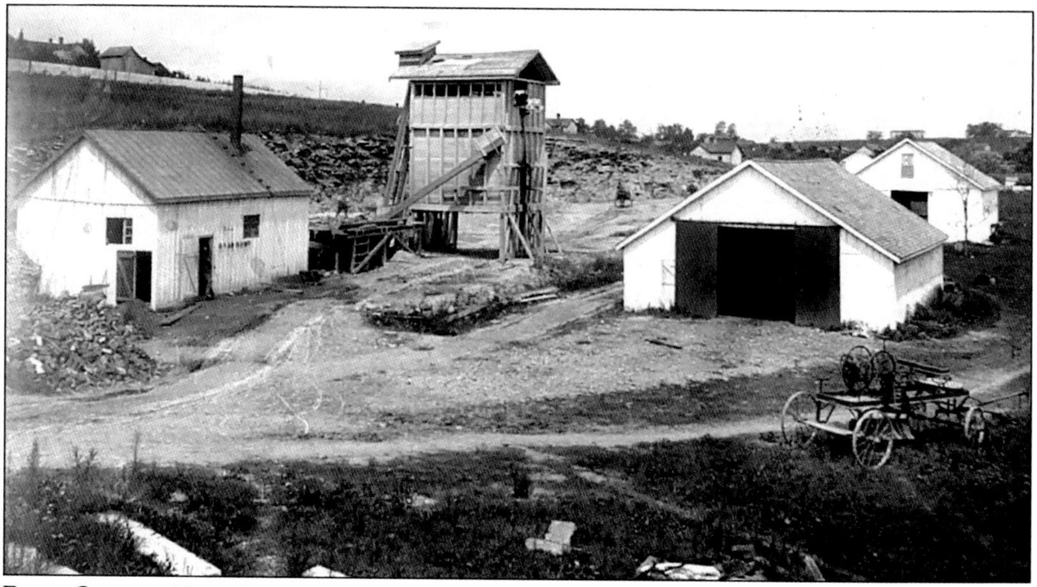

Rock Quarry Near Paris. Bourbon County, like most of Central Kentucky, lies on top of a thick crust of limestone rock. From the earliest days of settlement, Bourbon Countians mined the rock to build chimneys, foundations, and entire buildings as well as miles of stone fences. Crushed rock for road construction was also an important product. Pictured here in about 1905 is the quarry, now flooded, next to the present fairgrounds site.

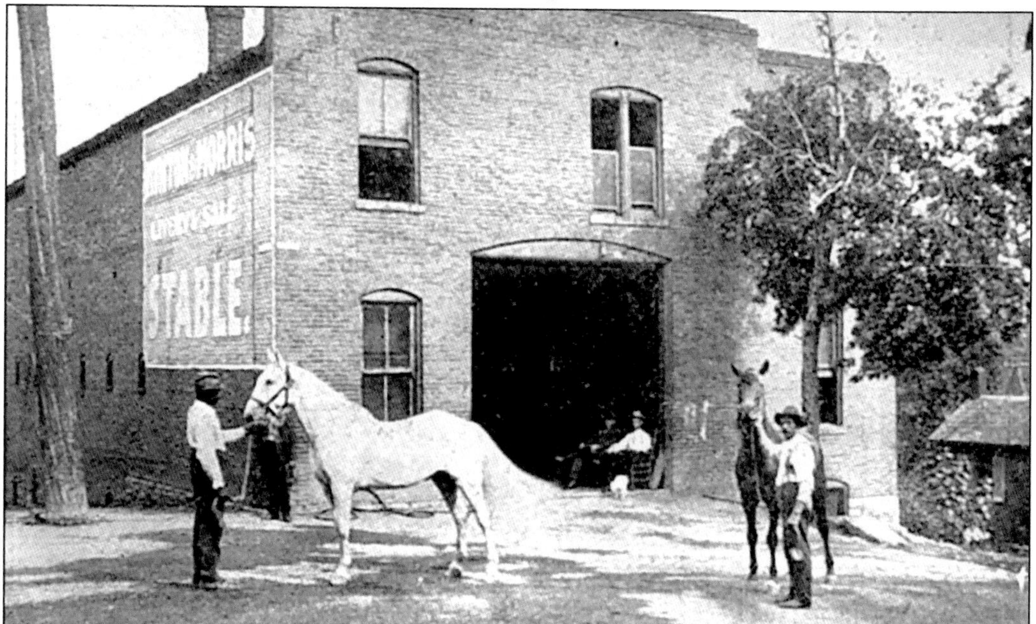

Will Hinton's Livery Stable Across From Windsor Hotel. The livery business consisted of maintaining and renting a wide variety of horses and horse-drawn vehicles. In a 1905 ad, Hinton claimed to have "a good horse or team of horses and comfortable, light, easy running vehicles at any and all times." Once the automobile came along, many local workers had to find new careers. Lost jobs included coachmen, hostlers, wagon makers, saddle/harness makers, blacksmiths, and teamsters.

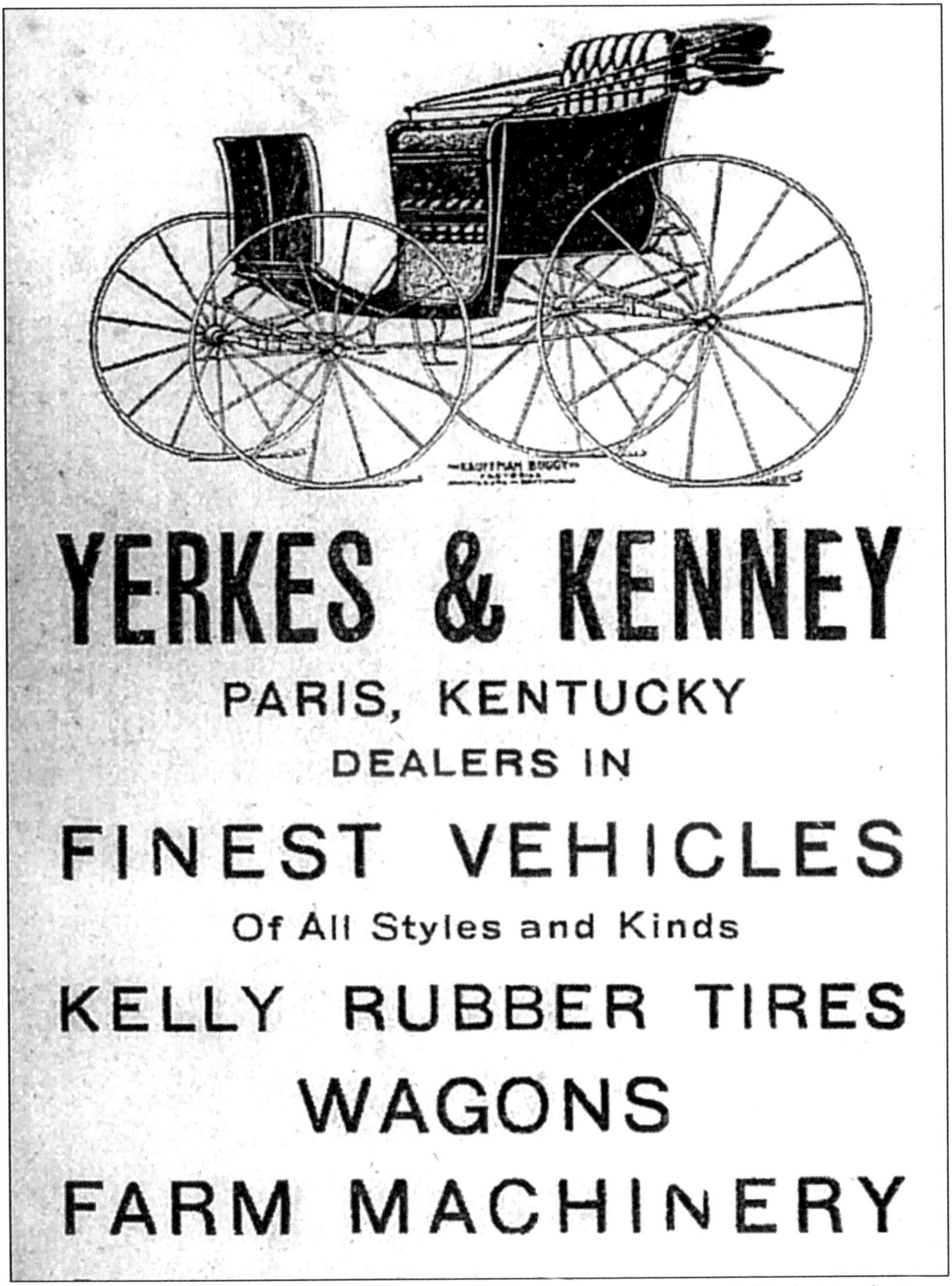

YERKES & KENNEY, A DISAPPEARING BUSINESS. Little did the proprietors of this thriving business at the corner of Fourth and Pleasant Streets know in 1908, when this ad appeared, that their industry would all but disappear in 10 to 15 years. In the meantime, the firm sold: "A full line of . . . Buggies and Run Abouts, Handsome Depot Wagons, Surreys, Phaetons and Stanhopes."

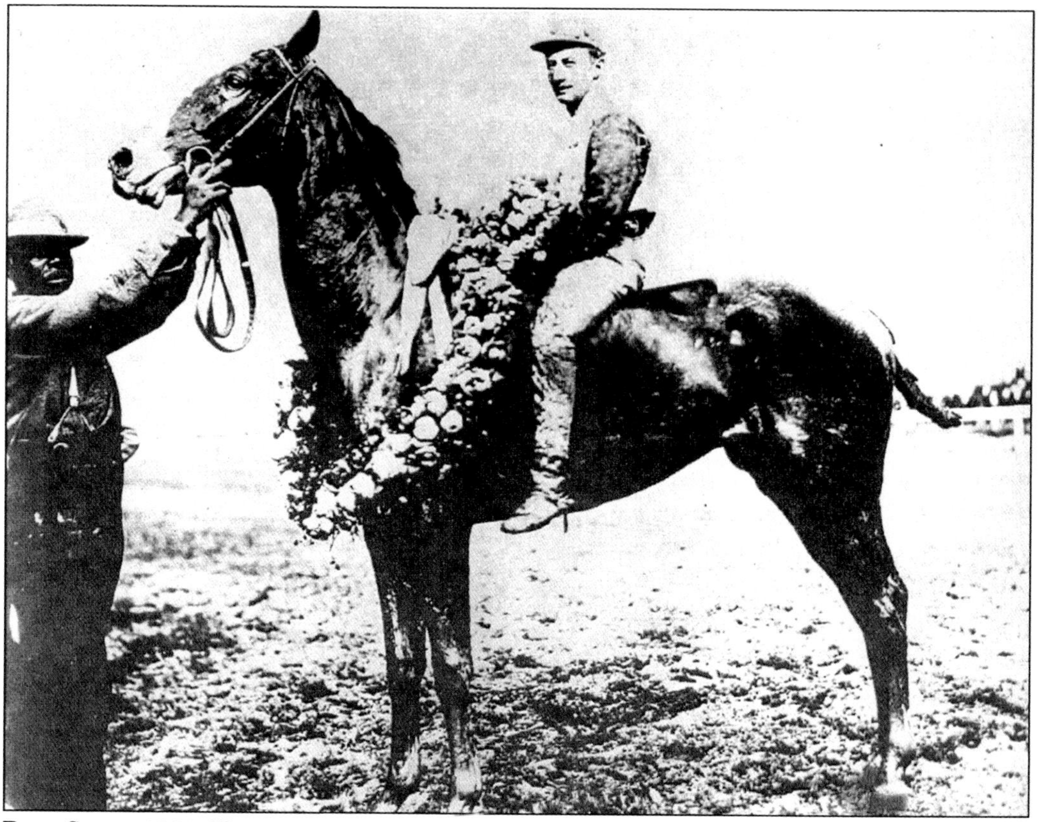

PINK STAR, 1907 KENTUCKY DERBY WINNER. The first Kentucky Derby winner owned and bred by a Bourbon County resident was Pink Star, who won in 1907. The bay colt was the only entry J. Hal Woodford ever had in the Derby. Pink Star developed a fever before the end of his three-year-old season and never went to stud. Woodford went on to raise other good horses and was elected state representative.

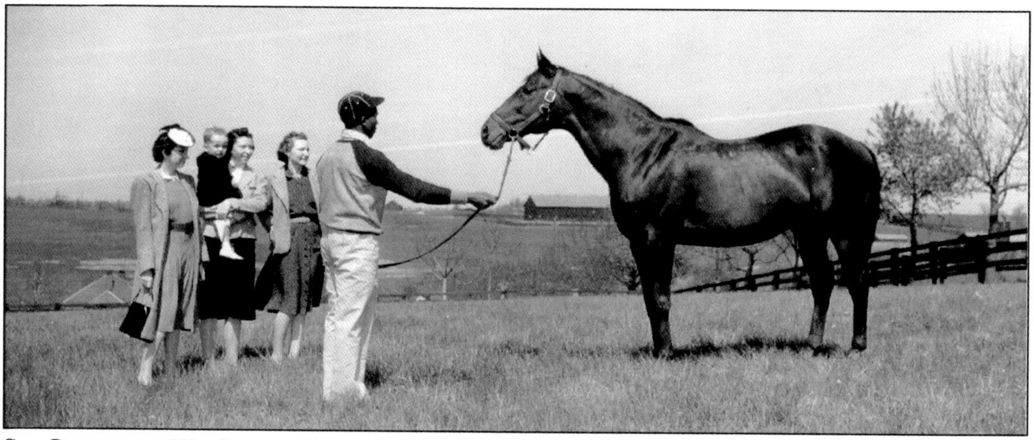

SIR GALLAHAD III, ONE OF CLAIBORNE'S MOST IMPORTANT SIRES. In 1925 when A.B. Hancock Sr., the founder of the world-famous Claiborne Farm outside Paris, purchased this French-bred stallion, he put together the first important syndicate in U.S. racing history. Sir Gallahad III led America's sires' list four times and the broodmare sires' list 12 times. As seen from this picture, Claiborne was as willing then to show its horses to guests as it is today.

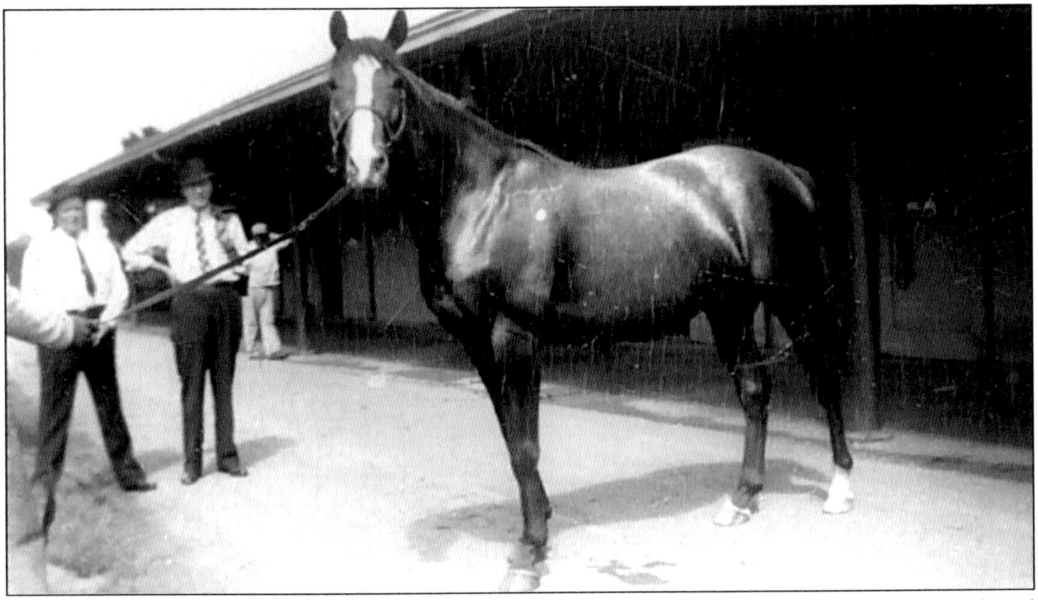

TRIPLE CROWN WINNER OMAHA SIRED BY GALLANT FOX. Sir Gallahad III's first crop produced the brilliant Triple Crown winner Gallant Fox. He became the only Triple Crown winner to sire another, Omaha, the stallion seen here in 1939. The man on the left is Fred Link, Paris's longtime police chief who was involved in a number of Prohibition-era shootings and also served as deputy coroner and police judge. The other man is Albert Johnson.

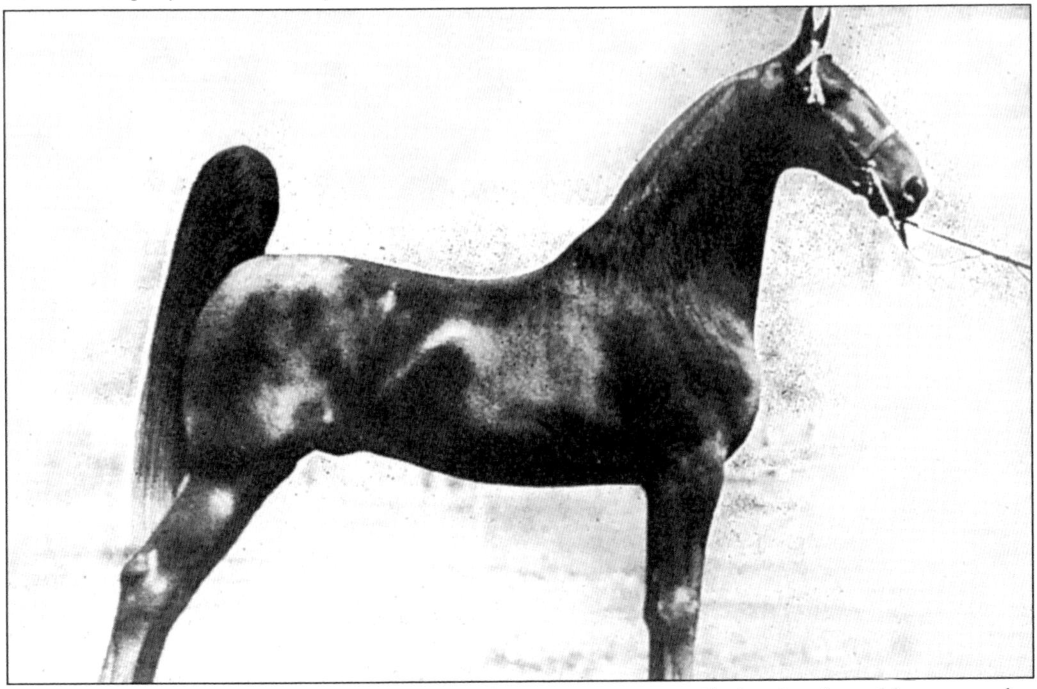

KING BARRYMORE. The saddlebred breed of horses were originally bred to be ridden every day and to draw buggies, and carriages. North Middletown was well known for producing some of the best saddlebred / show horses in the nation. King Barrymore 8861 was one of the greatest saddle horse sires of the 1930s and stood at A.G. Jones & Son Farm.

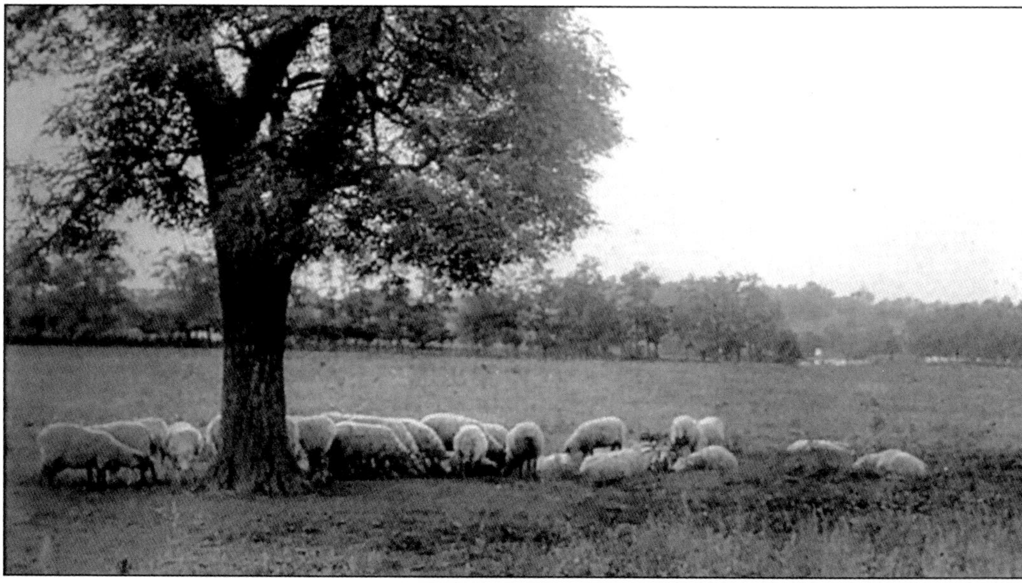

SHEEP PRODUCTION ONCE A MAJOR INDUSTRY. From pioneer times, sheep have been raised in Bourbon County. In 1880, 51,743 sheep were recorded in the county. By 1950, the number peaked at 81,000, but plummeted to 14,000 by 1970. Low market prices and the continuing threat of wild dogs hurt the popularity of sheep raising. Bourbon County mutton has won several ribbons at the State Fair.

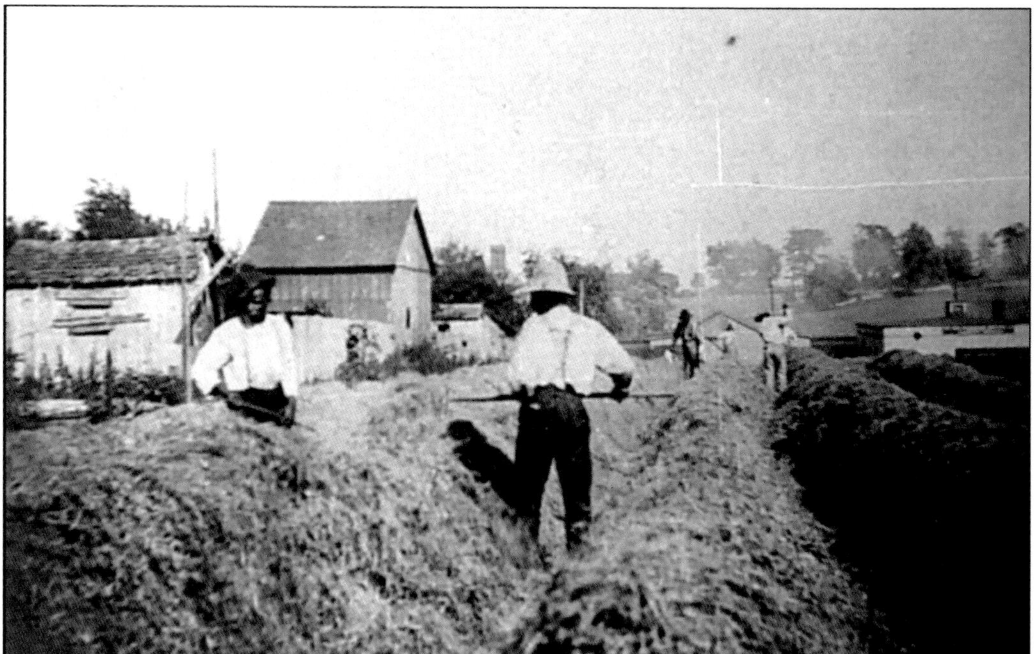

WORKING HEMP. Hemp production for the making of rope and sailcloth was one of Bourbon County's most profitable agricultural endeavors during the late 18th and 19th centuries. A very labor-intensive crop, hemp was the basis for a number of local fortunes. After a slump during the Civil War, local farmers produced a crop of 569 tons in 1870. By 1900, production had all but stopped, with a brief revival during World War II.

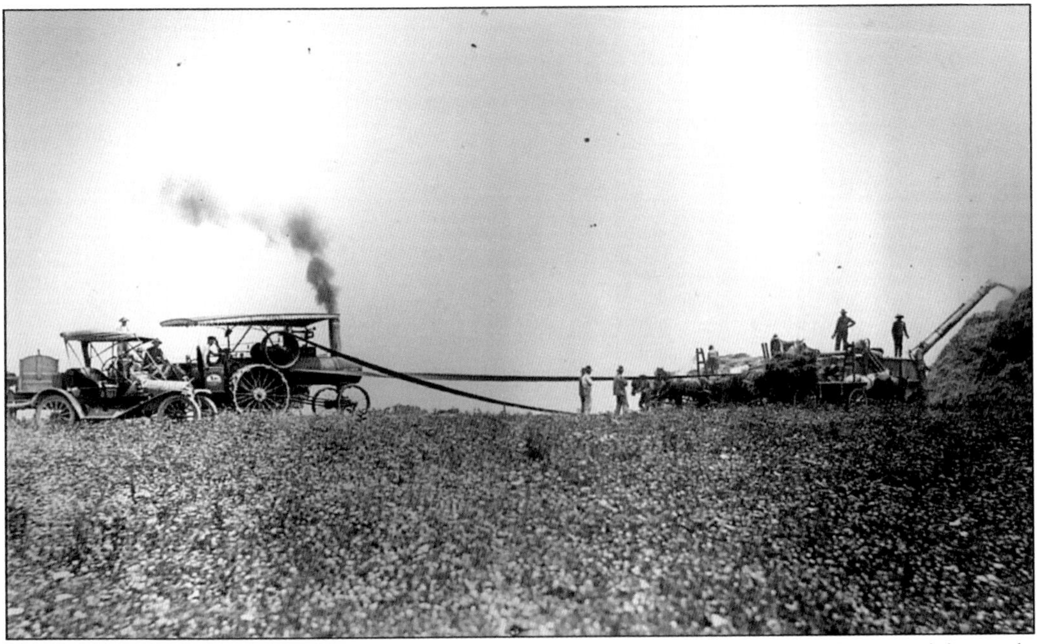

SEPARATING THE WHEAT FROM THE CHAFF. The process was made easier by the use of this early steam-driven threshing machine. The wheat was separated from the straw and bagged and then the straw was used for livestock bedding. This photo was probably taken before 1920—notice the early automobile in front of the thresher. Look very carefully; you can see that one of the men standing on the wagon is holding an oil can.

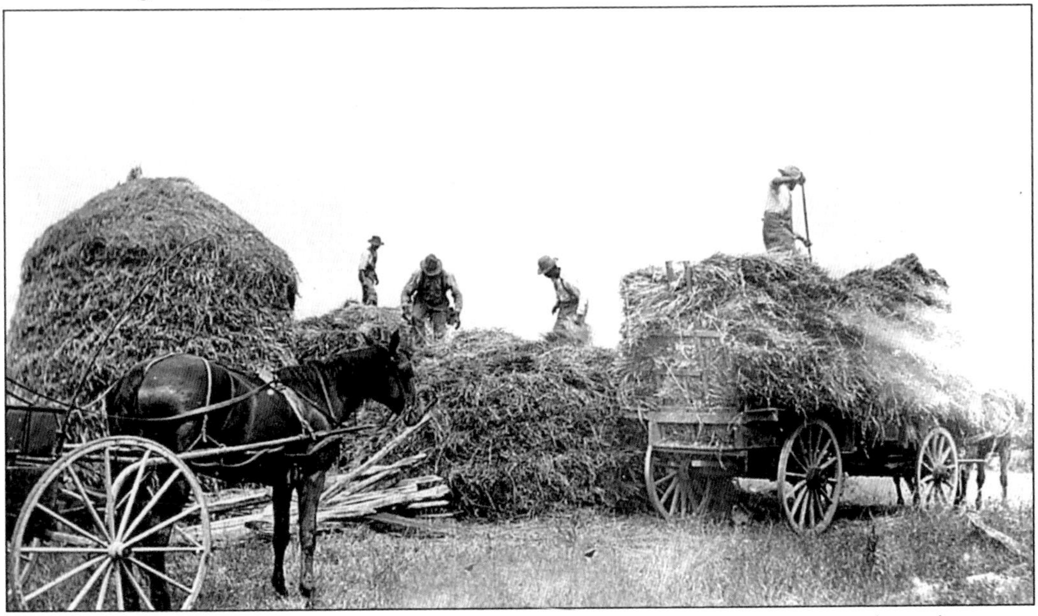

STACKING HAY WHILE THE SUN SHINES. These four men are busy stacking hay into neat haystacks like the one on the left that has been completed. The mare hitched to the buggy is identified as Blossom, dam of a filly named Lightsome. Lightsome was owned and trained by James L. Dodge who drove her to a win in the 1905 Two-Year-Old Futurity at the Red Mile in Lexington.

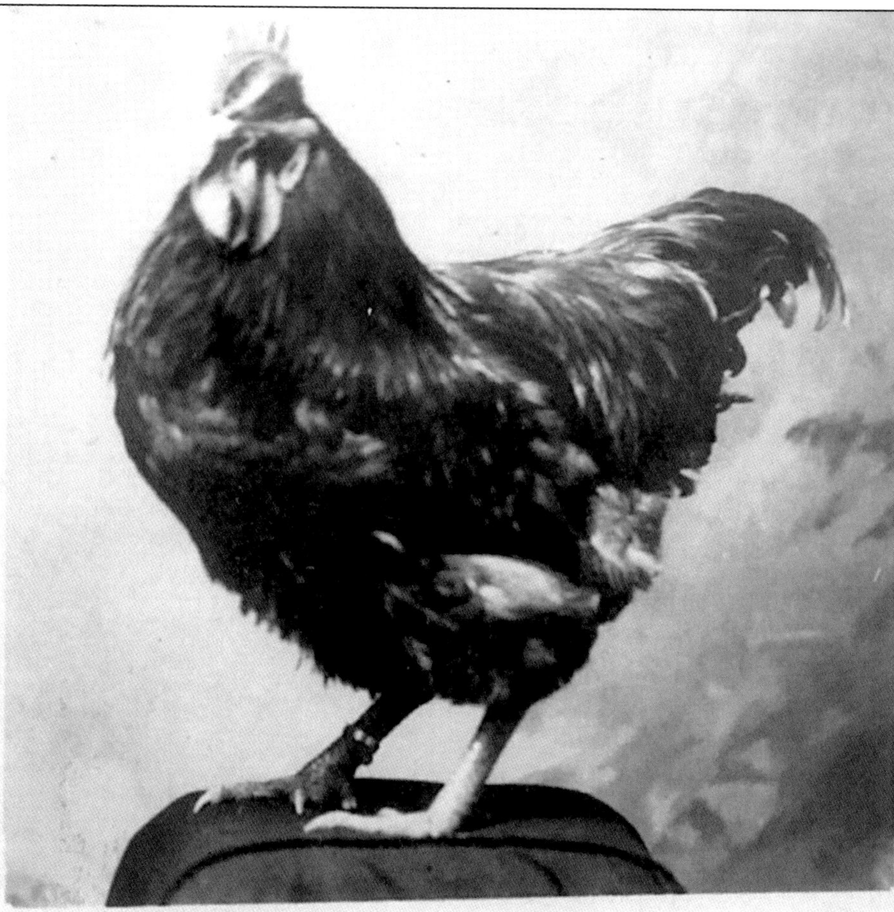

PRIDE OF PARIS.

First Chicago S. C. Buff Orpington Cockerel, Chicago 1910, and winner of Cup for best shaped male.

Mated to 4 grand imported hens of correct type and color, and four massive yearling hens, all several times winners.

EGGS, $12 FOR 15.

PRIDE OF PARIS. Horses, bourbon, and tobacco are not the only agricultural products Bourbon County was known for. Prized poultry became a major agricultural enterprise with chickens, geese, and turkeys predominating. Fighting cocks also had a long history in the county. This prize-winning rooster was owned by Mr. and Mrs. Duncan Bell who donated the land on High Street for the county hospital that is now the Municipal Building.

Seven

Sports and Leisure

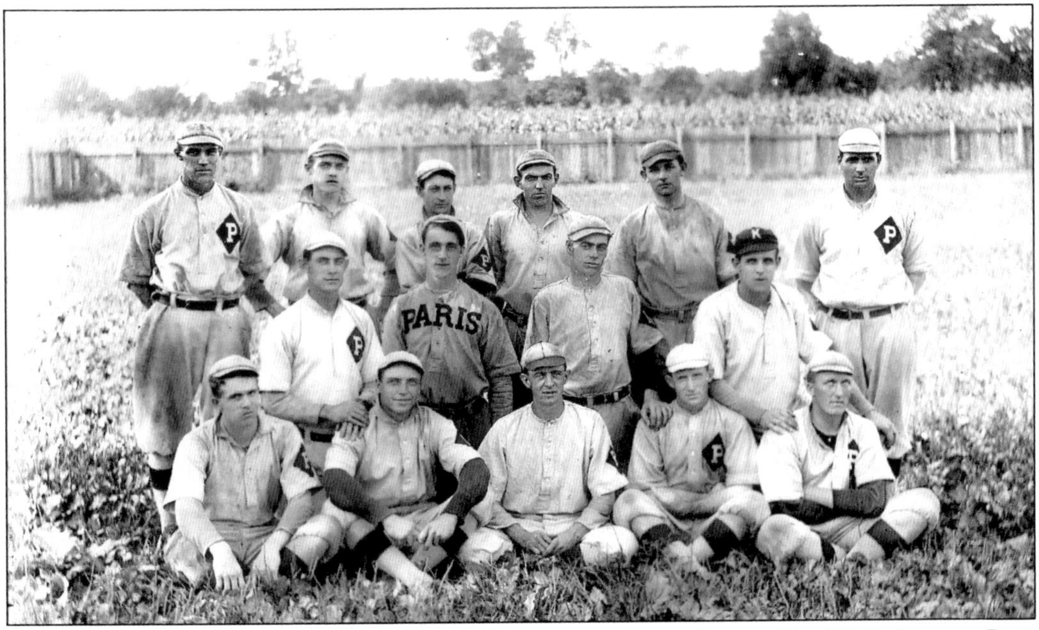

Paris team, 1910 Blue Grass League Champions. According to Dr. W.C. Ussery, Paris physician, who wrote the copy on the Blue Grass League for Spalding's Official Base Ball Guide, the Blue Grass League completed its third year of existence in 1910. "From its inception the league has provided high class ball, better, in fact, than the amount of money coming in at the gates justifies." The Paris minor league team went to the lead early in 1910 and never looked back. Another interesting item that Ussery mentions is that three Paris players from this team—outfielder "Deerfoot" Kaiser and pitchers Williams and Winchell were drafted by the majors. The players in the photo are identified from left to right as follows: (front row) Scott, Goodman, Chapman, McKernan (Mgr.), and Winchell; (middle row) Barnett, Scheneberg, Poole, and Williams; (back row) Kaiser, Kuhlman, Schmidt, Harold, Holder, and Maxwell.

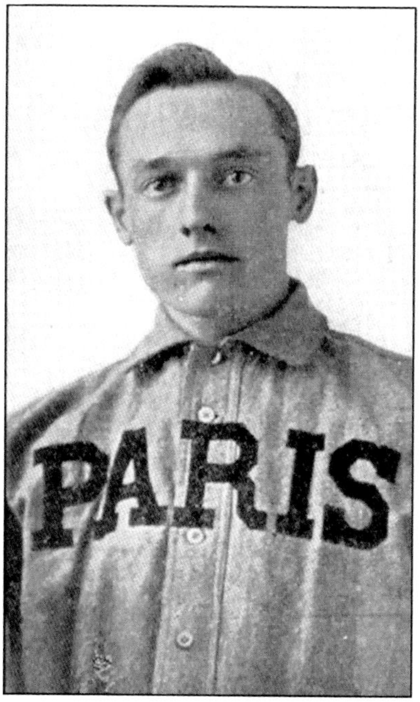

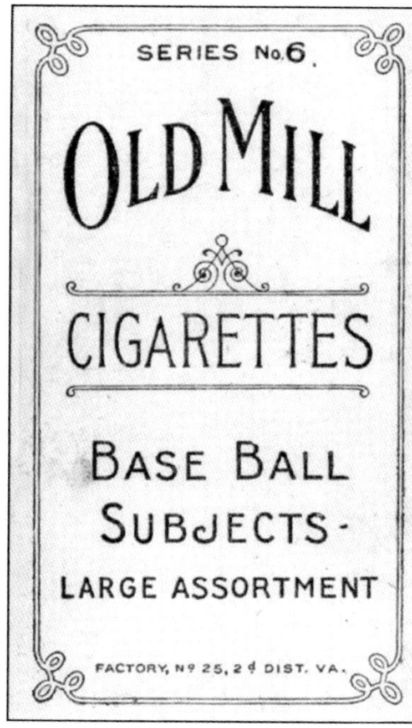

Old Mill Delivered Cigarettes and Local Baseball Cards. In 1910, when a pack of "smokes" was probably a nickel, the purchaser also received an extra bonus—baseball cards (or as they wrote the term: "base ball cards." Pictured are the back and front of one of the cards. The player shown is Kuhlman, a member of the 1910 Paris team who won the Bluegrass League championship. (U.K. Collection.)

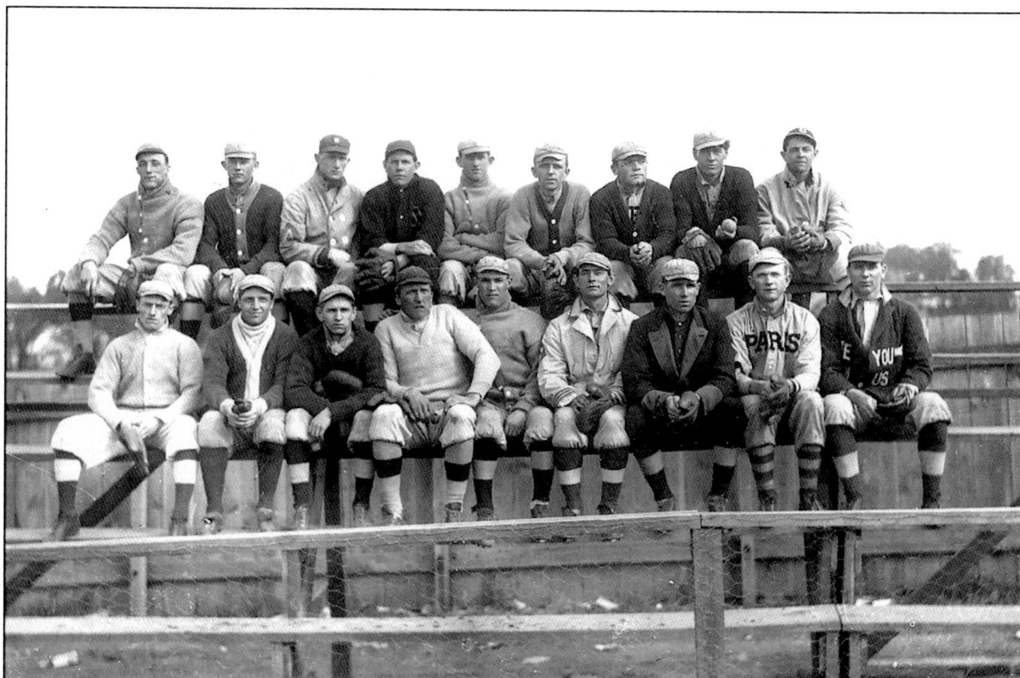

Bundled-up Baseball Players Indicate Early Spring Training. These Paris minor league baseball players are all bundled up in a variety of jackets and sweaters, so it was probably very early in the season. The local minor league team was named the Paris Bourbonites and they played the other teams in the Bluegrass League including the Lexington Colts, the Frankfort Lawmakers, the Shelbyville Millers, the Winchester Hustlers, and the Richmond Pioneers.

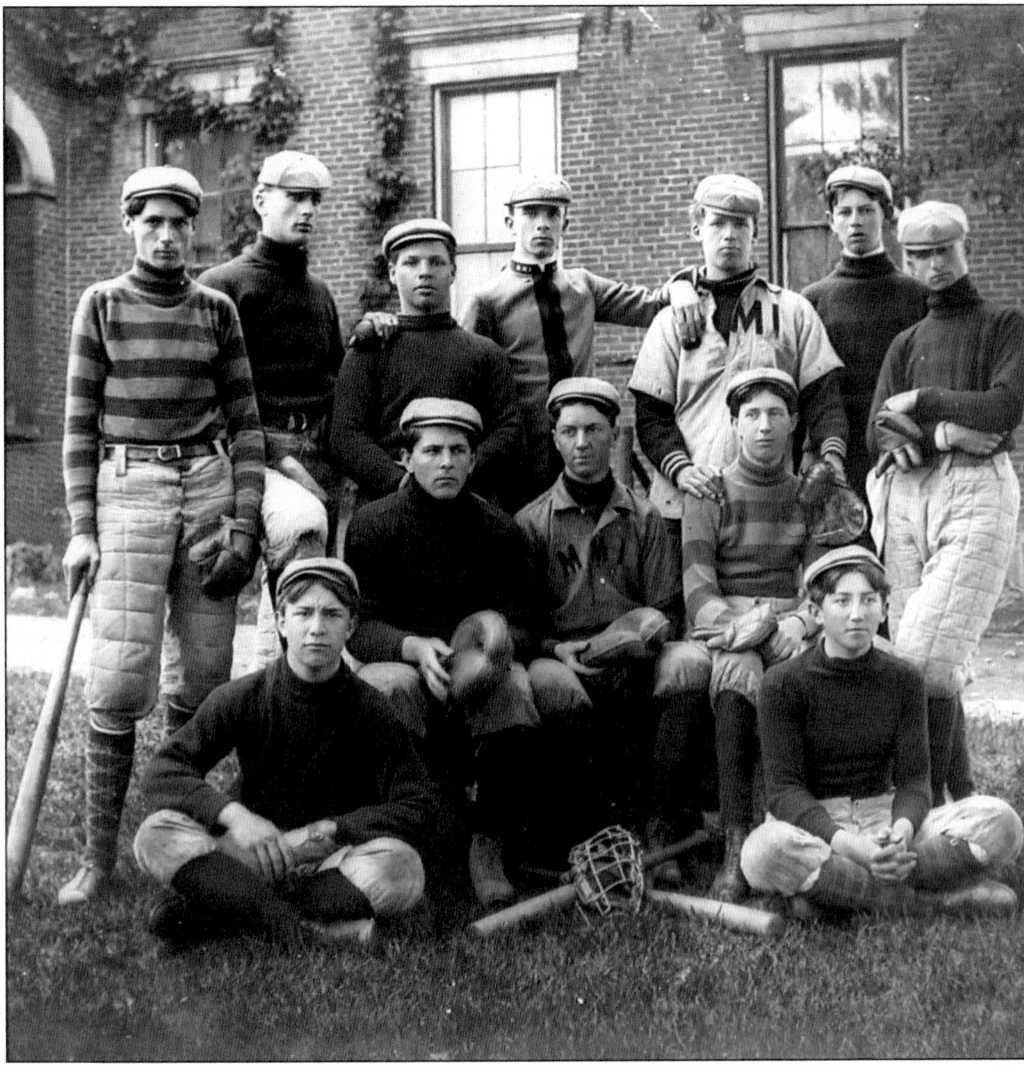

1890s Millersburg Military Institute Team Looks Serious. More than a century after this photo was taken, there is no information available on the record of this MMI team or the occasion for this picture, but the serious looks make it doubtful it was a photo to celebrate a championship year. MMI fielded strong sports teams including baseball, basketball, and football for decades. Note the early baseball equipment including quilted pants, bats, gloves, cleated shoes, and a catcher's mask. The boys are from left to right as follows: (front row) Jefferson and Coleman; (middle row) Coldwell, unidentified, and Arrowsmith; (back row) J.T. Judy, Boardman, Cantrill, Buck, Kemper, H. Judy, and Gamble. (U.K. Collection.)

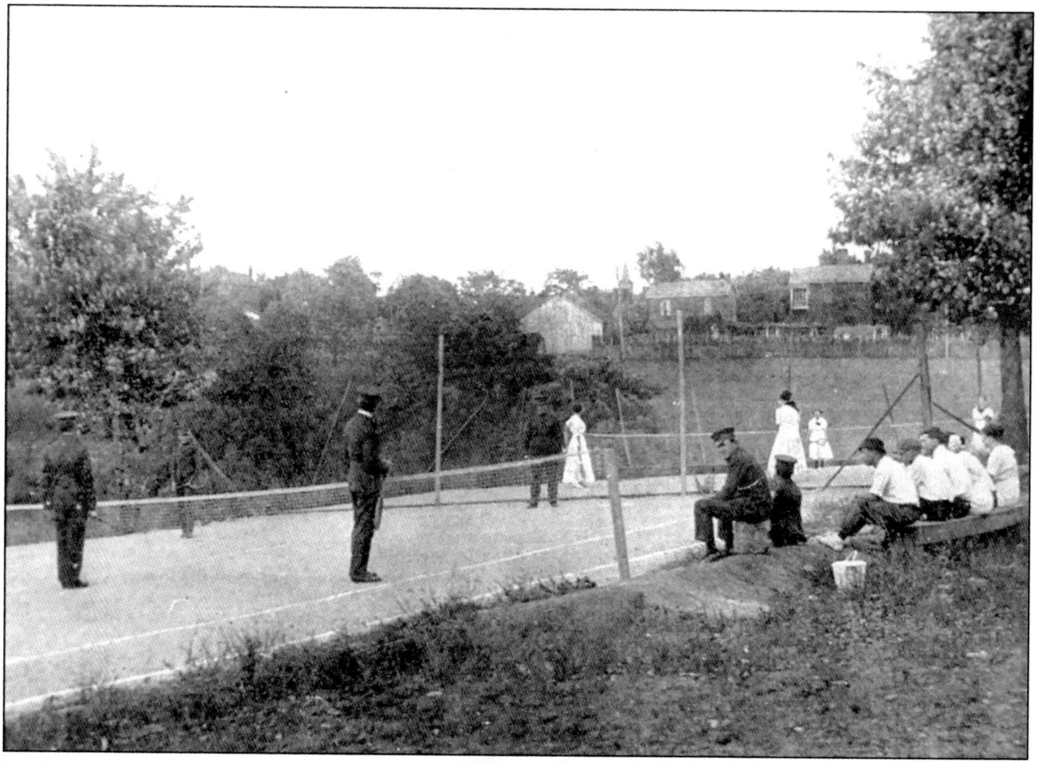

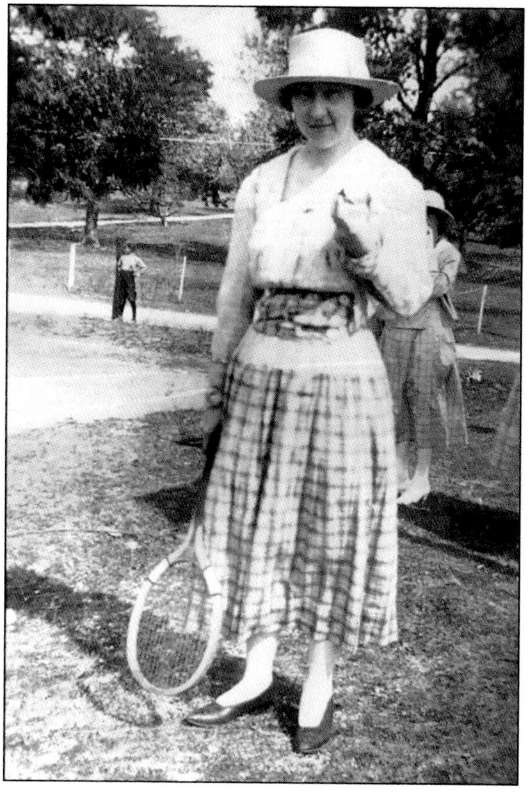

PARIS CITY SCHOOL'S TENNIS COURTS, 1912. It looks like boys' doubles in the near court and girls' doubles in the far court on this day in 1912. There is no information about where the courts were located, but they were probably clay courts and a bucket with chalk for the lines can be seen next to the bench. Many of the boys are wearing their cadet uniforms.

TENNIS A POPULAR SPORT FOR COUNTRY AND CITY DWELLERS. Paris residents could use the city school's courts but many farms and rural homes also had tennis courts. This is a photo of "Miss Pink" and her tennis racket taken in 1919. One hopes that she changed her shoes before she stepped out on the court, but women did play in long skirts during this era.

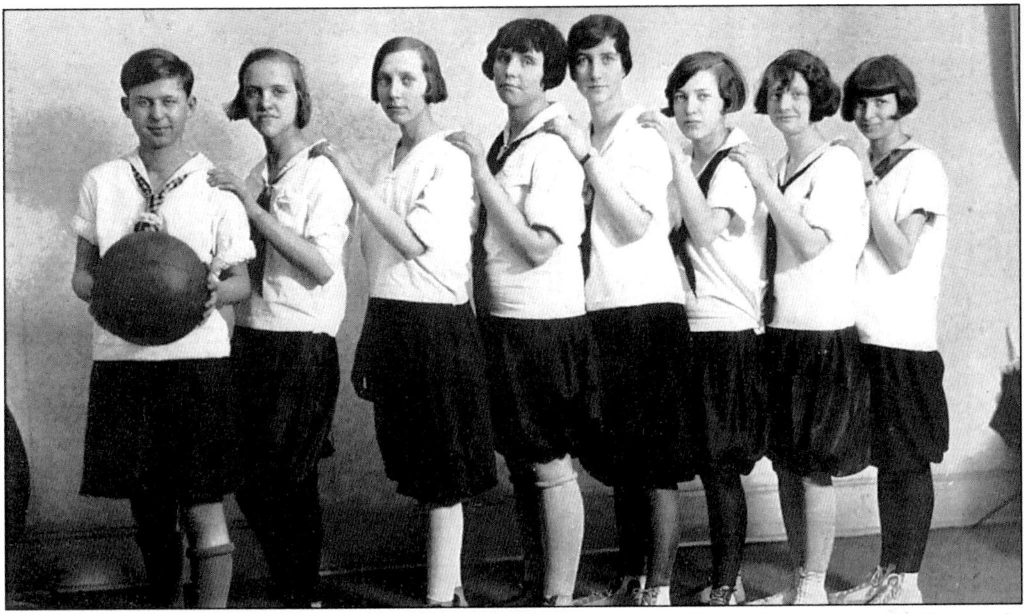

1925–1926 Paris Junior High School Girls' Basketball Team Undefeated. They only played seven games, but won six and tied Cynthiana once. There are 12 girls listed as members of coach Lula Batcheldor's team and only 8 girls in the picture. Members of the team included Elizabeth Anderson, Mary Bell, Naomi Cavanaugh, Laura Craft, Hillry Davis, Frances Dudley, Bourbon McCarty, Nancy Rankin, Caroline Reading, Vivian Smith, Shelby Spears, and Eleanor Swearingen.

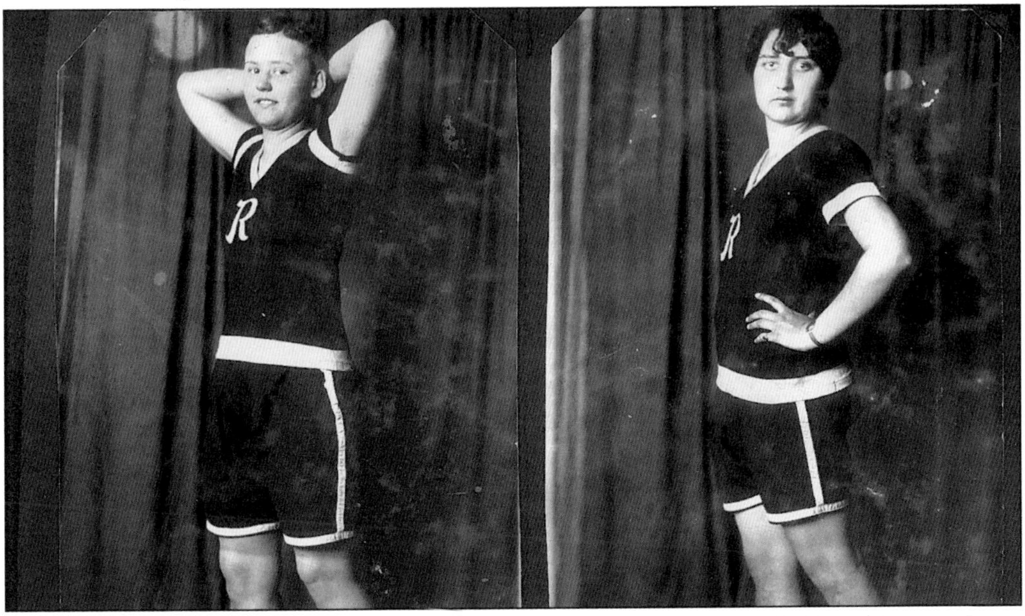

Two Members of 1932 Ruddles Mills Girls' Team. Elizabeth Hyatt (left) and Bernice Lowe show off their basketball uniforms for the camera. The team colors were wine and white for Ruddles Mills Consolidated School. The school did not have a gym until 1937, so the earlier teams played their games outside. That did not seem to bother them as the girls' basketball team rarely lost a game.

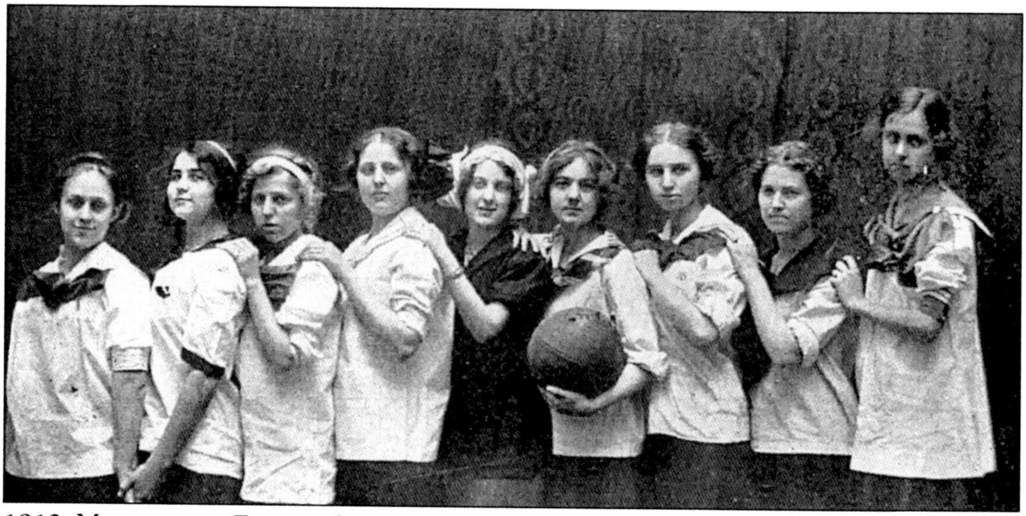

1912 Millersburg Female College Basketball Team. As discussed in the chapter on education, although MFC was called a college, it really just went two years beyond high school and the majority of the girls would have been high school and junior high school age. There is no information available about this team's record, but they look sharp in their "middy" blouses and their wide variety of ties.

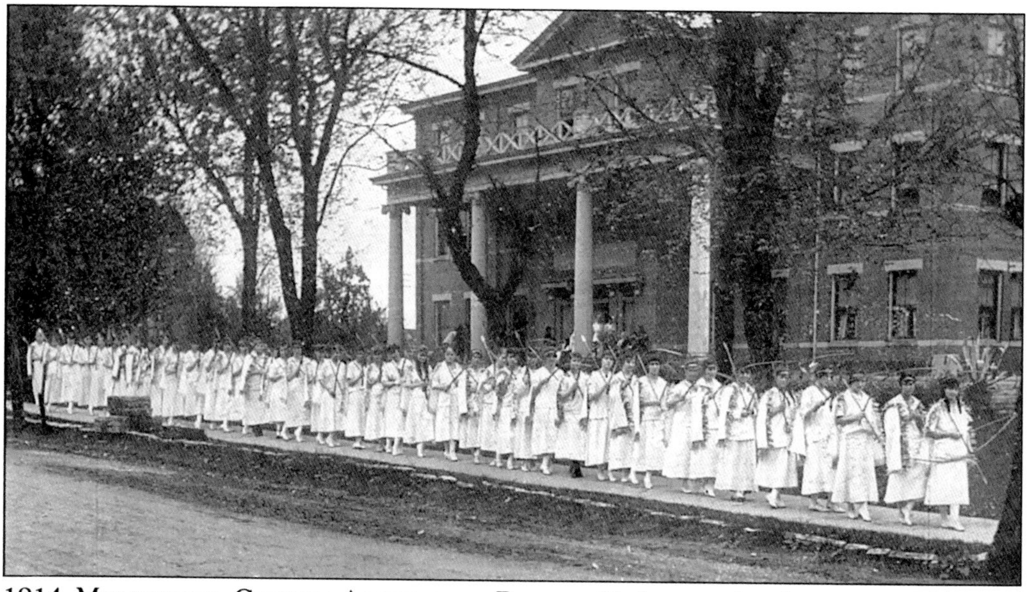

1914 Millersburg College Archers on Parade. Unfortunately, there is no additional information about where these archers are heading but there are more than 40 of them going somewhere. The handsome main Millersburg College (also known as Millersburg Female College before 1914) building can be seen in the background. Obviously, there were some types of recreational activities that have disappeared, as this is not popular today.

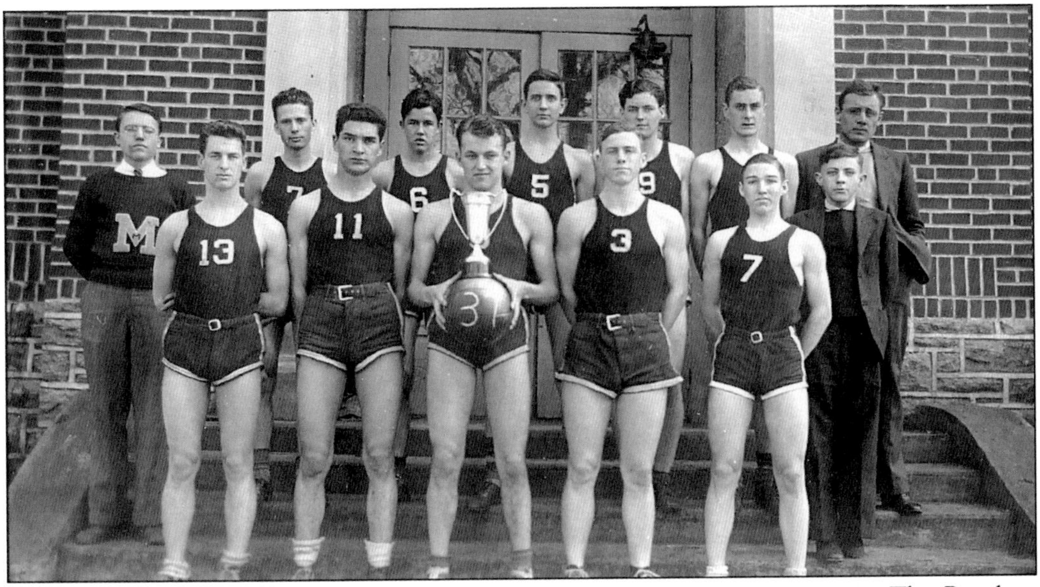

North Middletown's 1937 Boys' Basketball Team Won Championship. The Bourbon Kings that year went 18-3-1 and won the county tournament to claim the crown. Pictured from left to right are the following: (front row) James Meng, Henry Boardman Mark, Harry Richart, F.C. Bryan, and B.B. Bryan; (back row) manager John Heaberlin, Virgil Florence, John Thomas, Graham Jones, John Hinkson, J.F. Mark, asst. manager Kenneth Henry, and coach John T. Gentry.

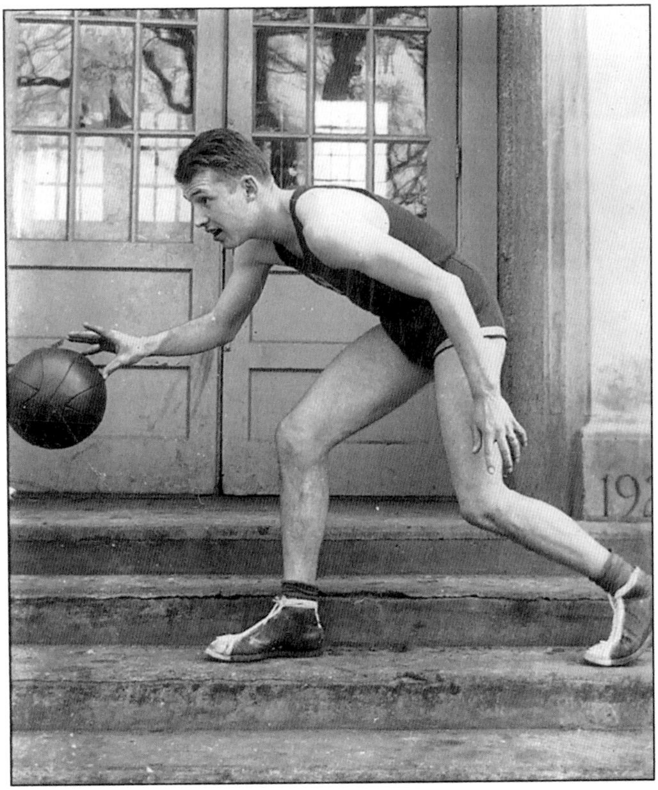

He Dribbles, He Scores!! It is obvious that Harry Richart, captain of the 1937 North Middletown Bourbon Kings, knows how to dribble. Since he was also the winner of the Most Valuable Trophy, one assumes he could score as well. During the 1936–1937 season, the team played 12 different schools, many of which are no longer in existence, including Bethel, Great Crossings, Trapp, Little Rock, Center Hill, and Ruddles Mills.

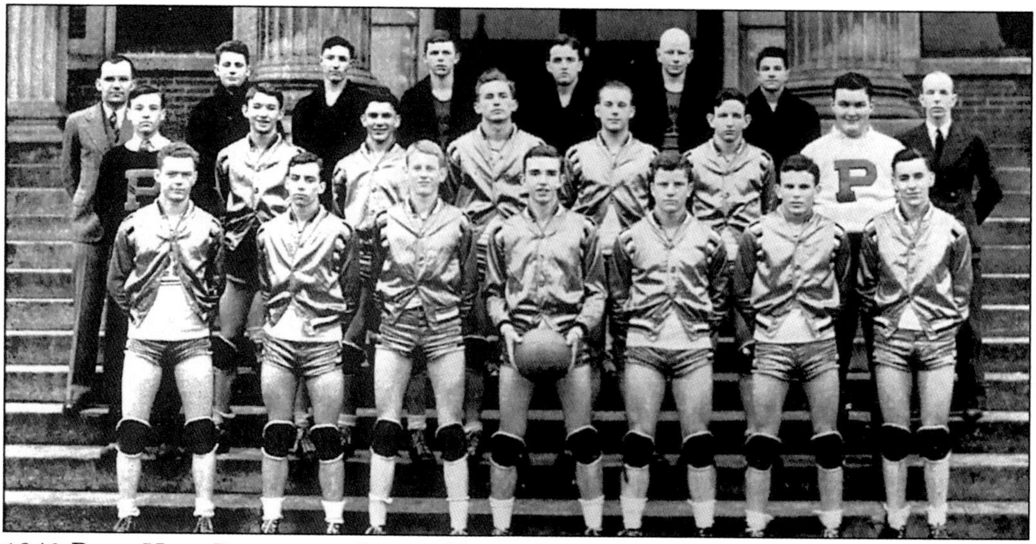

1940 Paris High Basketball Squad. Kneepads are now considered an unusual equipment item for basketball players, but all the teams of this era wore them. Pictured from left to right are the following: (front row) Red Barnett, Joe Goodman, Jim Parrish, Bill Price, Matt Lair, Dave Parrish, and Jack McKenzie; (middle row) Ed Sutherland, Bob Insko, Doug Williams, Jimmy Steele, Paul Kenten, Bill Thompson, and unidentified; (back row) Coach Blanton Collier, Bobby Ballard, Bobby Biddle, Hamlet Collier, Frank Shirley Dalzell, Francis Kennedy, Nick Nickolas, and Coach Dick Butler.

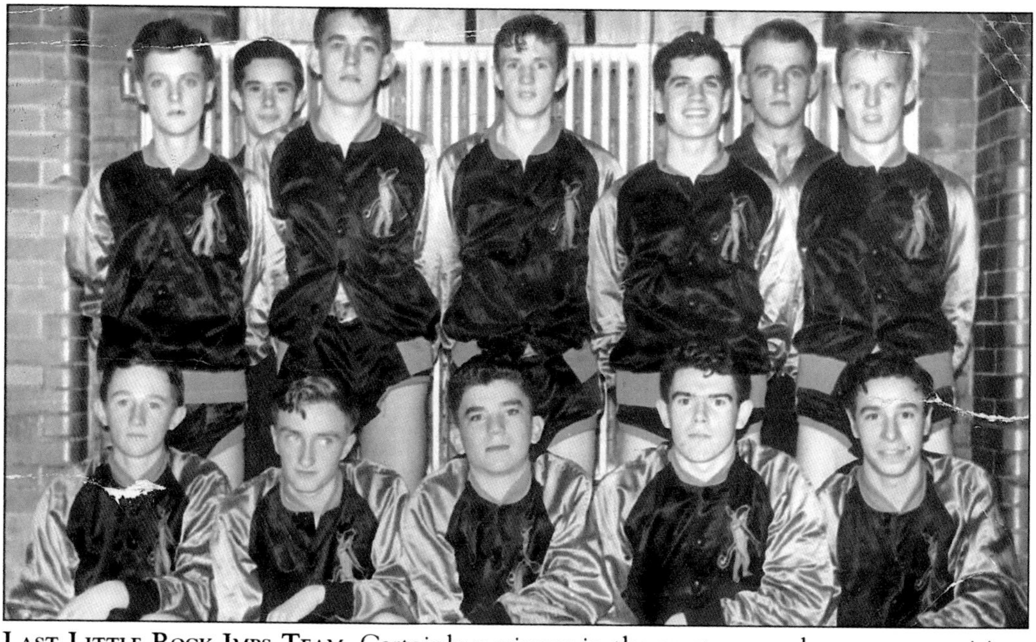

Last Little Rock Imps Team. Certainly a winner in the most unusual name competition, this team was the last to play for Little Rock as the students were moved to North Middletown in 1940. Pictured from left to right are the following: (front row): John Curtis Burris, Lowell Vice, Jimmy Banta, Charles Ray Hinkle, and Stanton Summay; (middle row) Templin Wasson, N.H. Fletcher, Turner Hinkle, Roger Lowry, and Bob Marshall; (back row) Frank Crouch and Loel Wasson.

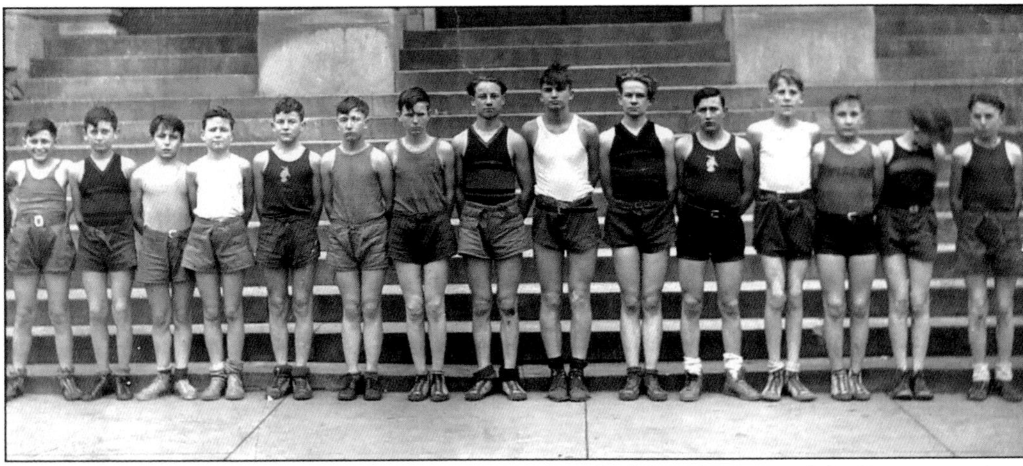

EARLY PARIS TRACK TEAM? This photo was not identified, but the steps of the Paris city school building are unmistakable as they appear in countless photos. The boys in this group vary in both height and age. One aspect that begs to be noticed is their footwear, especially their socks, which differ widely. The boys in this group vary in height and age. One interesting aspect that begs to be noticed is their footwear, especially their socks, which differ widely.

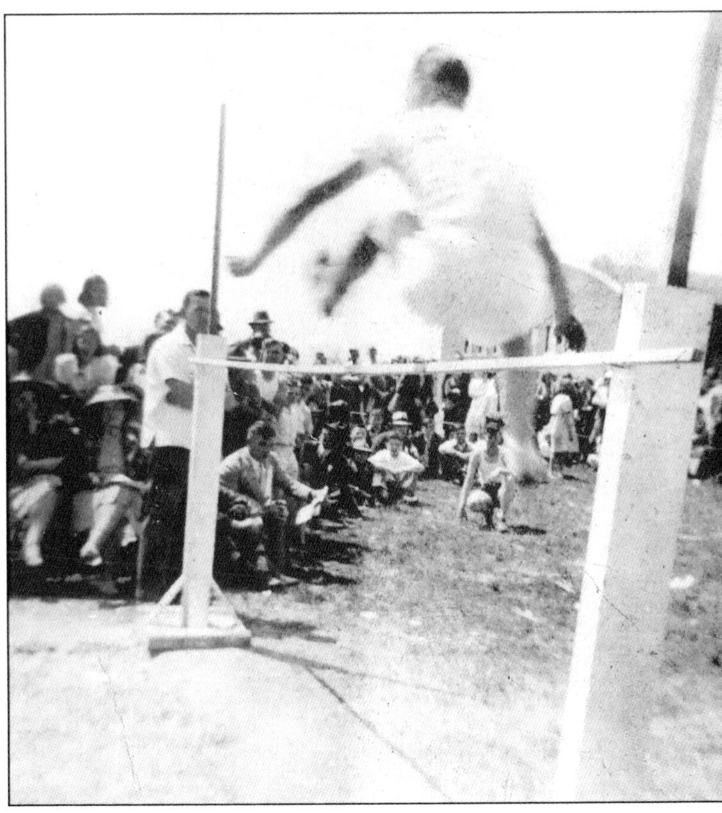

UP, UP AND OVER! Bill Burris Bryan sails over the bar at the 1939 Bourbon County Track and Field Day held at the Clintonville Consolidated School for children in the eighth through the twelfth grades in all six of the county consolidated schools: Little Rock, Clintonville, North Middletown, Center Hill, Bourbon County at Millersburg, and Ruddles Mills. As transportation became easier, smaller schools were closed and their students merged into larger schools.

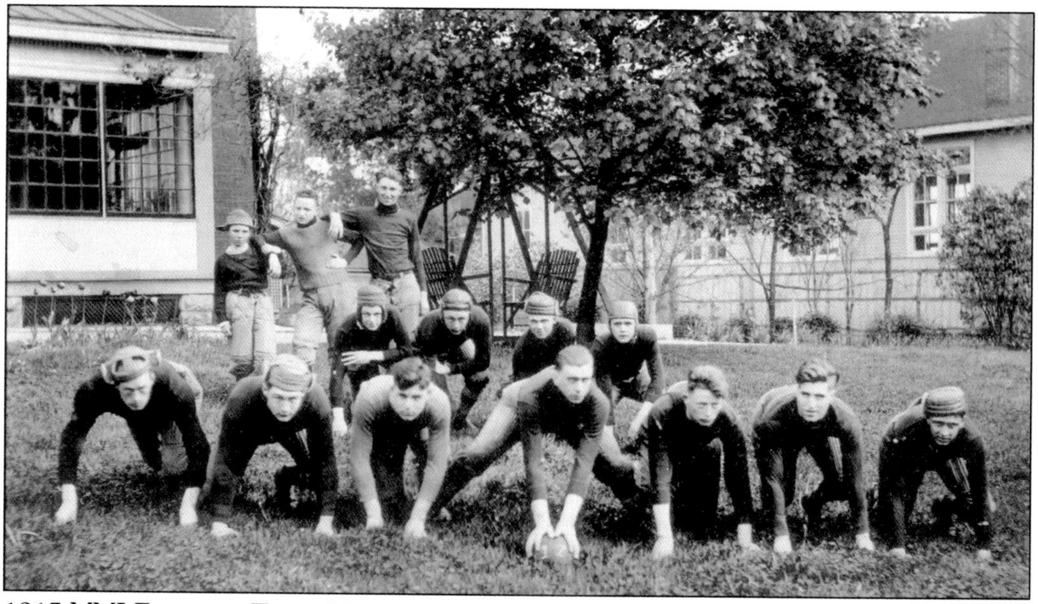

1917 MMI Football Team, May 1918. Maybe the team had spring training, as May is not a month that you would guess football team photos would be taken. Helmets seem to have been optional and even if worn do not look like they would have been much help in a collision. Identified team members include (not in order) Bond, Worwick, Cline, Stout, Woods, Baldwin, A. Hunter, Heuritze, Bruner, and Watson. (U.K. Collection.)

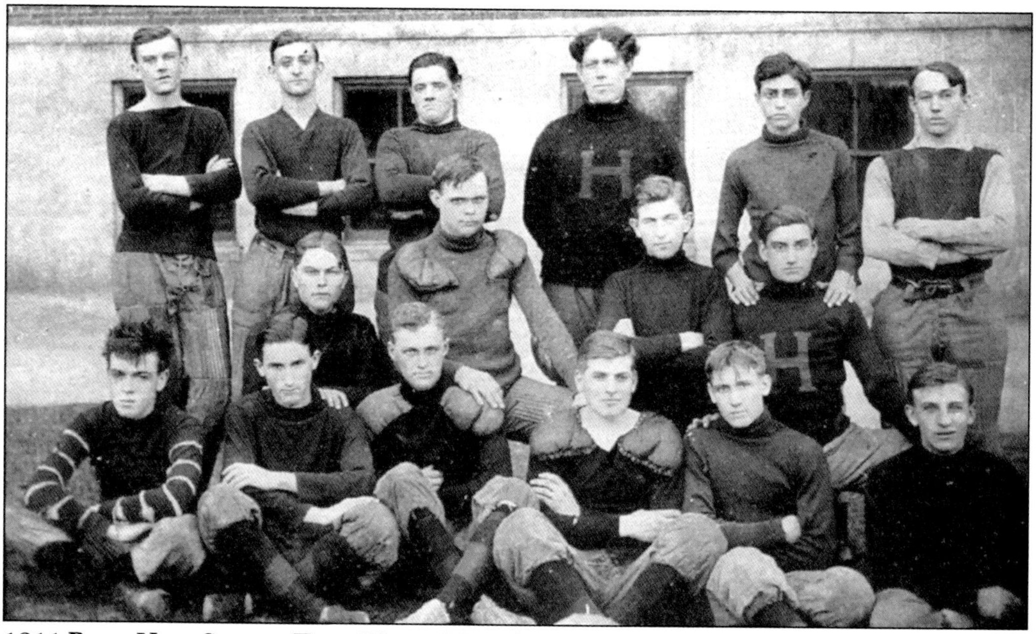

1911 Paris High School Team Wore "H." There is no information about why the lettermen earned an "H" instead of a "P," but the yearbook mentioned that in the last three years, the boys' football team had scored 207 points to 97 points by opposing teams. Pictured from left to right are the following: (front row) Lynch, Horton, Thompson, Link, Curtis, and Slicer; (middle row) Johnson, Templin, Arnsparger, and DeJarnett; (back row) Kerns, Friedman, Adair, Coach Johnson, Meglone, Mitchell.

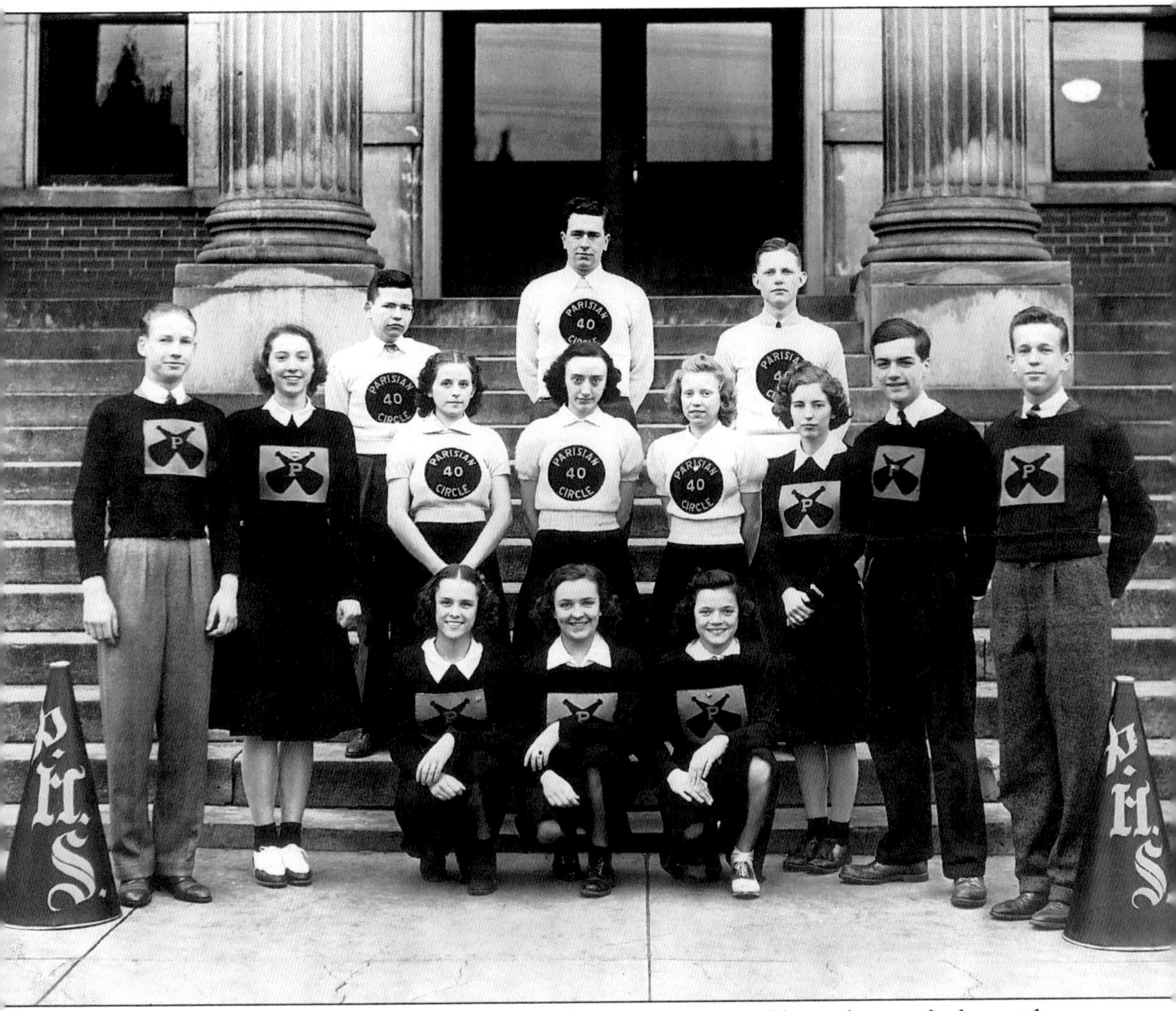

CHEERLEADERS AND PARISIAN CIRCLE. School team sports would not be much fun without the crowd and cheerleaders to cheer on their teams. At Paris High School, there was also another organization called the Parisian Circle made up of six seniors, four juniors, and two sophomores who were supposed to "put forth every effort to make PHS excel in scholarship and sportsmanship." The 1940 cheerleaders and Parisian Circle members are pictured here left to right (front row, kneeling) Betty Jo Denton, Nadine Baird, and Gloria Thompson; (middle row) John Gravitt, Kenney Shropshire, Joanna Maher, Gene Barr, Hazel Lyons, June Doyle, Withers David, and John Trimble Harris; (third row) Marion Snell, Archie Crump, and George Sidney Tate.

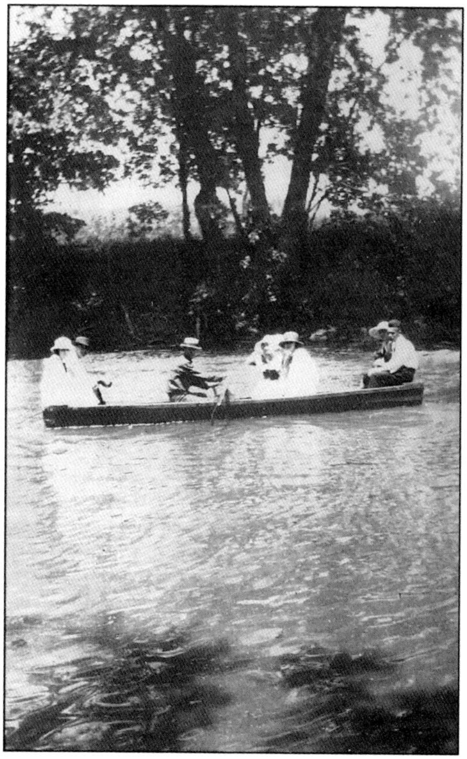

Enjoying a Row on Stoner Creek. Skimming down the creek on a summer day is fun today just as it was in 1921. This boat looks large and is carrying seven people, so perhaps "skimming" would not be the correct term. Countless lazy summer days have been spent in pursuits like these for the last century.

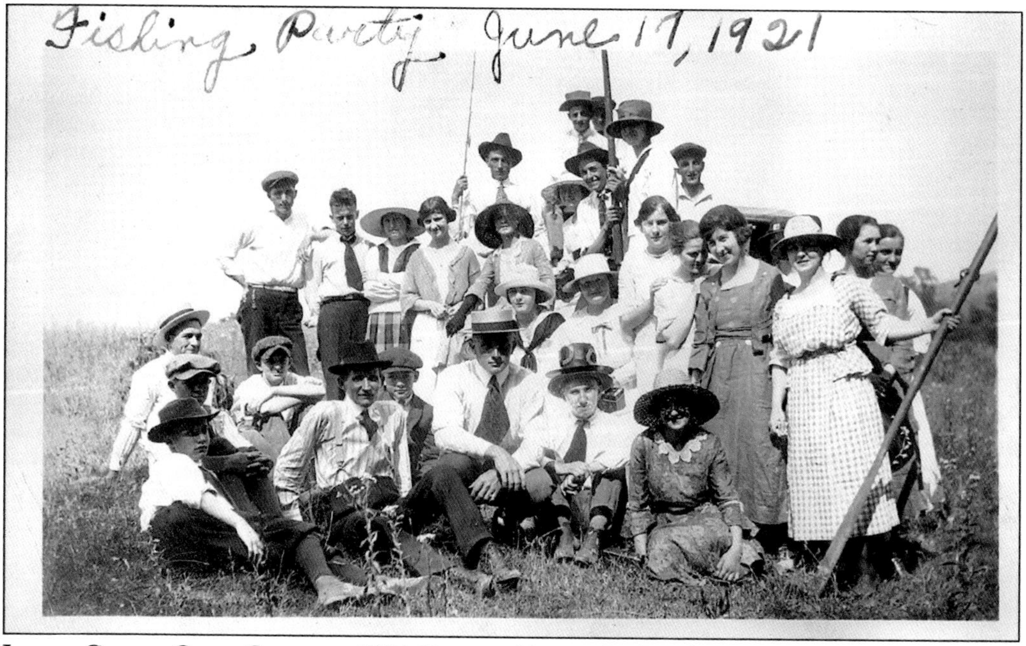

Large Crowd Came Out for 1921 Fishing Party. In Bourbon County, there are several navigable streams and creeks, and these waterways lend themselves to recreational activities like boating and fishing. This fishing party group looks like they are having a good time although only one person is holding a fishing rod. Notice the wide variety of headgear—the men are wearing everything from cloth caps to straw boaters to dark, felt hats.

Eight

Transportation

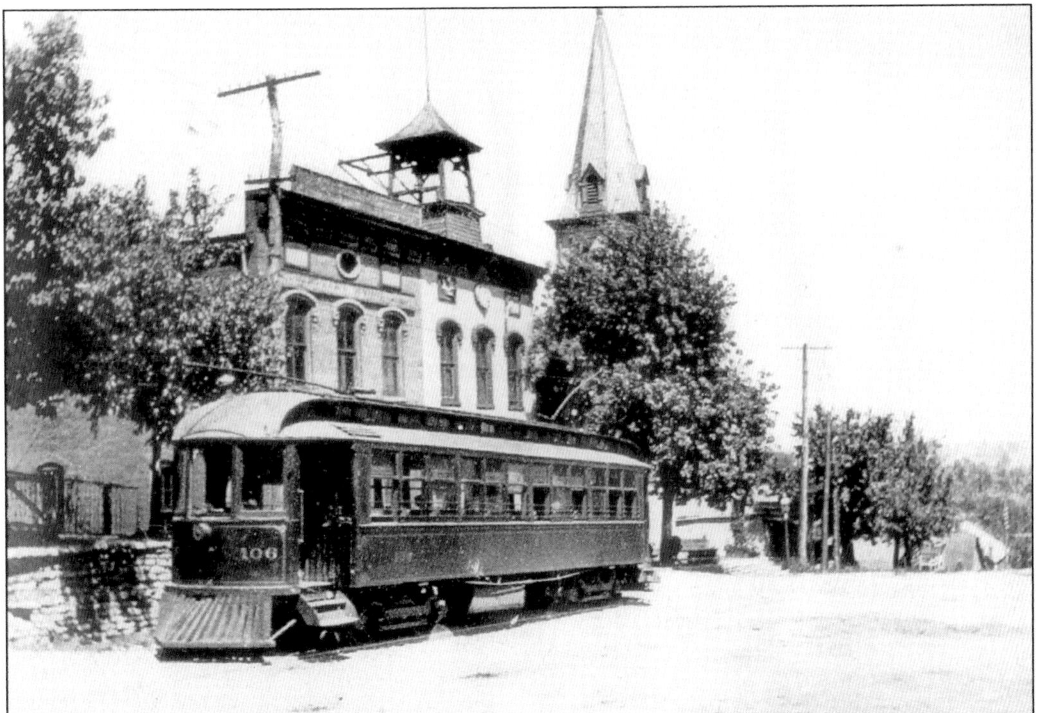

Interurban, from Paris to Lexington and Back. From 1902 until 1934, electric railway cars like this ran on tracks from a depot at the corner of Fifth and High Streets in Paris, along the west side of the Paris Pike, to downtown Lexington and back. This photo shows an Interurban car passing in front of the fire station and St. Peter's Episcopal church. The cars ran on an hourly schedule, from dawn to late at night, seven days a week and carried commuters, shoppers, college students, fresh eggs, and produce among other things. According to legend, during World War I when Paris was "dry" and Lexington "wet," it also carried a lot of bootleg whiskey. (U.K. Collection.)

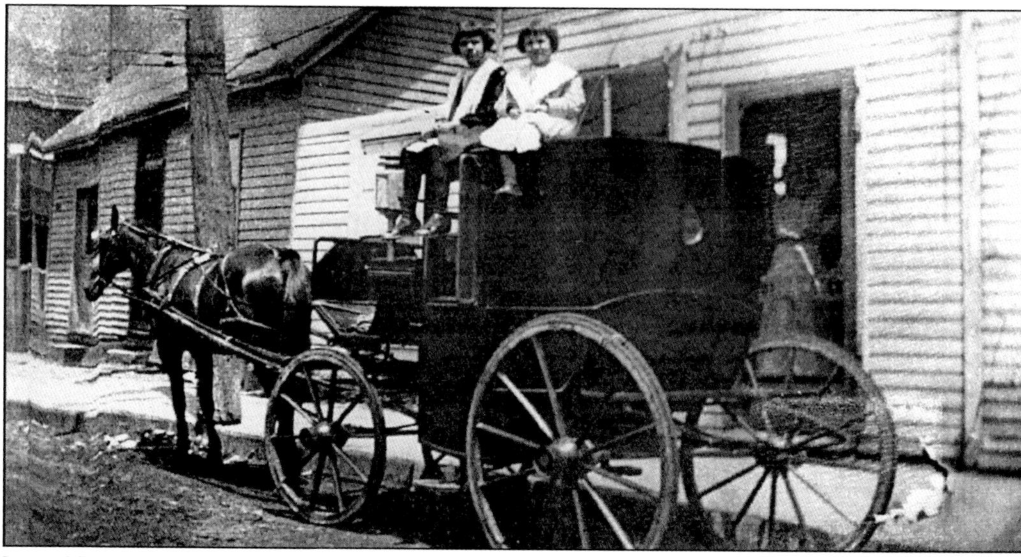

Last Horse-drawn Cab in Paris. When the gentle "clip clop" of horses' hooves provided the traffic noise in downtown Paris instead of the roar of squealing tires and broken mufflers, this carriage was one of the town's last cabs. Pictured in 1908, the two young girls are sitting where the driver Charles Coleman usually sat.

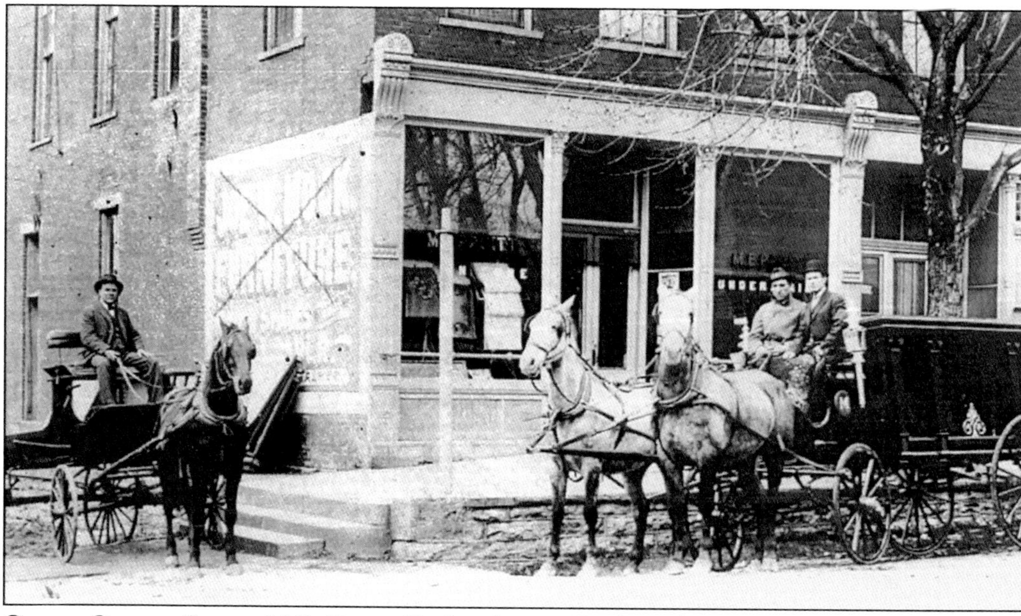

Going Out in Style. M.E. Pruitt Undertaker at Sixth and Main Street in Millersburg is thought to have utilized the last horse-drawn hearse in Bourbon County. Pictured here in 1913 are David E. Clarke, driving the flower wagon; William Baldwin, driver of the hearse, and M.E. Pruitt, undertaker. Pruitt, like many undertakers of the time, also ran a furniture store along with his funeral business.

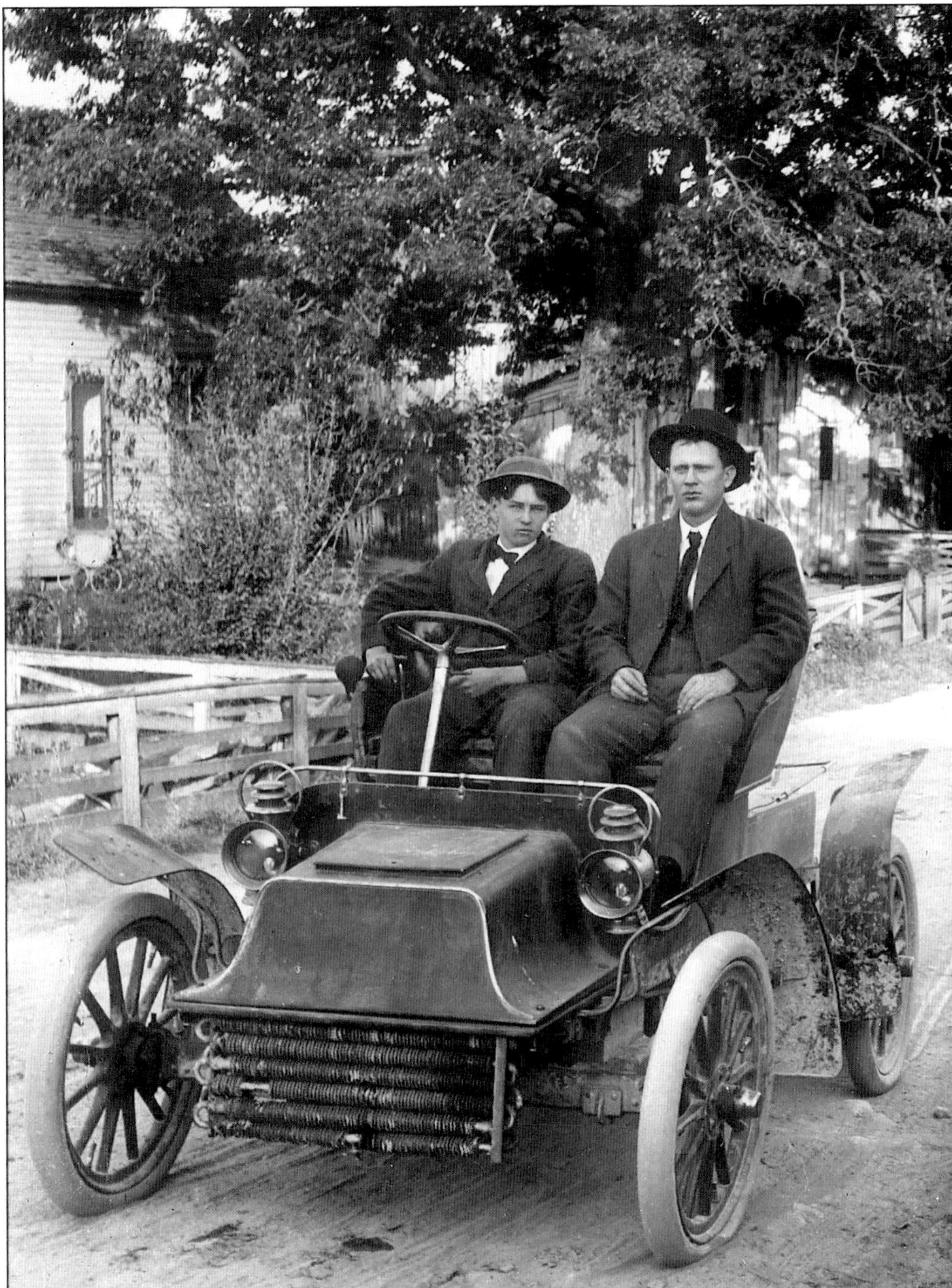

CADILLAC, COUNTY'S FIRST AUTOMOBILE? Paris residents, John Henry Richard (right) and his son Clyde Richard are seen here in a jaunty 1904, one-cylinder, "Model B" Cadillac. The 1904 product brochure states that this runabout "may be geared up until it is capable of speeds enough to satisfy the most reckless driver!" Tools, tire pump, and repair kit were the standard options; the costly brass gas lamps (seen here) had to be ordered from a separate manufacturer.

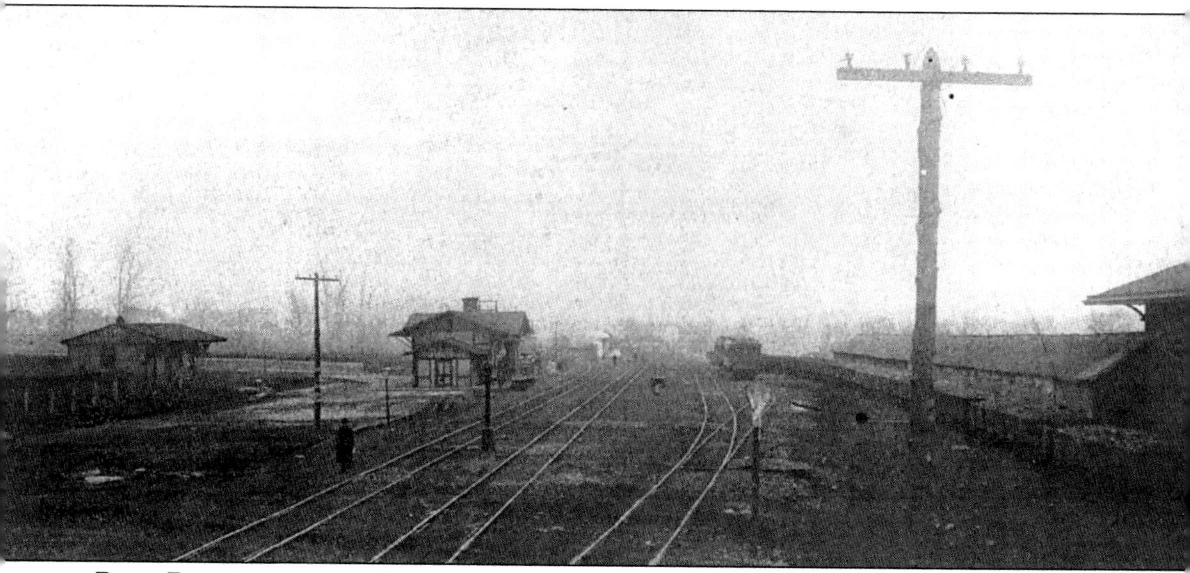

PARIS RAIL DEPOT IN 1888. Shortly after the Civil War, Bourbon County became embroiled in the "railroad fever" that swept the state. Individuals as well as local governments invested in the competing rail lines that began to spider-web across the state. Political battles over railroad taxes and right-of-ways divided Bourbon Countians nearly as much as the late war had. By 1888 when this photo was taken, Paris was considered a "rail hub" and was a major repair yard for the Kentucky Central Railroad and three other railroads that ran through Paris. In 1890, the depot and most of the yards seen here were sold to the Louisville & Nashville Railroad. The building seen left of the depot was a very profitable saloon run by Dick Alexander.

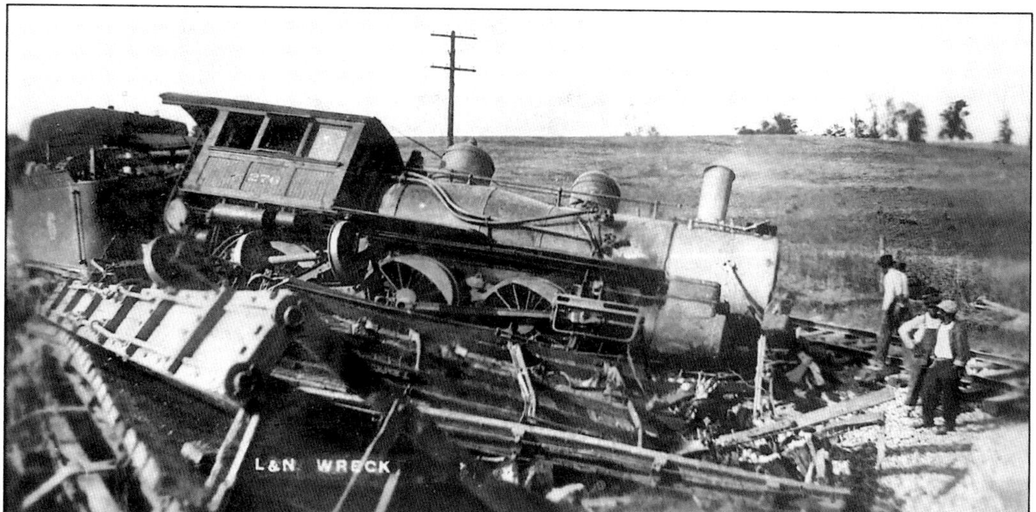

1912 TRAIN WRECK. Back when a community depended on its railroad connections to provide it with mail, transportation for commuters and travelers, fresh produce, and all kinds of goods and information, a train wreck was taken even more seriously than today. This derailment of a Louisville & Nashville passenger train just south of the Paris city limits in 1912 killed the engineer and permanently crippled the fireman.

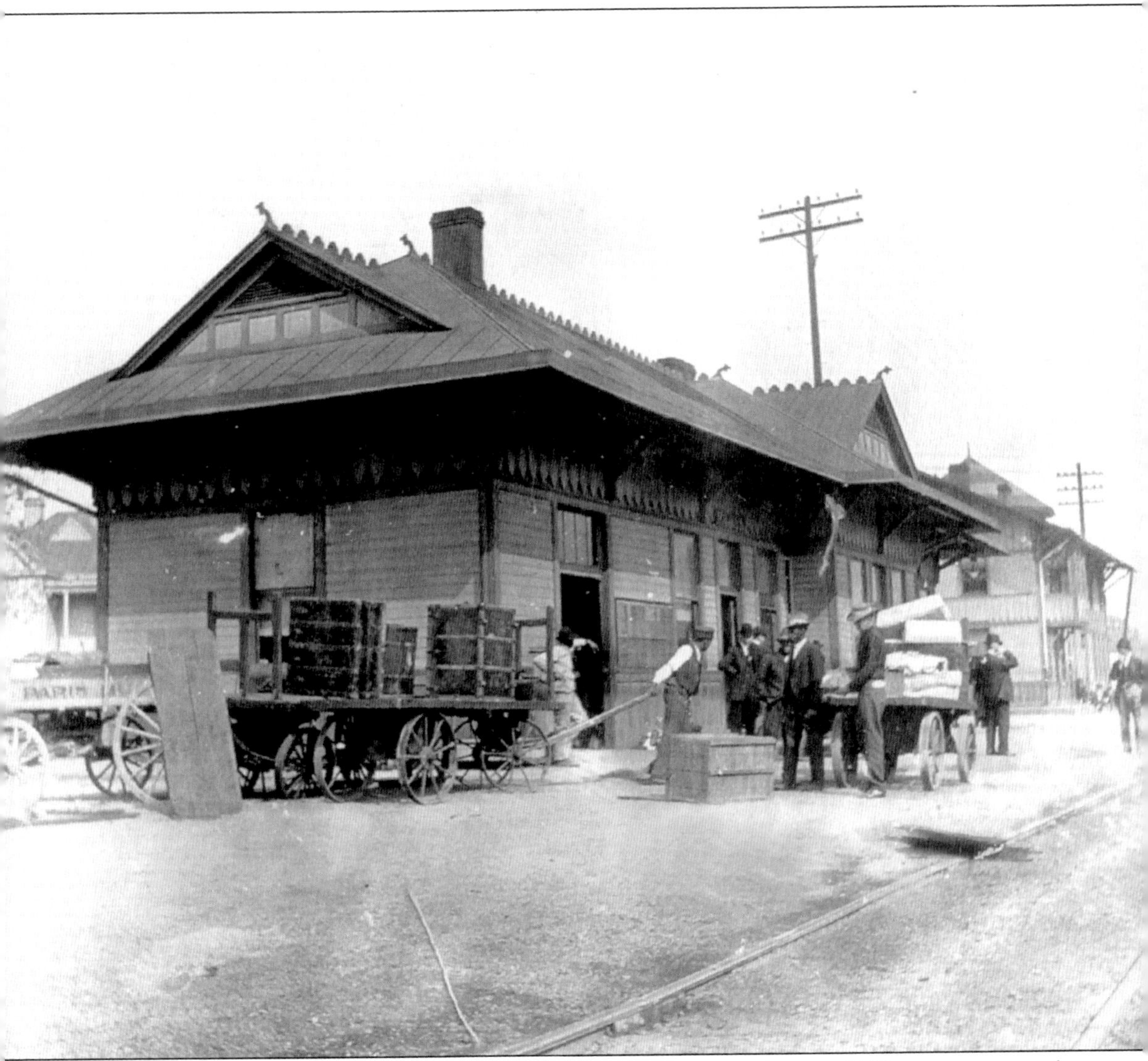

L.& N. PASSENGER DEPOT IN 1900. The Paris railroad station seen here in 1900 was constructed in 1872. The covered platform later generations are familiar with had not yet been constructed. This depot replaced the city's first train station located at Second and Pleasant Streets behind the Windsor Hotel. The first passenger train arrived in Paris in December 22, 1853, from Lexington as a part of the Lexington & Covington Railroad. The last passenger train left Paris on March 7, 1968. (U.K. Collection.)

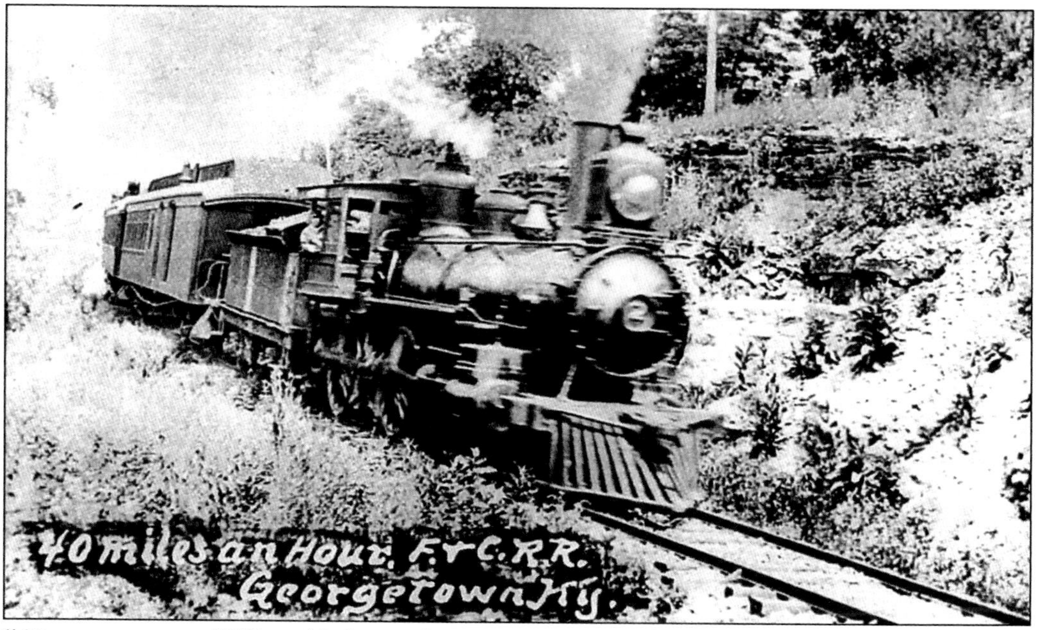

“40 Miles an Hour!” This old photo of a steam engine seen between Georgetown and Paris has “40 miles an hour” written on it; that was probably an amazing speed for the time. The train ran on what was begun in 1888 as the Kentucky Midland Railroad and later became the Frankfort & Cincinnati Railroad.

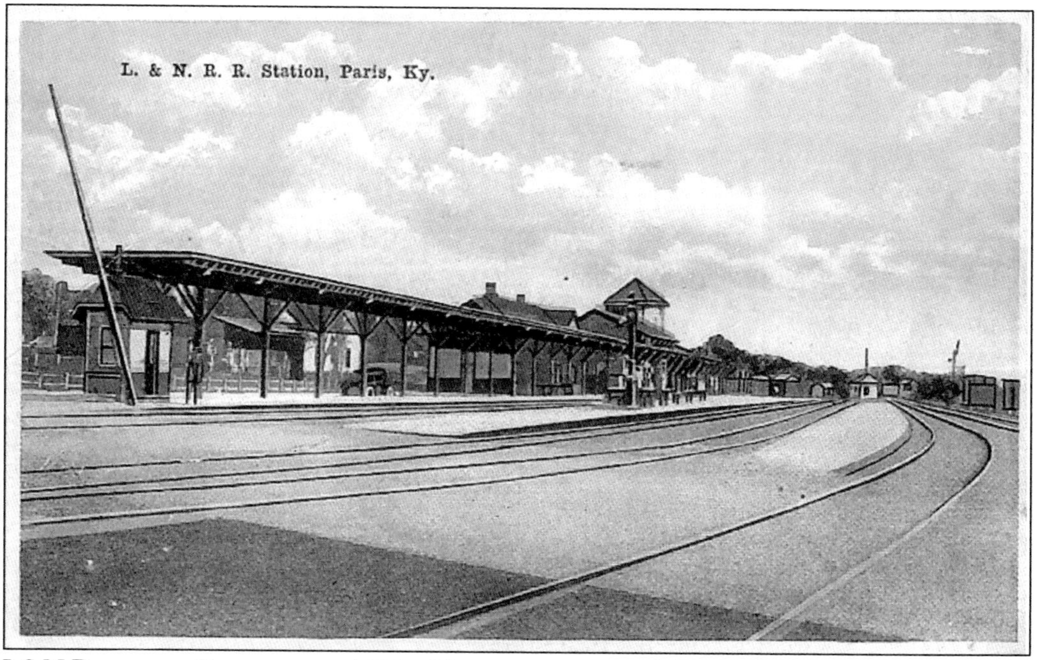

L&N Passenger Depot in the 1930s. This picture postcard shows what the Paris train station looked like beginning in 1927 when the L&N Railroad covered the long passenger platform. Countless Bourbon Countians went off to school and war from this depot, many never to return. The building was slated for demolition in the 1970s, but local preservationists had the property listed on the National Register of Historic Places and saved the site.

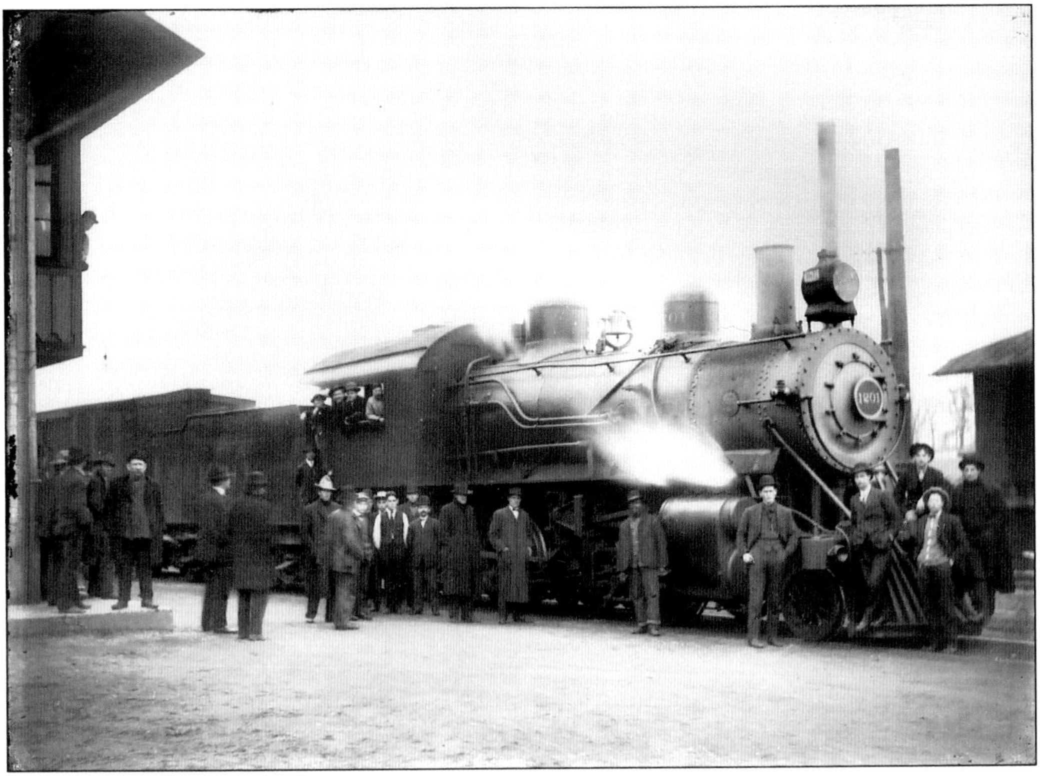

Steam Locomotive was a Powerful Mover. Around 1900 when this photo is believed to have been taken, a steam locomotive was considered one of the most powerful forces and complex pieces of machinery there was. The men clustered around Engine No. 1201 in this photo were probably part of the crew as well as admirers of this awesome technology. Notice the man leaning out of the bay window in the Paris stationmaster's office.

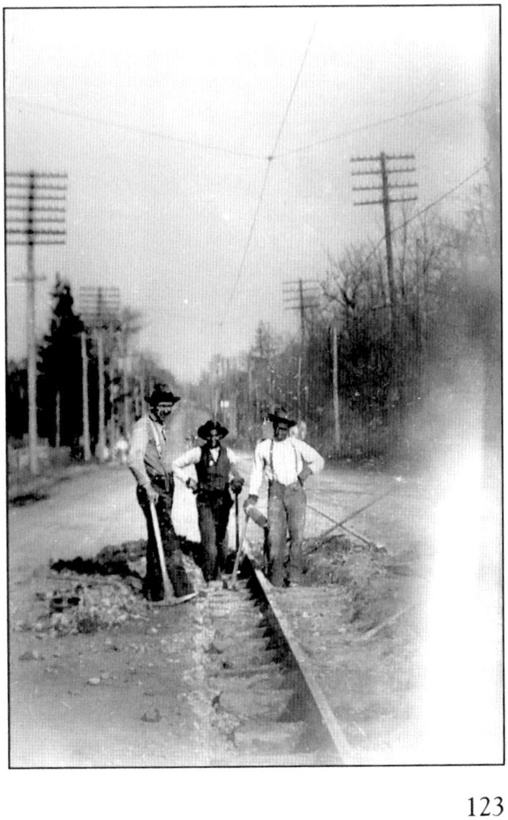

Track Workers on Interurban Line. The rails that the interurban traveled on were in the middle of the road down High and South Main Streets as it headed to and from Lexington. It was not until it reached the country that it traveled along the west shoulder of the Paris Pike. Pictured is a crew some time in the early 1920s working on the tracks in the city.

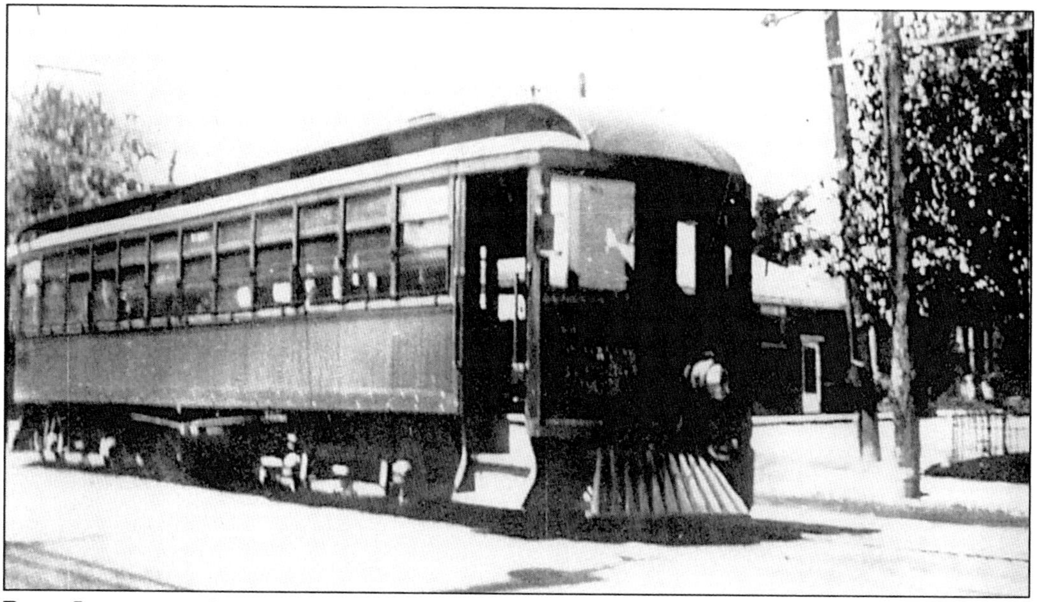

Paris-Lexington Interurban. A convenient and dependable (but slow) light rail service linked Paris and Lexington from 1902 until 1934. Operated by the Kentucky Traction & Terminal Company, the single car trains ran from a terminal at Fifth and High Streets, down High till it crossed over to Main Street at Fourteenth. It went to downtown Lexington and then returned. This 1905 picture shows the car turning on to Main Street. (U.K. Collection.)

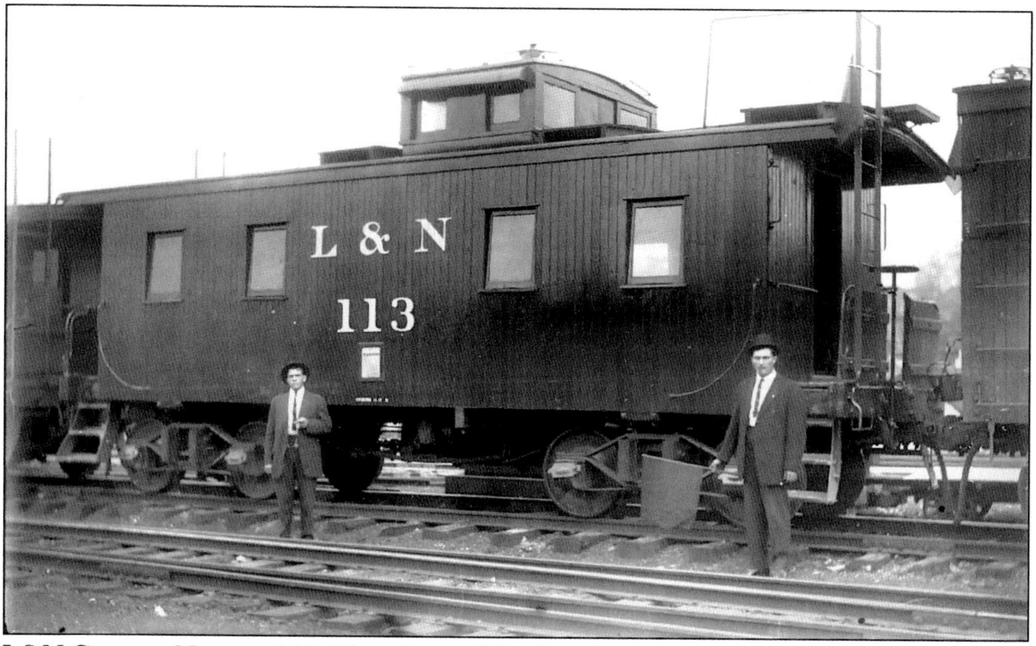

L&N Caboose Number 113. The caboose, like this one in the Paris rail yards about 1900, was a freight train crew's traveling galley and sleeping quarters. The flag men in the photo seem to be unusually well dressed. Perhaps it was a special occasion or we are underestimating the dress code of the time. The Louisville & Nashville began in 1850, but did not come to Paris until 1893 when it acquired Kentucky Central's main line.

INTERURBAN SERVED MANY PURPOSES. Originally organized as the Blue Grass Traction Company in 1902, the Interurban line between Paris and Lexington was later absorbed by the larger Central Kentucky Traction Company that also ran interurban lines into Lexington from Versailles, Frankfort, Nicholasville, Georgetown. There were three basic types of cars, the large city to city passenger cars, the freight cars that carried everything from mail to produce to ice, and the smaller "city streetcars."

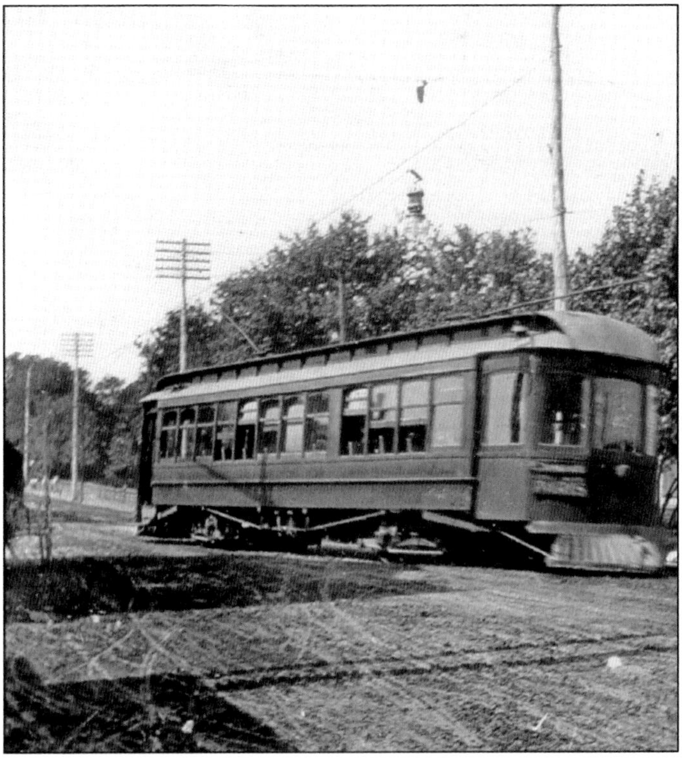

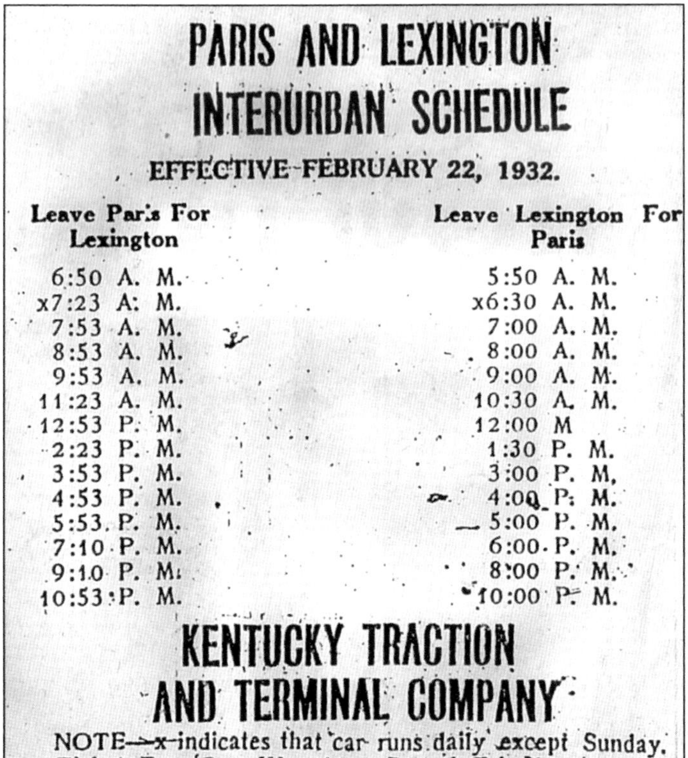

PARIS AND LEXINGTON
INTERURBAN SCHEDULE

EFFECTIVE FEBRUARY 22, 1932.

Leave Paris For Lexington	Leave Lexington For Paris
6:50 A. M.	5:50 A. M.
x7:23 A. M.	x6:30 A. M.
7:53 A. M.	7:00 A. M.
8:53 A. M.	8:00 A. M.
9:53 A. M.	9:00 A. M.
11:23 A. M.	10:30 A. M.
12:53 P. M.	12:00 M
2:23 P. M.	1:30 P. M.
3:53 P. M.	3:00 P. M.
4:53 P. M.	4:00 P. M.
5:53 P. M.	5:00 P. M.
7:10 P. M.	6:00 P. M.
9:10 P. M.	8:00 P. M.
10:53 P. M.	10:00 P. M.

KENTUCKY TRACTION
AND TERMINAL COMPANY

NOTE—x—indicates that car runs daily except Sunday.
Ticket Fare One Way 40c—Round Trip 70c.

INTERURBAN SCHEDULE. The Interurban's 1932 itinerary is pictured at left.

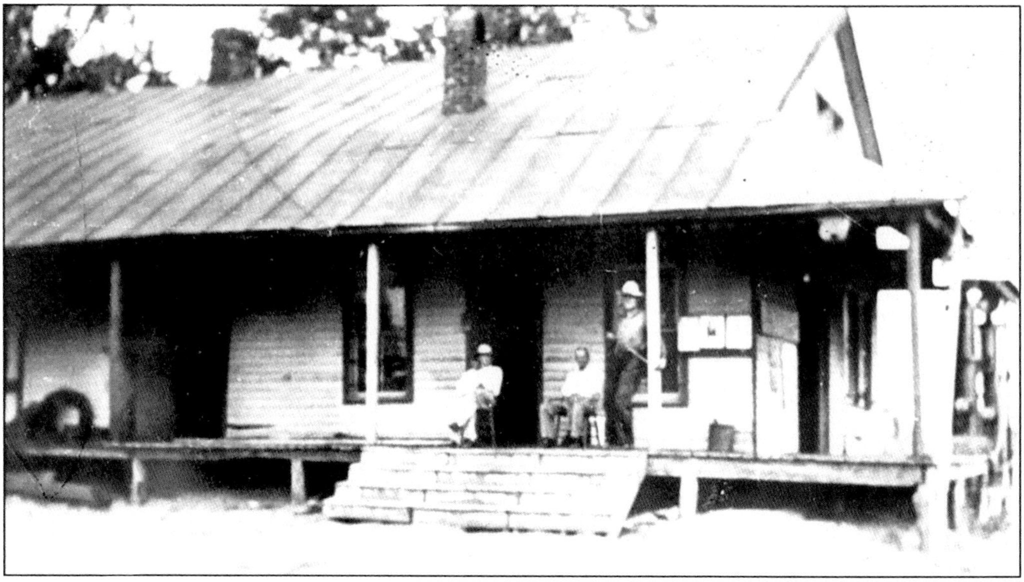

CENTERVILLE TRAIN STATION. Long a community meeting place, the Centerville train station also served as a general store, and later a gasoline station. The men seen in this early photograph are identified from left to right as George R. Burberry, Clyde Burberry, and Jim Ryles. Both the "dinky" and full-sized trains passed by and utilized the station.

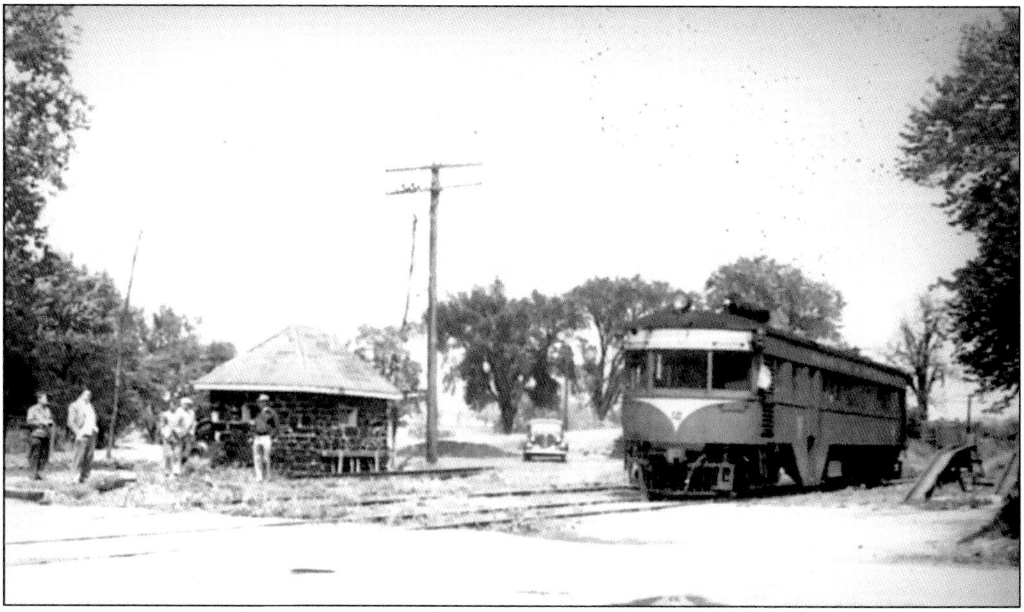

"DINKY" TRAVELED THROUGH CENTERVILLE. The Frankfort & Cincinnati Railway connected Centerville to Paris, Georgetown and Frankfort. This photo taken sometime in the late 1920s shows the single car "dinky" train passing by the Centerville station that is just out of the picture to the left. The small building in the picture housed scales and was built out of blocks of coal.

GREYHOUND BUS IN PARIS. With the passing of the interurban rail lines and the improvement of highways, buses became the transit alternative between towns in the Bluegrass. The ubiquitous Greyhound Line stopped in Millersburg and Paris daily for many years. For those without automobiles or, for those who wanted to "Leave the driving to us!" it was popular right up to the end of the 20th century.

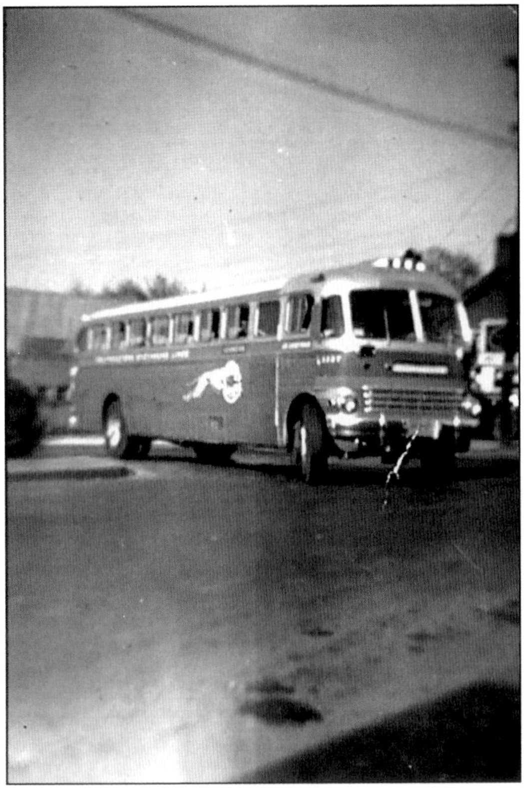

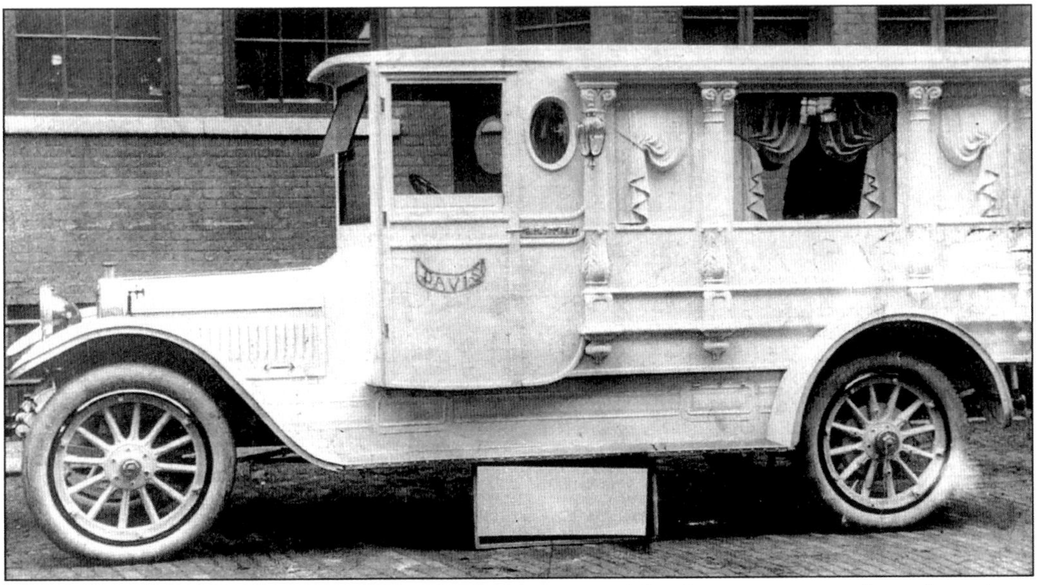

COMBINATION HEARSE AND AMBULANCE. This was one of the first automotive funeral carriages in Bourbon County. Also used as an ambulance, or "invalid wagon," it was first used in the funeral of Madie Jordan in July of 1917. It was operated by George W. Davis Funeral Director at the corner of Fifth and Main Streets in Paris. He advertised his services saying, "Disinfecting a specialty."

ACKNOWLEDGMENTS

Compiling a book of historical photographs is a project that requires the cooperation of a great many people. We needed input and assistance from many people so that this book could be representative of Bourbon County people and events before 1940. This is our second volume of historical photographs covering approximately the same period, making our task more difficult in some ways.

Many of the images in this volume came from two sources—the Audio-Visual Archives in the Special Collection at the University of Kentucky Library and the Pittenger Collection of historical photographs collected by Dr. B.N. Pittenger in the 1960s and donated to the Paris-Bourbon County Library. We have indicated the photos that came from UK so that anyone interested could request a copy of any of the photos by calling Special Collections at 859-257-6311.

Special thanks are due to Bobby Shiflet from Frames on Main. Many of the photographs in this volume were in large, antique frames that had to be carefully removed and replaced. Without Bobby's help, we would not have been able to use some of the best photos in this book.

We also owe a "thank you" to Betsy Kephart at the Hopewell Museum. The Hopewell Museum and the University of Kentucky Library's Special Collections both provide an invaluable service by serving as repositories for wonderful old photographs. Anyone who has old photographs should consider donating them to either of these organizations. Even so-called "family photos" are welcomed. Many of the photos in this volume came from family scrapbooks, which provide a wonderful resource for historians.

We are deeply grateful to all the people who loaned photos or who helped in other ways with this book including Bill Marshall, Lisa Carter, and Jason Flahardy at UK Special Collections; Ann Rogers, Joe Larry Eads, Susan Eades, Suzanne Rogers and all the rest of the wonderful staff at the Paris-Bourbon County Library; Kevin Crump, Tug Wilson, Kay McLaughlin, Joe and JoAnn Ewalt, Dan Graham, Ric O'Connell, Dave and Susie Parrish, Lida Soper, Betty Allman, Laura Minnick, Betsy Kuster, Ann Butler Burroughs, David Dick, Wanda Richard, Robert and Diane Steffer, Victor McLain, Scott Doyle, Bill Buckner, Jeff Bell, Dorothy Vactor, Margaret Watkins, Barbara Straus, Virginia Downey, Jerome Harney, Mary Clay, Patty Biddle, Manes and Nana Hazzard, Nancy Mason, George Sydney and Charleen Tate, Catherine Lytle, Nornie Adair, Jean Wallen, Louise Ott, Patsy Baldwin, Ken Hixson, Mary Ida Linville, Ora Mae Jacobs, Jack Shout, Bill Burris Bryan, Louise Alverson, Charles Ramsey, Wally Shropshire, Bud Butler, Belva Chamberlain, Dudley Forsythe, Jane Hansen, and Martha Clark.

And last, but certainly not least, thanks to our family—especially Sean, Rob, Becca, Daddy, Pat, and grandson Noah, for their love and support!